THE RIOT A

THE RIOT
AT CHRISTIE PITS

CYRIL LEVITT AND WILLIAM SHAFFIR
With a new Foreword by Marcus Gee

NEW JEWISH PRESS

SECOND EDITION

Copyright © 1987, 2018 Cyril Levitt and William Shaffir

This edition published in 2018 by
New Jewish Press
Anne Tanenbaum Centre for Jewish Studies
University of Toronto
170 St. George St., Room 218
Toronto, Ontario M5R 2M8
www.newjewishpress.ca

Book design: Mark Goldstein

LIBRARY AND ARCHIVES CATALOGUING IN PUBLICATION

Levitt, Cyril, 1946–, author
     The riot at Christie Pits/Cyril Levitt and William Shaffir.

Previously published: Toronto: Lester & Orpen Dennys, 1987.
Issued in print and electronic formats.
ISBN 978-1-988326-08-5 (softcover).—ISBN 978-1-988326-09-2 (PDF)

1. Riots—Ontario—Toronto—History. 2. Christie Pits (Toronto, Ont.)—History. 3. Jews—
Ontario—Toronto—History. 4. Antisemitism—Ontario—Toronto. I. Shaffir, William, 1945–,
author II. Title.

FC3097.9.J5L48 2018   971.3'541004924009046   C2018-900005-8
                                                             C2018-900006-6

PRINTED IN CANADA

To the memory of Ben Levitt, who first told his son about the exploits of those who fought in the battle of Christie Pits
C.L.

To the memory of my mother
W.S.

Contents

Note to the Reader

With the exception of the Foreword and Postscript, this publication is a reproduction of the original text of *The Riot at Christie Pits*. Any temporal references such as "at present," "today," "now," or "currently" refer to the period of its original publication, circa 1987. There will also be minor changes in copy style that have evolved between the first publication and this one.

Acknowledgments

It is perhaps a testimony to the ethnic mosaic that is Toronto that this book about events in the city in the summer of 1933 was written in Berlin, Tel Aviv, and Hamilton, Ontario. The idea for the project arose during an exhibition concerning the history of prejudice and racism in Canada in which a newspaper clipping from the *Toronto Daily Star* of 17 August 1933 about the riot at Christie Pits called to mind the stories that one of the authors had heard from his father in the 1950s. Subsequent discussions with Tony Hyde in Ottawa helped to give the project a clearer focus.

There are many, many people to whom we are indebted for their help in bringing about this book. Robert Fulford suggested that we write up our research findings in the form of a book and put us in touch with Malcolm Lester, who was enthusiastic in his support of our work. Ben Kayfetz was always ready to fill in gaps in our knowledge about Toronto in the early thirties, and his interpretation of certain events and phenomena proved to be most helpful. Alan Shefman, of the League for Human Rights of B'nai Brith, and Stephen Speisman, Director of Archives at the Toronto Jewish Congress, were untiring in their assistance. David Rome, the indefatigable researcher on antisemitism in Canada, helped us to put the events of the summer of 1933 into historical perspective. Judy Nefsky provided us with every assistance during our research at the Canadian Jewish Congress Archives in Montreal. Lawrence Tapper and Myron Momryk, of the National Archives of Canada, were most helpful to us on the question of ethnic violence. We would also like to thank Victor Russell, Supervisor at the Toronto City Archives, and staff members Elizabeth Cuthbertson and Alan Meisner for their patience and expert guidance through the material relevant to our study. Frau Dr. Keipert and the staff at the Archives of the *Aussenamt* in Bonn also provided important assistance. Our thanks go as well to the staff at the American Documentation Center on Nazi War Criminals in Berlin for its co-operation and help. Jim Ingram at Robarts Library, University of Toronto, was of tremendous assistance in obtaining reproductions of newspapers for the photo section and cover.

We were indeed fortunate in having colleagues with whom we could discuss various aspects of our research. Especially helpful were Irving Abella, Ray Breton, Howard Brotz, Jean Burnet, Yaakov Glickman, Louis Greenspan, Robert Harney, David Kirk, Graham Knight, Michiel Horn, Frank Jones, Jim Lemon, Peter Pineo, Malcolm Spector, Henry Trachtenberg, and Harold Troper. Without the assistance of the scores of people who agreed to be interviewed by us for the book, the contents would have been much less compelling. Several people were interviewed many times. We thank them for their patience with us and for sharing their information. We also thank, for reading the manuscript and assisting in our research, Harry (Burke) and Saul Bergstein, Louis Greenspan, Irv Lasky, Sammy Luftspring, Jack Rosen, and Stephen Speisman.

This book would not have been possible without the generous financial assistance of the LaMarsh Programme for Study of Violence and Conflict Resolution at York University, and of the Secretary of State, Multiculturalism Directorate. We also wish to thank the Alexander von Humboldt Foundation for enabling one of the authors to conduct research relevant to this book in the Federal Republic of Germany. And finally, we are gratefully appreciative of financial assistance provided by McMaster University's Arts Research Board and Peter George, Dean of the Faculty of Social Sciences, McMaster University.

Our wives—Angelika Levitt and Rivka Shaffir—deserve very special mention for always enabling us to travel to Toronto, Ottawa, and Montreal to conduct interviews and library research in connection with the writing of this book.

We wish to thank Margaret Woollard for skilfully copy-editing the manuscript. Special mention must be made of the essential contribution of Janet Hamilton, without whom this book would have been much poorer in structure.

Foreword

An ethnic riot in Toronto? A clash between Jews and Gentiles in a public park? It seems hard to fathom today. Modern Toronto is a multicultural marvel. People come from around the world to study how people from so many backgrounds can live together in such harmony. Canada has no anti-immigrant party braying for the ejection of unwanted newcomers. The city's Jewish community is secure, established, and highly successful.

The Toronto of 1933 was a very different place. It was a British city, a loyal daughter of the Empire. Four in every five Torontonians were of British descent. The Orange Order, that Union Jack-waving bastion of Protestantism and jingoism, was a dominant force in the political and cultural life of what was once called Toronto the Good.

Newer immigrant groups—the Jews, the Italians, the Ukrainians—lived largely apart, excluded from many jobs and looked down on by the majority. About 45,000 Jews lived in Toronto in 1931, the authors of this book report. They made up 7.2 per cent of the population, but a much higher proportion in parts of the west end, like the districts around Christie Pits (18.6 per cent) and Kensington Market (30.5 per cent). In the ultra-British district around the eastern beaches, which were to play a big part in the tensions that lead to the riot, they made up just 0.08 per cent. Fights sometimes erupted when Jews and others ventured out of the relative safety of their neighbourhoods.

The spark that turned fighting into rioting was news from across the sea. The rise of Hitler was well covered by the Toronto press. Both the Jewish papers and the mainstream dailies ran big headlines about Nazi outrages against German Jews in 1933. (Say goodbye to the notion that the Western world didn't know what was happening in Germany.) So imagine the indignation of the Jewish community when residents of the Beach neighbourhood formed something called the Swastika Club and held a march on the boardwalk. They said they weren't antisemitic—

perish the thought. They just wanted to keep "obnoxious visitors" from fouling their lovely beaches. Jews often came to the Beach for weekend picnics. Some locals wished them gone. They liked their beaches "clean and nice."

Tensions rose through the summer of 1933. A clash broke out in the big park called Kew Gardens in the Beach area, a tune-up for what was to happen later in Christie Pits. On August 16 the riot began with the unfurling of a big swastika flag at a softball game between teams of the Harbord Playground (which had many Jewish players) and St. Peter's. Jewish fans attacked those who brought it. Fighting spilled into the streets. Youths armed with broom handles and iron bars battled hand to hand. Italian youths from the surrounding neighbourhood came in on the Jewish side.

Faced with an outrageous provocation, Toronto Jews defended them-selves. They knew what was going on in Europe. They were not going to stand by and have the Nazi symbol waved in their faces. The robust response of the Jewish street—youths piling into trucks to rush to the scene—showed that, in the New World, they would not accept the big-otry and ostracism that were the lot of many European Jews. Refusing to be victims, they fought back. The riot shocked the provincial Toronto of those years. It revealed a city divided—on one side, the old British city, fearful of the newcomers in its midst and eager to preserve its way of life; on the other, the struggling immigrant city, shut out and resentful.

Christie Pits has nagged at Toronto's conscience ever since. There were complaints when, in 2008, authorities put up a plaque at Christie Pits Park to mark the 75th anniversary of the riot. Some asked whether the city should commemorate such an ugly event. Of course it should. Christie Pits happened right here in Toronto. It is important to under-stand why, which is why this book is still worth reading.

One way to look at the riot is as a warning, evidence that even in a staid and peaceful place like Toronto, the beast is always lurking. It startled everyone how quickly the violence erupted, how readily the us-against-them impulse burst to the surface. We see that impulse at work even now. In the wake of Donald Trump's accession to the most power-ful office in the world, hundreds of hate incidents were being reported across the United States. Shouts of "Hail Trump! Hail Victory!" rang out at a far-right gathering. There have been faint echoes in Canada, too, like the antisemitic message on the window of a Toronto library.

Another way to look at Christie Pits is as a sign of how societies can evolve. Toronto was changing even then and the pace of change would quicken in the decades to come. After World War II, a wave of immigrants from southern Europe gave the city new variety and vigour. Toronto got its first Jewish mayor, Nathan Phillips, in 1955. Freed, over time, from the blackballing and quotas of the Christie Pits years, Jews advanced in the professions, in business, in the arts. A neo-Nazi crank who came to town in 1965 "encountered practically unanimous hostility from all sectors of the population."

When the first edition of this book came out in 1987, the authors concluded (with some understatement) that the Christie Pits riot was "a rather unpleasant chapter" in Toronto's history. It exposed the prejudices of a society that had closed its doors to pre-war Jewish immigration—the shameful "None is Too Many" episode that authors Irving Abella and Harold Troper uncovered in 1983.

"And yet," Cyril Levitt and William Shaffir continue, "the book is a tribute to the city today, for Toronto has become a human success story measured against other cities the world over. Although a product of human artifice and thus fraught with problems, Toronto has taken great strides towards making the scores of different ethnic groups who constitute the multicultural mosaic of the city feel safe, secure, welcome, and at home."

Three decades on, as this new edition of their book appears, that verdict seems even more fitting. Christie Pits was the beginning of the end of old Toronto. Nothing like it ever happened again. Whether it is good management or just luck—Canada is nicely insulated from the waves of migrants that have whipped up the haters in Europe and the United States—this country has made a brilliant success of its experiment in mass legal immigration. Tens of thousands arrive in its biggest city every year from Africa, China, India, the Philippines, Venezuela, Vietnam, the Caribbean, and scores of others places. There is no end of the flood in sight. Nobody can ride a Toronto streetcar or visit a suburban Toronto mall without being astonished at the mix of peoples—every complexion, every language, every religion.

When my son played little league baseball in Christie Pits, the boys he played with came from all over (or their parents did). In his elementary school class, it was he—a pale-skinned, red-headed boy—who was the visible minority. It would never have entered his head that things should be any different. The idea that people should club together by skin colour and ancestry, or, worse, fight over it, would have left him bewildered.

Though no one makes them conform, immigrant kids, plunged into the integration machine of the public schools, become little Canadians at light speed. The main complaint of immigrant parents today is not that they aren't accepted by their new country but that their children become thoroughly Canadian too quickly, forgetting the language and customs of the old country.

If Christie Pits was a shameful episode, it was also the dawn of some- thing new and really quite wonderful. It is no exaggeration to say that the city where Jew and Gentile once beat each other bloody is now the hope of the world.

That doesn't mean that hate has been banished from our midst. Trump's rants about banning Muslims and expelling Mexican "rapists" brought the hate-mongers scurrying forth. But as odious as they are, they are on the losing side of history. Look at Toronto then. Look at it now. Christie Pits is both a warning of hate's power and a reminder that it can be overcome.

Marcus Gee
Toronto
April 2018

Introduction

Mid-summer 1932. The fire crackled in the clearing, sending pungent smoke upwards to the starlit heavens. Around the flames sat several hundred Jewish youths who had gathered at these camping grounds in the forest on the outskirts of town. This was their celebration of the sabbath in which they mixed religious tradition and secular Zionism. The leaders, facing the sea of blue-shirted boys, alternately chanted ancient, mystical sabbath hymns and recited modern Hebrew verse bearing a message of enlightenment, progress, and secular liberation.

Suddenly, the trance was broken by cries from the surrounding woods: "Down with the Jews! Death to the Jews!" Hundreds of teenage boys rushed from behind the trees armed with clubs and knives and attacked the sabbath gathering. One of the Zionist leaders, a young man who had seen combat in Palestine, attempted to rally his lads in self-defence. The fighting was furious. One of the blue-shirted youths managed to break through the cordon around the camp and alert the police in the nearby town. The police, however, were slow in responding to the call for help, and many of the youngsters had to be hospitalized with serious injuries. In the aftermath of the fighting the police closed the camp and advised the Jewish lads to return to their homes. The next day, as the column of blue-shirted boys wound its way down the streets of the town towards the railway station, the townsfolk heaped verbal abuse upon the already disheartened juveniles.

Summer 1933. The weather had been hot and humid with only inter-mittent relief. Several thousand people were gathered in a city park to watch a playoff game between rival teams, one of which had a majority of Jewish players. Antisemitic incidents had occurred at the previous meeting of these two clubs, and today anti- and pro-Jewish forces had gathered in strength. The crowd was tense and a few minor incidents occurred during the earlier part of the contest, but the game was played to its conclusion without major disruption. Suddenly, in the middle of the park, a group of some twenty youths raised a large white sheet upon which had been painted a black swastika. "Heil Hitler," cried nameless voices from the crowd. Jewish supporters rushed the flag-bearers, and pandemonium broke out. Spectators yelled "Kill the Jews" as youths made after one another with clubs, chains, bats, and broom handles. The two policemen on duty in the park were simply overwhelmed. They sent for reinforcements, which were slow in arriving. Scores of youths were injured; several were rushed to hospital.

The two incidents, taken out of their larger contexts, are nevertheless representative of the *Zeitgeist* (the spirit of the times) in which they occurred. The first took place in the woods outside of Dessau, about one hundred kilometres south of Berlin, Germany, the city in which Moses Mendelssohn was born.[1] The second occurred in Willowvale Park, popularly known as Christie Pits,[2] in Toronto, Ontario, Canada. The first incident was an expression of the growing antisemitism in Germany and of the relative impunity with which antisemitic attacks were carried out by Hitler's followers. The second was an expression of the hostile atmosphere surrounding the Jews in Canada in the thirties and earlier, and an example of the abuse and violence, both verbal and physical, to which they were sporadically subjected.

This book is not about the Holocaust, but about the violent expression of antisemitism in Canada in the shadow of the beginnings of Jewry's darkest hours. It was not the usual antisemitic fare in Toronto that led to the riot at Christie Pits. There had been antisemitic violence long before and there would be such violence long after the riot. Only when local antisemitism became symbolically linked with German National Socialism did the anger of large numbers of Jewish youth erupt violently.

In order to understand this process, we have to consider the way in which the news of events transpiring in Germany between January and August 1933 became known to the residents of Toronto. To our surprise, we discovered that Toronto newspapers had been full of stories describing the Nazi rise to power. They carried horrifying front-page reports of the atrocities against Jews during the first months of Hitler's rule. The *Toronto Daily Star*, for example, referred to the burning of the books in May 1933 as a "holocaust," and repeated references were made in both the English and Yiddish press to the "destruction," "annihilation," and "extermination" of the Jews in Hitler's power. Pictures of roll calls from German concentration camps were published prominently in Toronto newspapers that same spring. In fact, because of the censorship of the media by the Hitler regime, Torontonians probably knew more about what was occurring to Jews in Germany during those fateful months than did most Berliners.

For the Jews of Toronto, the swastika immediately became the symbol of persecution, torture, and death. And yet large sections of the British majority, encouraged in part by the reports and editorials of some newspapers, especially the *Evening Telegram*, showed considerable ambivalence towards this symbol of German Fascism. Everyone in Toronto knew that the swastika was an antisemitic symbol, but the perception of the seriousness and depth of that antisemitism differed between Jews and large numbers of Gentiles in the city. The calls of "kike" and "sheeny" may have occasioned schoolyard brawls, but the showing of the swastika in a Toronto park led to a full-scale riot. Without the atrocity stories coming out of Germany, without the editorials and letters to the editor on Hitler's rise to power, and without the examples of resistance and protest that the newspaper reported, it is highly unlikely that the riot at Christie Pits would have happened.

Detailed review of the coverage of the Nazification of Germany reveals a fascinating connection with the present—the careful imitation of the Nazi technique of denial by such Holocaust revisionists as Ernst Zundel. Whereas the reports, editorials, and letters to the editor that challenged the atrocity stories emanating from Germany in 1933 show that the denial campaign was taken seriously by some "responsible" segments of the population then, the current campaign of Holocaust denial has met with universal rejection from all sober quarters today. But the denial reports are important, too, for the quasi-legitimacy they gave to the youthful swastika bearers of Toronto. Simply by suggesting, as the Toronto *Evening Telegram* did on numerous occasions, that the reports of anti-Jewish terror in Germany were exaggerated, the media opened the way for young people at the Beaches and at the Pits to "play" with the swastika as a symbol without having to identify directly with torturers and murderers.[3] In fact, the swastika was adopted not because these young people were Hitlerites and Nazis, but as a way of saying symbolically that Jews were not wanted in their neighborhoods.

Thus, there are two interwoven themes throughout this book—the events in Toronto during August 1933 that led up to the riot at Christie Pits and the influence the Nazi rise to power in Germany had in the shaping of those events. In presenting the material covering the reporting of German events in the Toronto papers, we hope to show the reader the nature of the process whereby Torontonians became aware of the new meaning of the swastika.[4]

The story that follows is about Toronto as it was in 1933. The analysis of the events themselves will reveal much about the nature of the city at that time. The story not only concerns an isolated incident of ethnic violence, but also has much to tell us about the ongoing relations between ethnic groups, the role of the police force, the power of the Orange Order, the debilitating effects of the Depression, the nature of the British connection and the British sense of "fair play and justice," the character of civic politics, the slant of the press, the suppression of Communist and socialist organizations, the fight for freedom of speech, the xenophobia of large sections of the Anglo-Saxon majority, the pervasiveness of antisemitic feeling, and the impact of the rise of Hitler on various groups in the city. As A. M. Klein recalled:

> In certain presumably respectable, and indeed intellectual, quarters admiration was being expressed, as if fairly to give the devil his due, for Hitler's achievement. Here and there the Nazi dementia was exalted—not with malice, but as it were scientifically—to the status of a philosophy. Even men of the best of will began to speak—as though they were but acknowledging the unpalatable but inexorable fact—of the "wave of the future."
>
> All the Nazi agencies of corruption were now busily engaged in world-wide distribution of the Judeophobic poison. The period of the dumping of antisemitism into Canada had begun.[5]

Measured against conditions in Europe, the development and maturation of antisemitism in Canada was marginal. However, antisemitism, a term invented in the late nineteenth century, served as an important component of the Jewish experience in Canada from the time that Jews began to immigrate to this country in increasingly large numbers. While the term "anti-Semitism" implies the presence of something called "Semitism" to which one can be opposed, such a thing is simply unknown to science or scholarship. Often written "anti-Semitism," this spelling both avoids the more vulgar term "Jew hatred" and provides its users with a seemingly scientifically credible concept. We have, therefore, chosen to write the word "antisemitism" (in lower case, without a hyphen) to avoid lending scientific legitimacy to the "Semitism" concept. The English word "antisemitism" is derived from the German, *Antisemitismus*, a term coined by the notorious antisemite Wilhelm Marr in 1879 to replace the word *Judenhass*—"Jew hatred." The term itself can have several nuances, and the differences among them require clarification if we are to appreciate the Canadian, and specifically Torontonian, experience. Arnold Ages has called attention to the crucial difference between what he terms "mild" antisemitism and the more "diabolical" variety:

> In its most innocent form, antisemitism is a manifestation of the kind of ethnic prejudice that is widespread throughout the human race. In a particular individual, antipathy towards Jews can be a mild hostility resulting from an unfortunate contact with an unsympathetic Jewish merchant or simply a vague negativism imbibed from the font of anti-Jewish teachings transmitted by Christianity.
>
> Both cases differ from diabolical antisemitism, which sees Jews not as human beings suffering from the foibles that characterize men and women in their weaknesses but as agents of an international conspiracy, sinister forces in a campaign to dominate the world....
>
> The distinction between mild antisemitism and its more malignant expression is not a mere exercise in semantics but a differentiation that is germane to the Canadian experience.[6]

Although we agree in general with this distinction, it should be noted that the "mild" form of antisemitism has been extremely pernicious, limiting accessibility for Jews in housing, employment, education, and recreation during the 1930s. The "diabolical" variety, which is really congruent with political antisemitism, has never had much electoral success in Canada. Fred Egan, the reporter for the *Evening Telegram* who covered the antisemitic incident at the Beaches in 1933, indicated that the antisemitism in Toronto at the time was largely of the mild variety.

> Well, as I told you before it was sort of...I don't think it was antisemitic, I don't think that anybody intended to be really antisemitic. But those were the days when the Jewish pedlars—we called them sheenies—came around to the door collecting your garbage, not garbage, but things that were thrown out, everything like that. And there was a feeling there, but it wasn't vastly different from the feeling about Catholics, that I told you. I don't think it was what we think of as antisemitism now. See, Toronto at that

time was largely British ... Anglo-Saxon. There were hardly any people other than that and perhaps the Jewish community. I don't remember it being any real serious antisemitism. There was, oh, I don't know what you call it. There was a feeling that any foreigner, anybody that wasn't just like them, came into your neighbourhood, you know. It was that parochial an existence then.

But in spite of the fact that the mild form of antisemitism tended to predominate, for a brief period during the 1930s the spread of Fascist ideology and the general social, economic, and political turbulence of the period occasioned a lapse into the virulent form by a noisy if small minority of the population. It is precisely this period of the early 1930s that provides the immediate context for understanding the formation of the Swastika Club in Toronto, its activities at the Beaches, and the riot at Christie Pits.

Following the appearance of the swastika at the eastern beaches and at Christie Pits, many Jews perceived that a change had begun to take place among the British majority: a shift was in the making from a mild form of antisemitism, based largely on xenophobia, to the more virulent variety.

Neither Quebec nor Ontario Jews faced organized antisemitism of the malignant strain until the early 1930s, when Adrian Arcand's populist political cadres began to stir up anti-Jewish feelings among French Canadians. As Lita-Rose Betcherman has shown in her survey of Fascist movements in Canada in the 1930s,[7] Arcand orchestrated a campaign of antisemitism through public pronouncements and through the press. As the editor of three weekly newspapers, *Le Goglu*, *Le Miroir*, and *Le Chameau*, he was instrumental in promoting French-Canadian chauvinism and spreading anti-Jewish propaganda.

Initially, only traces of antisemitism were noticeable in Arcand's writing, but after a few months, lead articles and editorials against the Jews appeared with regularity. In January 1933, when Hitler became Chancellor of Germany, no one was more jubilant than Arcand. Immediately predicting that the anti-Jewish Hitler government would help create similar governments in fifteen other countries, he exhorted his readers to stand up and be counted:

What about us, Goglus, do we know what to do as well as the young patriots in the European countries? Are we going to roll back the Jewish invasion more each day? Are we going to spread the word as much as we can about boycotting Jewish merchants and products? Are we going to convince our merchants not to receive Jewish travelling salesmen and not to buy anything from Jewish suppliers?[8]

In March 1933, when other Canadian newspapers were reporting on the perils facing German Jews and the atrocities committed against them, Arcand informed his readership that "if it was good for Germany to get rid of its Jews, it would be even better for Quebec and Canada."[9]

Not surprisingly Arcand's open antisemitism caused grave concern. Addressing a Zionist convention, E. F. Singer warned: "Unless something is done quickly the Jewish people may well meet the same fate in Canada that the Jews are meeting in Germany.... No fire is so easily kindled as antisemitism. The fire is dormant in Canada, it has not yet blazed up, but the spark is there. Germany is not the only place with prejudice. Look at Quebec."[10]

Singer was not alone in his view. In a speech read before the members of Shaare Zion Congregation in Montreal in 1932, a community leader maintained:

> I am not an alarmist, but as a student of the Jewish phenomenon in Canada, and particularly in the Province of Quebec, I feel it is my duty to draw your attention to a series of facts....
>
> Antisemitism in its rudest form is foreign to British ideals and to British liberalism, yet in this British country of ours, violent explosions of antisemitism manifest themselves in various parts of this fair dominion, and cause great anxiety. Newspapers [are] published and distributed freely, accusing us of the most unspeakable crimes and disseminating amongst the French population hatred against us.[11]

Clearly, Hitler's propaganda had struck deep roots in Quebec, where antisemitism was blatant and enjoyed both the overt and the covert support of journalists and clerics. The situation in Ontario was also degenerating. In that province, the Canadian Jewish Congress reported in 1937 that "during the past four years we have witnessed an amazing growth of antisemitism. Manifestations of an intensified anti-Jewish sentiment have been springing up everywhere."[12]

Summarizing the specific areas in which Jews had encountered discrimination, the report continued:

> The truth is that during the past four years an entirely new type of antisemitism has assumed prominence in this country. There has been a transition from the sporadic and unorganized type of anti-Jewishness to national organizations directed by professional agents. It is this professional aspect of anti-Semitism which has given an entirely new status to anti-Jewish functions, has aroused unprecedented anti-Jewish feeling, and has brought the Jewish community face to face with a situation somewhat familiar: the situation in Germany in the early years of the Nazi movement.[13]

A specific disillusionment that the Jews of Ontario and Quebec suffered in the thirties was the defeat of legislation in the provincial legislatures to curb the spread of racism and discrimination. On 24 February 1933, an editorial in *Der Yiddisher Zhurnal*, a Canadian Yiddish-language daily, welcomed the introduction of a private bill to ban the spread of race hatred in Ontario. The editorial is interesting in two respects. First, it provides us with information on the extent and character of antisemitism in Ontario.

Second, it shows us that the Jewish community did not feel that its members were "100% Canadians."

> The proposed legislation is aimed not only against the Ku Klux Klan in Ontario, but against every form of discrimination, which we have recently had in our province, where hotel owners have dared to put up signs with the inscription: "No Entrance for Jews" or "Jews and Dogs Not Allowed." Or [they add] such postscripts as: "Jews Need Not Apply."
>
> If one considers that the proposer of the legislation is not an extreme radical, is not a Jew, but a 100% Canadian and, moreover, a member in good standing of the Conservative Party, one is forced to conclude that the existing sort of discrimination and race hatred which is so maliciously spread touches not only Jews and foreigners in general, but the entire population of the province. It will suffice to recall the evil deeds of the Klansmen in Oakville, Ontario, a while back. The whole province suffered and suffers still from the "gowned" defenders of the night who are afraid to show themselves in the light of day without masks. Peo-

ple of Martin's pedigree [Argue Martin, MPP for Hamilton West, who was introducing the bill] understand that the whole province is getting a bad reputation on account of the few fanatics who have appointed themselves defenders of Canada and patriotism.[14]

The bill had no chance of passing, although it did make it to a second reading. On 14 March, the *Toronto Daily Star* reported that the government was willing to give it a hearing but wanted to make sure that it did not become law. The *Star* cited Premier Henry: "'I think,' said Hon. G.S. Henry...'that this is a matter that deserves discussion.' His emphasis on the last word indicated that that was about all he thought it deserved."[15] The *Star* went on to explain: "Members' laughter indicated that sending a bill to the legal committee was, in their opinion, on par with sending a man to Siberia."[16] E. F. Singer argued that the legislation would not interfere with private communication between resorts or hotels and their clientele with regard to the barring of certain racial or minority groups, but would merely stop "'gratuitous insults' being offered to certain citizens in public." He too referred to signs that read "Jews and dogs not allowed," and further suggested "that a community of dogs would perhaps be more charitable toward Jews and Englishmen."[17]

On 11 April the *Zhurnal* reported that both the Martin bill in Ontario and a similar bill introduced by Premier Taschereau in Quebec had been thrown out. Martin's bill did not get support, it was reported, because members were afraid that it would be a threat to freedom of speech. Premier Taschereau himself rescinded his bill, arguing that the antisemitic attacks in Arcand's papers had been toned down and that it was not worth putting freedom of expression at risk. These explanations notwithstanding, the Jewish community was disappointed and suspected that the lawmakers were not really interested in helping prevent the spread of race hatred, especially if the hatred and discrimination were directed at Jews. In fact, many Jews believed that the defeat of the Martin bill in the legislature gave a certain impetus and licence to antisemites to spread their poison. As an editorial in the *Zhurnal* stated:

The rejection of the Martin bill in the last session of the Ontario legislature gave the antisemites a kind of unofficial licence for their ugly antisemitism and discrimination....

As everyone knows, M.P.P. Martin of Hamilton, Ontario, introduced a bill to ban discriminatory writing or announcements with regard to race, nationality or creed.... In summer resorts around Toronto the signs "Gentiles Only" are very familiar.

XXVI   THE RIOT AT CHRISTIE PITS

In dance areas and at beaches on the Lakeshore Highway they were present only in exceptional cases and those few who put up such signs were looked upon with repulsion. But now with the rejection of the Martin bill they have received a stamp of approval saying "one may."

... On Lakeshore Road, on the side from which American tourists come, a sign was put up at a beach stating that this beach is for Gentiles only. Two years ago the Toronto City Council, not caring that the sign was on land which didn't belong to the city, protested against it with the result that the sign was taken down.

Now after the Martin bill has failed, the same sign has reappeared with an even greater brazenness, just as though the owners wanted to say thereby that they have permission to do it. The legislature certainly knew that such discrimination predominates and was satisfied with scolding the owners of such places. In fact they are looking through their fingers at them because they didn't want to intrude upon the "hundred percent Canadians" under the pretext that that would limit personal freedom.[18]

The failure of the authorities in Quebec and Ontario to take official action against the spread of racist propaganda and practices heightened the tension among Jews at a time when antisemitism was on the rise both at home and abroad. Any analysis of antisemitism in Canada during the early 1930s must emphasize both its scope and its intensity. Although frequently camouflaged as nationalism, particularly in Quebec, and disguised and justified in terms of rising unemployment and economic uncertainties, the effects of antisemitism for the Jews were unmistakably clear: increasingly stereotyped by media attacks as "radical, disloyal, unbelievers, domineering, cosmopolitan, and otherwise as being a danger to Canadian society,"[19] Jews encountered growing prejudice and discrimination because of their religion or ethnicity. The consequences of this had their most serious impact during the 1930s, as officials in the highest reaches of Canadian government, succumbing to various internal pressures, pursued a systematic policy of barring Jewish refugees from entry into Canada, thus ensuring their deaths at the hands of the Nazis.[20]

Certainly, the presence of Nazism in Europe had a spillover effect on the Canadian scene with "a flood of anti-Semitic and Fascist pamphlets pouring into Canada through the mails...and the forming of English-

and French-language groups modelled after Hitler's troops."[21] But as David Rome observed:

> In spite of the strong imported influences upon this movement from parallel European anti-Semitism, the Canadian mania was largely just that—Canadian. Its own scholars developed its world view and dogma and preached it by virtue of their own authority.... [They] needed no foreign references. It was to Canadian nationalism that they attached and from Canadian history they sought their examples.[22]

The antisemitism of the early 1930s, then, was not a new phenomenon for Canada, although its scope was suddenly intensified. But the younger generation's sensitivity to and awareness of this rising tide of anti- Jewishness differed from that of its parents. Rome has aptly captured this difference:

> A generation of refugees from Czarist Russia, accustomed to the hostile glance of the passerby and of the official, is not as likely to be injured by a similar meeting in Montreal. But his [sic] son who was taught in school and by his juvenile reading of the decent expectations of western European and American equality, whose life is less tightly limited even by the invisible ghetto walls—this generation is likely to be stunned even by a static measure of hostility, especially when sensitized by shocking happenings overseas which can readily be transposed to this country.[23]

It was therefore not at all surprising that members of this younger generation refused to tolerate the more blatant displays of antisemitism in Toronto and were determined to react against them by the use of force.[24]

The structure of this book and our conclusions about the causes and significance of the riot at Christie Pits are shaped by a number of methodological considerations.

Our study makes no claim to be a fully objective account of the Swastika Club and the Christie Pits riot. Any account may be accused of bias by the members of one side or another who claim that their views were either misrepresented or not fully represented. For the most part, those with whom we spoke about what occurred at Christie Pits were Jewish.

Not surprisingly, their accounts were heavily coloured by recollections of the prevailing antisemitism, which, they maintained, lay at the root of the tension and conflict.

Unfortunately, with only a few exceptions, we were unable to locate individuals from the "other side"—members of either the Swastika Club or the Pit Gang—who were in a position to provide us with an alternate perspective for appreciating the formation of the Swastika Club and the conflicts between Jews and Gentiles that culminated in a riot. One individual who was in an excellent position to shed light on the matter adamantly refused to speak with us. Perhaps other researchers will be more successful in this area.

Our conversations with participants in the riot occurred in 1984 and 1985, more than fifty years after the event. We are aware that the passage of time clouds memories and that the more remote the event the greater the potential distortion. Two examples will suffice:

"Do you remember who played in the ballgame?"

"I think the Lizzies were playing McCormicks. It was either McCormicks or it was…."

"Ever heard of a team called St. Peter's?"

"St. Pete's was in a different league."

[St. Peter's was one of the teams playing in the ballgame.]

"Do you remember Rabbi Sachs?"

"Ya, I remember, but I don't remember him having anything to do with it [Christie Pits]."

"Do you remember something called the League for the Defence of Jewish Rights?"

"Not in those days, no sir. We were the defence, but there was no organization."

[A second respondent:] "There was no League."

[At the time the League for the Defence of Jewish Rights served as the representative voice of the Jewish community.]

A further complication was the almost universal tendency on the part of witnesses to compress the period 1933–45 into an undifferentiated whole in which events were recalled out of their natural sequence. At the same time we were impressed by the range of detail that most of those interviewed offered, indicating the special place held by the

Christie Pits riot in their memories. The indelible impression left by this event, we will suggest, has coloured these commentators' views about the nature of Jewish life in Toronto to this day. More specifically, the phase of antisemitism that culminated in the riot served as the main focal point around which they organized their subsequent views both about antisemitism and about the level of tolerance accorded Jews in Canadian society more generally. Their thoughts about the current manifestations of antisemitism in Canada, most notably the events surrounding the Zundel and Keegstra trials and the rise of anti-Zionist sentiment, seem to be directly influenced by their experiences in Toronto some fifty years earlier.

Perhaps because most were between thirteen and twenty-five years old in 1933, or because of the simple passage of years, their recollections of that period were highly specific. All recalled the antisemitism of the day with apparent ease, but few remembered the formation and activities of the Swastika Club some two weeks prior to the riot. The presence of the club was at best only a vague memory, another instance, but not a qualitatively different one, of the prevalent anti-Jewish sentiment among the larger population. Attempts to jolt their memories met with little success.

In light of these commentators' chronological distance from the period of this study, the most credible accounts of the events in question are to be found in contemporary newspaper reports. From 1 August until 24 August, reports about the Swastika Club, the reactions of Toronto Jewry, and the riot and its aftermath appeared in the Toronto press daily, virtually always on the front pages and, on more than several occasions, as headline news. In short, Toronto's four English dailies—the *Toronto Daily Star*, the *Globe*, the *Evening Telegram*, and the *Daily Mail and Empire*—as well as the daily Yiddish paper—*Der Yiddisher Zhurnal*—provided extensive coverage of the unfolding events. As would be expected, these newspapers varied in both the range and the depth of their coverage. However, by synthesizing the various reports we believe that we have succeeded in reconstructing a credible account of the period in question.

Each of the newspapers slanted its coverage according to its respective political bent. In sifting through the numerous reports, we made no deliberate attempt to adopt any particular version. Instead, we tried to incorporate the details provided by each to fashion a comprehensive story. By quoting extensively from these reports, we have allowed the story to tell itself.

We have, however, intentionally quoted most extensively from *Der

Yiddisher Zhurnal. Far more than any other Toronto daily, this paper interpreted the swastika-related activities within the most relevant socio-political context of the time: as an extension of the rampant antisemitism that was wreaking havoc in Nazi-governed Germany. For this newspaper, it was simply impossible to separate one set of events from the other. Unlike the English press, the *Zhurnal* not only reported on Swastika Club activities but continuously editorialized on the club's alleged connection with Fascism in Canada and the sinister spectre of antisemitism here. The *Zhurnal's* readership was more directly affected by the antisemitism of Hitler's Germany than any other group in the city and accepted the paper's point of view without serious challenge.

The accessibility of the newspaper accounts contrasted sharply with the paucity of available police reports pertaining to the Swastika Club's activities and the Christie Pits riot. Checks of their files by the RCMP, the Ontario Provincial Police, and the Metropolitan Toronto Police were all but fruitless. The Metro Police supplied us with the minutes of a special meeting of the Board of Commissioners of Police held on 17 August 1933 at 10:00 a.m. (see Appendix A), but the information contained therein is scanty. The City of Toronto Archives did not include any information bearing directly on our interests. Quite surprisingly, our review of history books about Toronto, even those dealing with the 1930s, made little or no mention of the Swastika Club or Christie Pits. The two notable exceptions are Lita-Rose Betcherman's *The Swastika and the Maple Leaf* and Stephen Speisman's *The Jews of Toronto*. However, both of these are studies of larger topics and thus provide only the barest details about the events that are the focus of this book.

At one level, this study traces a brief but dynamic segment in the history of Toronto Jewry. The events surrounding the Christie Pits riot were for many a dramatic confirmation of what they already knew or at least deeply suspected: that support for anti-Jewish activities among the Gentile population could be marshalled with apparent ease. But the story of the swastika provocations that exploded into the riot serves as a landmark in the history of Toronto Jewry for yet another reason. The Jewish response to the deeply offensive activities of the swastika groups included not only verbal protestations, but, for the first time, collective physical violence as well.

At a broader and deeper level, this book is as much about Canada as about Toronto. In fact, the ethnic violence in Toronto tells us something about Canada as a whole in the early thirties. Our study details how antisemitism manifested itself in a Canadian city during a brief period in the summer of 1933. To be sure, the quality of life for Jews in Canada, and more specifically in Toronto—which had one of the largest concentrations of Canadian Jews—was superior to the uncertainties and pogroms that Jews experienced in eastern Europe. But the relative freedom and opportunities enjoyed in this country notwithstanding, Jews, especially younger Jews, discovered that antisemitism was woven deeply into the fabric of Canadian society. As Irving Abella and Harold Troper revealed in their landmark study of the Canadian government's reaction to the plight of Jewish refugees between 1933 and 1948,[25] antisemitism was entrenched in the attitudes of some of the country's most influential bureaucrats and politicians during this period. The "genteel" antisemitism of some of the highest officials in the land was perched upon the shoulders of the cruder antisemitism of the street.

CHAPTER 1 Toronto the Good—1933

Widespread disorder raged over the vast area of Toronto streets for hours last night when rioting broke out following the display of the swastika emblem on a white quilt at a baseball game in Willowvale Park.

In the disturbance which flared up like a spark among tinder, scores were injured; five were removed to hospital. Lead pipes, baseball bats, broom-handles and clubs were freely used. Police at times were almost overwhelmed or out-numbered; reserves were called out and batons were drawn.

Long after midnight the reserves were still patrolling the affected area as groups of rioters armed with broom-handles hid in alleys or made sorties therefrom to beat up foes.

The disturbance became largely racial in character, bands of Gentiles and of Jews apparently taking up opposing sides in the battle. So far as could be deemed, no arrests took place arising from the disorders, the police apparently devoting their major attention to breaking up the several serious melees which developed, in which hundreds appeared to be fighting at once. More than 8,000 persons were involved or enmeshed in the disturbances shortly after they began.

One Jewish youth was struck over the head with a baseball bat, dozens of others received less serious injuries, fistfights and free-for-alls raged all over the park, police billies were used and for half an hour the situation threatened to get out of hand.

Cries of "The Swastika! The Swastika!" rose in various parts of the park as soon as the taunting emblem made its appearance.

In one confused mass, in sections of the crowd, more than 3,000 surged across the park and over the hill toward the emblem. Fighting broke out as Jews recognized Gentiles.

—*Daily Mail and Empire*, 17 August 1933

Toronto, in 1933, was not about to become a Nazified city in a country terrorized by storm troopers and blackshirts. But of Toronto it might be said that the year 1933 was both the best of times and the worst of times. If you were among the fortunate 60 per cent or so of the bread-winning population who had steady work, hunger would probably not have taken the edge off your pride in a city that boasted the new Canadian Bank of Commerce, the tallest building in the British Empire. If you weren't preoccupied with finding fuel to provide heat during the winter months, you could marvel at the recently completed Maple Leaf Gardens and vicariously share the fate of the local hockey club. If your clothes were not too shabby, you might dine at the luxurious Royal York Hotel, recently constructed on the site of the former stately old Queen's Hotel. And if you had some money tucked away in the family teapot, you could purchase clothing, furniture, appliances, china, silverware, and what have you at Eaton's new College Street store.

For those who had the two bits for a ticket, the Toronto movie theatres were presenting the latest Hollywood fare. In February, Cecil B. DeMille's *The Sign of the Cross*, starring Fredric March, Elissa Landi, Claudette Colbert, and Charles Laughton, was playing at the Uptown. If a stage show was more to your liking, the opportunity was there to view Eddie Cantor hosting the Ziegfeld Follies' *Whoopee* on stage at the Imperial Theatre. In April, John, Ethel, and Lionel Barrymore were starring in *Rasputin and the Empress* at the Loew's theatre, and in July, Warren William, Ruby Keeler, Joan Blondell, Ginger Rogers, and Dick Powell were on the silver screen in the musical revue *Gold Diggers of 1933*.

Those who couldn't come up with the money for a theatre ticket could listen to the radio, which was at the centre of family entertainment in the pre-television era. A poll conducted by the *Evening Telegram* in March 1933 discovered that the favourite Canadian radio program of Torontonians was the *Neilson Hour*. (The favourite American program was the *Chase and Sanborn Hour*.)[1]

For baseball fans the entire decade was a disappointment (with the exception of Ike Boone's 1934 ball club), but there were a number of colourful players who enlivened the game: pitchers Hot Potato Hamlin, Peanuts Pezzullo, Steamer Lucas, Bots Nekola, Hoot Gibson, Skabotch Samuels, Gunner Cantrell, and Izzy Goldstein, and infielders Stinky Davis, Lu Blue, Porky Howell, Poosh 'Em Up Tony Lazzeri, Twinkletoes Selkirk, Ollie Sax, Flea Clifton, Tubby Reiber, and Oreb Hubbell.[2] The lack of success plaguing the Toronto Maple Leafs and the often superior talents of the best players in the amateur hardball and softball leagues caused amateur teams like the Lizzies (Elizabeth Playground) to have a minor following in the city and star players like Harold "Whataman" Sniderman to attain minor celebrity status.

The Toronto Argonaut football club won the Grey Cup in 1933 for the first time since 1921. But the Toronto Balmy Beach team had captured the cup twice in the past ten years. The condition of professional hockey in Toronto was better than in pro baseball. The famous "Kid Line" of the Leafs—Harvey "Busher" Jackson, Joe Primeau, and Charlie Conacher—was red hot on offence, and King Clancy and Red Horner provided a solid defence. Although the Leafs didn't win the Stanley Cup in 1933, they finished first in the Canadian division.

Looking back at the early thirties from the present, it is difficult to believe that prices could have been so low! An unskilled labourer today would count himself a millionaire if he could purchase commodities at 1933 prices:

A six room house on Boulton Avenue was advertised for $15 a month and for $50 a month you could rent a 10-room house at Bloor and Spadina Avenue. Bungalows were being sold for $150 down and prime sirloin beef from prize stock that had been exhibited at the Royal Winter Fair could be had for 25 cents a pound. Sugar was 10 pounds for 46 cents; tea was 35 cents a pound and coffee 39 cents. A young fellow could take his girl to the movies and have a dish of ice cream on the way home for a total expenditure on the whole night of not more than 50 cents.[3]

Eaton's was selling back bacon at twenty-two cents a pound; a twenty-four pound bag of pastry flour could be had for fifty-nine cents; two dozen oranges were forty-nine cents; butter was twenty-one cents a pound; six sixteen-ounce tins of pork and beans could be had for twenty-five cents; fifteen pounds of potatoes were going for thirty-three cents. Eaton's Grill Room was advertising a luncheon special: tomato-juice cocktail, jellied-chicken-and-ham mould salad with sliced tomato and celery curl, mayonnaise, ice cream with cake, tea, coffee, or milk. All for the magnificent sum of thirty-five cents!

Big-ticket items, too, seem a giveaway by our present standards. Gas ranges were selling for $37.95; a four-piece bedroom suite could be had for $80.75; a new Plymouth four-door sedan could be driven away for $730; a steel bed with spring and mattress was $12.95; a wood stove, $13.75. Canada Steamship Lines was offering a holiday cruise from

Toronto to Montreal and Quebec City, including sightseeing and first-class hotels for the eight-day trip, for $95 return. A house in the Annex could be bought for $2,000; a mansion in Forest Hill was, of course, more expensive, at $15,000.

The list of "bargains" could go on and on. But the fact is that Toronto was then living through the worst phase of the Great Depression. Unemployment, poverty, and hunger were the lot of millions of Canadians and about one-third of Torontonians. There were no unemployment insurance, medicare, family allowance, or other social programs to cushion the shock. There was only "relief." But though tens of thousands availed themselves of it,[4] there was a tremendous sense of shame attached to being on "pogey." Novelist Hugh Garner catches the mood of those standing in line to receive their hand-outs:

> "Look at some of these people carryin' club-bags and paper to wrap their stuff up in. They don't fool nobody. I seen a man last week walk back two car stops along Dundas before he got in a street car goin' the other way, just so's people wouldn't know he'd been here. He had his rations in a suitcase too. It's gettin' so everybody that carries a suitcase on the street get the name 'Pogey Stiff'" .... He waited for his packages to be placed in a large paper bag by a man across the counter, and watched several other people shoving their supplies into old army kitbags or suitcases. The bolder ones walked out to the street with their stigmata held out for all the city to see. It wasn't only Cabbagetown and the West End slums that were represented in the relief lines now. It seemed that the depression, as it was beginning to be called, was, like a war or revolution, a leveller of the population.[5]

Unskilled labour, lucky to be employed at all, could be paid as little as a dollar a day—or even less. Skilled labourers still employed would take home fifteen or twenty dollars a week. Toronto geographer James Lemon points out that in "sweatshops like Eaton's, which had earlier been a model for the industry, piecework wages were cut drastically, and the women were forced to work faster, with their pace being timed by stop-watches. They could expect to be fired if they did not reach the production level of the minimum weekly wage of $12.50 established in the 1920s."[6] In light of these wage rates, the "bargain" prices that existed then no longer seem such bargains.

Toronto in the early thirties was a parochial, provincial, and puri-
tanical city that still felt a strong attachment to the British Empire.
The ethnic minorities—Jews and Italians for the most part—were
tolerated and, officially, treated according to the tenets of British
fair play and justice; but they were outsiders ethnically, religiously, linguistically, culturally, and economically.[7] Politically the city
was dominated by the Orange Order. Socially and economically
it was led by wealthy Tories with long pedigrees. Official Toronto
went through the Depression in a rather self-satisfied manner. It
relied upon the police and the courts to keep Communism and
socialism in check.

Not surprisingly, the Depression polarized society into warring
camps. A number of unemployed and working-class people joined or
passively supported radical movements, although electoral support for
radical parties was not very great. Both the Communist Party of Canada
(CPC) and the newly organized Co-operative Commonwealth Federation (CCF) enjoyed a certain popularity among some groups in the
city. A far larger number of the British majority in Toronto, however,
had become fearful of Communism, which it identified largely with the
eastern- and southern-European immigrants who had come to Canada since 1880. After the Bolshevik Revolution in Russia in 1917 and the
General Strike in Winnipeg in 1919, majority sentiment in the country
turned against "foreign" (i.e., non-British) immigrants. This xenophobia
was in part responsible for the closing off of Canadian immigration in
the 1920s, and it played a not insignificant role in the "none is too many"
policies of the Mackenzie King government.[8]

In Toronto, anti-Communism was thus inextricably intertwined
with xenophobia and antisemitism. As Michiel Horn suggests:

It is hard to escape the conclusion that anti-Communism in Toronto was linked not only to a general dislike of foreigners but
also to a more specific dislike of Jews.… The linking of Communists with foreigners had some evidence to support it, though for
most Torontonians it was probably a canon of faith not requir-
ing evidence. While much of the leadership of the CPC was Brit-
ish-born and of British stock, some 95 percent of the members
were of non-British extraction, most of them European-born. The
largest foreign group was Finnish, but there was also a sizeable

Ukrainian and a smaller Jewish element. The last of these was particularly noticeable in Toronto.[9]

Rick Salutin recalls that one of the Toronto papers "editorialized that though not all Jews were Communists, all Communists were Jews."[10]

On 1 May 1928, Brigadier-General Dennis ("Dennie") Colbarn Draper became Chief of the Toronto Police Department.[11] Draper's official assumption of duties as Chief Constable on this date is ironic, since the first of May is considered the international day of labour by radical parties and trade unions, a day they mark with parades and speeches. It was this "red" assembly and speech making that Draper was determined to prevent.

The first official shot in the anti-Communist crusade was fired by the Toronto Board of Commissioners of Police in the fall of 1928 when it adopted new guidelines concerning meetings held in public. From this point on, it would be unlawful for a speaker to address an audience in public in a foreign tongue. The board argued that police officers, unable to understand what was being said, would be forced to assume that appeals to sedition and treason were being made. Chief Draper therefore announced: "Hereafter all proceedings and addresses at all public meetings are to be in the English language, and no disorderly or seditious reflections on our form of government or the King or any constituted authority will be allowed." As Michiel Horn reports:

> No prohibition of French or of church services in foreign languages was intended, the chief explained. The real purpose soon became clear with the arrest of Philip Halperin, editor of the Yiddish Communist weekly *Der Kampf* [*sic*], on a charge of disorderly conduct after he addressed a Lenin Memorial meeting at the Standard Theatre in Yiddish. "We are determined to stamp out this communist menace," Chief Constable Draper told a *Star* reporter, adding that although the constable who had arrested Halperin did not understand Yiddish he was sure that British institutions were being attacked.[12]

In a further decree the commissioners threatened to revoke the licences of halls, theatres, shows, etc. that rented their facilities to those organizing "Communist or Bolshevist public meetings."

The free-speech issue typified the narrowness of the city administration in those years. This narrowness extended far beyond the political realm. With regard to public morality, Chief Draper's tactics were quite ludicrous, according to the recollection of John Gray: "I remember in the 1930s when the police chief General Draper stationed constables with stop-watches in the wings of the Royal Alexandra Theatre, timing the kisses in the Lunts' production of *The Guardsman*, ready to bring down the curtain if they lasted more than 20 seconds."[13]

Harry Rasky tells of his own run-in with the blue laws of Toronto in the thirties:

> Once on a Sunday I was picked up by the police for breaking the Lord's Day Alliance. I don't know with whom the Lord was allied. But in Christian Canada and proper Toronto, I was a criminal for helping collect bills that would pay for the next week's supply of chickens…. After the collection period on Sunday, there was the question of what to do in Toronto. Fear of the Lord was every-where. At Earlscourt Park there were tennis courts; no nets could be hung. There were sandboxes and swings; the swings were padlocked. Padlocked! Once, when I found one free and began swinging, a policeman in his bobby hat grabbed my shoulder. His words have never left me: "Nobody swings on Sunday!" Amen.[14]

Toronto, which he believed was a paradigm for the country, had the kind of moral stuffiness that caused Aleister Crowley to write: "Toronto as a city carries out the idea of Canada as a country. It is a calculated crime both against the aspirations of the soul and the affections of the heart."[15]

The anti-Communist crusade started a chain reaction that created some of the pre-conditions for the Christie Pits riot five years later. First, it intensified the identification in the minds of many between Com-munism and Jews.[16] It emphasized the foreignness of the immigrants, their supposed ungratefulness to Canada, their alleged unwillingness to adopt British ideals and values, and their seeming lack of appreciation for the British tradition. Three of the four Toronto daily papers support-ed the Commissioners of Police and the Toronto Police Department and cultivated the image of the foreigner as a radical and the radical as a foreigner. As Stephen Speisman points out:

> There were disturbing signs, especially in newspaper comments stereotyping the Jew as a radical and otherwise as being a dan-ger to Canadian society. Postwar economic difficulties, coupled

with the "Red Scare," produced widespread paranoia and xen-ophobia in Toronto. Moreover, because Jews had been active in movements for social change in Europe and because Yiddish was so closely related to German, the language identified in the local press with Bolshevism, some Torontonians began to see all Jews as revolutionaries.[17]

As well, the need for forcible prevention or disruption of radical assemblies and speeches meant that the police had to divert sizeable numbers of men to this purpose. (Some observers, in the aftermath of the Christie Pits riot, blamed the lack of prompt police reinforcements for the spread of violence at Christie Pits. Police were out in force, as we shall see, breaking up a meeting of unemployed in Allan Gardens at the same time as heads were being cracked at the Pits.) Several meet-ings in the summer of 1929 were either prevented by a show of police force or violently stopped.[18] By the summer of 1933, there were regular clashes between police and various unemployed and workers' groups in several Toronto parks. For example, on Saturday, 3 June 1933, police clashed with about five hundred members of the Unemployed Workers' Association at Trinity Park. As the *Evening Telegram* described the en-counter: "Meeting the 'ganging' tactics employed by the demonstrators, the police asked no quarter and gave none."[19]

On 25 July, police broke up a meeting held by a radical group in Trin-ity Park and on the following day police on motorcycles dispersed a much larger crowd that had again gathered in the park. According to the *Toronto Daily Star*, "Dense clouds of smoke which came from exhausts on machines of a squad of motorcycle officers was [*sic*] the main expe-dient resorted to by city police last evening to break up an unemployed demonstration at Trinity Park which had attracted between five and six thousand people…."[20]

Several things emerge here: that from 1929 a pattern of violence had been established in the city parks, and that in the eyes of most of the Toronto press, the instigators of the violence were radical organizations composed almost entirely of foreigners—read "Jews." Finally, although three of the daily papers stood squarely behind the city administration in relation to the free-speech issue, the *Toronto Daily Star* distinguished itself as a champion of the right to freedom of speech and assembly in public areas for all law abiding groups. For its supposed "softness on Communism" the *Evening Telegram* referred to the *Star* as "the Big Brother of the Little Reds."[21]

Although the polarization between the *Star* and *Tely* has a long history and extends far beyond this single issue, it was to become extremely important in the months prior to the formation of the Swastika Club and the Christie Pits riot. During this period public opinion concerning Nazism in Germany was being shaped in Toronto. When we recall that the violence both at the Beaches and at the Pits was occasioned by the display of the swastika emblem, we can see just how important the press reports concerning the German Nazis were. The *Star* was the outspoken champion of the Jewish minority; the *Tely* was the most anti-Jewish of the Toronto newspapers. In a sense, the Beaches incidents and the riot at the Pits may be seen as clashes between *Star* and *Tely* readers and, ultimately, between the differing views of Toronto and Canada of the *Star* and *Tely* themselves.

In 1904, in a speech before the Empire Club in Toronto, Frederick Barlow Cumberland said, "We are trustees for the British race. We hold this land in allegiance."[22] He was, in the context of the city at the time, merely stating the obvious. Even twenty-seven years later, in 1931, people of British descent constituted more than 80 per cent of the city's population. And a goodly number of these "British" Canadians identified closely with the Motherland and with the British Empire. Each week in its Saturday edition, the *Evening Telegram* included a page of news entitled, "Echoes from the Motherland." Support for Canada's participation in both the Boer War and the First World War was motivated to a large extent by concern for the fate of Britain and the Empire. But the "Britishness" of the majority of Torontonians was in fact an exaggerated display, a kind of play-acting at being more British than the British. The well-known tendency of colonials or ethnics living away from the *Heimat* (native country) to distort certain aspects of nationality or ethnicity leads to an unintentional caricature of the manners of the mother country. In the case of Toronto, along with this hyper-Britishness went a suspicion of foreigners, hostility to groups conceived to be potentially subversive of British ideals (e.g., Communists, socialists, anarchists, etc.), conservativism in politics, public celebration of the Protestant religion, and an attempt (largely successful, in spite of the fact that they couldn't stop the streetcars from running on Sunday) to constrict the social life of the city by means of blue laws and social pressure. Hugh Garner describes the example of "Mabel's family," which "had been Conservative for generations, and like most of the Cabbagetowners she was still a rabid Conservative, as well as a monarchist, an antiforeigner, a passive anti-Catholic, and more British than the people of the British Isles."[23]

Not all the people of British background in the city were puritan jingoists suffering from xenophobia. However, there was a sizeable number of them, and they were largely able to have their way. As D. C. Masters suggests:

> All Torontonians, of course, were not strict Protestant moralists, but there were enough of that type to fix the tone of the city. The constant insistence of a strict observance of Sunday was one indication of their attitude. For many citizens, to be on the streets on the Sabbath, for reasons other than church-going, placed their souls or their social position in jeopardy, and whether or not streetcars would run was a hot subject of debate during the 1890s. In this respect Toronto was a mirror image of Belfast blueness. The common epithets of "Toronto the Good" and "British Town on American Soil" were extended by most to include the "Belfast of Canada" and "the bush metropolis of the Orange lodges." The conservative and ultra-Protestant Orange society was an integral component of the city's flavour, or flavourlessness, as many would say.[24]

The young people at the Beaches who donned swastikas and "mixed it up" with Jewish youths, for example, or those who went to the aid of the members of the Pit Gang at Christie Pits, holding aloft the swastika flag, were overwhelmingly Anglo-Canadians. Many would have come from homes where the transmission of "Britishness," xenophobia, and antisemitism were part of the process of socialization. Most were probably readers of the *Evening Telegram*, and many were from families that had some involvement with the Orange Order. "We Beaches people," Robert Fulford recalls, "we *Telegram* readers, were loyal in the way that only the petty bourgeois can be loyal: we accepted England and the King as fixed stars in the heavens; when we sang 'There'll Always Be an England,' as we did on every conceivable occasion, we believed it firmly."[25]

If there was a centre of Protestantism and the British connection, it was the Orange Order in Toronto. The Order had been founded in 1795, in the village of Loughgall, in the county of Armagh, after a violent clash between rival Protestant and Catholic groups, "to better coordinate local Protestant defences."[26] Of the many local Protestant societies at the time, the Orange Order was the one that succeeded in organizing itself nationally and, ultimately, internationally. Brought to British North America by Irish colonists and Irish military personnel,

Orangeism in Canada grew with the country, developing along lines dictated by the unfolding settlement geography of a new society. It assumed a rural and small town character. Protestant Irish immigrants, the largest group moving to that essentially empty land, not only brought Orangeism with them as part of their Orange cultural baggage but insured by their numerical preponderance that their Orange institution would not go unnoticed. Neither could it be suffocated by preexisting political and social alignments.[27]

Toronto was one of the largest centres of Orange strength. Although Orangeism was not able to attract many members of the Family Compact that ruled Toronto and Upper Canada before Confederation, or to bring into the fold prominent members of the economic elite in the late nineteenth and early twentieth centuries, the Orange lodges had enough support in Toronto to be kingmakers in civic politics. Having successfully shed its exclusively Irish character (although the Irish still predominated), the order was able to attract Protestants from a variety of ethnic backgrounds. To be sure, their reasons for joining were not always the purest, for the order had control of the patronage positions in the city.

In Toronto the increase in the number of Orange lodges, from seventeen in 1870 to fifty-nine in 1920, reflected the population growth of the Protestant city.... The order was a powerful force in the city's administration and the sense of power and its control of patronage made its strength self-perpetuating. Many of the newcomers were attracted to the fraternity by both an appreciation of its principles and motives of opportunism.[28]

Many of Toronto's policemen and firemen were members of Orange lodges. A good number of its civic workers were also Orangemen. It was difficult for a Jew or a Catholic to get one of the patronage positions from the city government. The mayor of Toronto and most of the aldermen were either Orangemen or had the support of the Orange lodges. The *Telegram* championed lists of candidates for civic elections, and most of those it supported were Orangemen, who were duly elected. The parade on 12 July, commemorating the victory of the Protestant troops of William of Orange over the Catholic army of James II at the Boyne River, was a major event in the life of the city. Coverage of the Orange parade, even in the "liberal" *Star*, was spread out over several pages. As the *Telegram* quipped, in 1894:

> Like the temple of old Egypt
> Empty as a noxious mine
> Stood the City Hall deserted
> For "the byes" were all in line.

And on 12 July 1933, Toronto's Mayor Stewart, Chief Constable Draper, and the city dignitaries were all there, following King Billy's white stallion, which bore the Orange motto "No Surrender." Civic workers, too, were out in force.

The Orangemen were charged above all with defending the interests of the British Empire. As part of the Orange oath, a new recruit had to swear to "steadily maintain the connection between the Colonies of British America and the Mother Country, and be ever ready to resist all attempts to weaken British influence, or dismember the British Empire."[29] In the Canadian context it meant primarily opposing the spread of the French language and blocking the extension of the Catholic separate schools. (It is one of the ironies of history that a Conservative premier of Ontario, William Davis, a good Orangeman from Brampton, should have initiated a move to provide full government funding for the Catholic Schools in the province of Ontario. *Paris vaut bien une messe!*)

Orange antisemitism was inextricably bound up with xenophobia, anti-Communism, and Protestant moralism, fed by negative stereotypes of the Jew, and tinged with racism. It was quite different from Catholic antisemitism in the province of Quebec where, as David Rome has argued, the Jew, among other things, was hated because he was seen as part of the English community.[30] In Toronto, and elsewhere in Orange circles, the Jew was hated because he was most definitely not British! The *Evening Telegram* was forever complaining about the fact that some Jews, and certainly not the best examples "of their race," according to the *Tely*, were unwilling to accept British ideals, British institutions, and British manners.[31]

What did it mean to be Jewish in the "Belfast of Canada" in 1933? What did it mean to be a Jewish youth then? Where did the Jews live? What did they do for a living? What kind of lives did they lead? How did they relate to "British" Toronto and to other ethnic groups? How did they cope with antisemitism?

There were 45,305 Jews in Toronto in 1931, and this represented about 7.2 per cent of the total population of the city (excluding the suburbs). In no area of the city did the Jews constitute a majority, although Jews made up 30.5 per cent of the residents of Ward 4 (which included the Spadina Avenue area south of College Street and Kensington Market) and 18.6 per cent of the residents of Ward 5 (which contained Christie Pits). Jews constituted the smallest percentage of the population (0.08 per cent) in Ward 8 (which contained the eastern beaches). Nevertheless, the Jews were the largest minority group by far in the city (the Italians were next with about 2.6 per cent of the city's population) and, at that time, the most visible minority.[32] (Appendix B, Table 1 shows the distribution of British, Jewish, and Italian residents of Toronto by ward.)

Of the 45,305 Jews in the city in 1931, only 18,612 were born in Canada; 1,400 were born in the UK, and 25,264 were "foreign born." Of the latter, 12,933 were born in Poland, 8,717 in Russia, and 1,216 in the United States. For the Jewish population ten years of age and over for Canada as a whole, Yiddish was the mother tongue of 124,408 or 95.54 per cent of the total. English was the mother tongue of only 1,547 Jews or 1.18 per cent of the Jewish population of the country. In Toronto in 1931, 1,366 Jews ten years of age and older spoke no other language than Yiddish. (See Appendix B, Tables 2 and 3.)

Although the vast majority of Jews in Toronto in 1931 (92.8 per cent) spoke both English and Yiddish, there were slightly more Yiddish than English speakers. (97.87 per cent of Toronto's Jews could speak Yiddish; 96.38 per cent could speak English.) However, since we know that for the country as a whole Yiddish was the mother tongue of 95.54 per cent of Jews, we can safely assume that most bilingual Jews (Yiddish-English) learned English as a second language. Furthermore, since a majority of Toronto Jews were foreign born, we can assume that those who immigrated as adolescents or adults were not entirely fluent in English.

On the occupational front, most gainfully employed Jews—66.86 per cent of the total—were working either in manufacturing or in merchandising. This was in sharp contrast to the population as a whole in which 33.48 per cent of the total had occupations in these areas. The discrepancy was especially pronounced in the manufacture of clothing and fur products. More Jews in Toronto earned their livelihood in the needle trades than in any other single branch of the economy. And most of these Jews were wage earners, not employers. Of the 12,371 Jews in Canada who were engaged in the making of clothes in 1931, 90.2 per cent were wage workers. In Toronto, they worked for the most part in small shops and factories along Spadina Avenue and along the thoroughfares that intersected it from King Street north to Dundas Street.[33] At the best of times they worked long hours for relatively little pay; during the Depression, wages were cut, and conditions of employment worsened. Dissatisfaction with the evils of such a system spurred trade unionism and encouraged radical political groups—anarchists, Communists, and socialists of a variety of stripes. Socialism, trade unionism, and Yiddishism underlay the character of the secular Jewish culture of the Jewish community in the Spadina area.[34]

Jews were over-represented in commerce, manufacturing, laundering, entertainment, and sport, and under-represented in everything else. (See Appendix B, Table 5.) Indeed, the image of the Jew in the public mind—as the tailor, presser, cutter, and cap maker on or off Spadina, the retailer of dry goods, shoes, confections and condiments, haberdashery, poultry, broadloom, and hardware in many areas of the city; the ubiquitous rag "n bones man, junkman, peddler, or "sheeny"; the newspaper boy, street hawker, or huckster; and the boxer, comedian, agent, or manager—was based on the fact that one encountered higher percentages of Jews in these occupations than in other areas.[35]

In Ontario, discrimination in housing and recreation was blatant as Jews were barred from certain occupations and were either refused admission or made to feel increasingly unwelcome in certain social and recreational circles. Ben Kayfetz has attested to discrimination against Jews in medicine, engineering, and education in the thirties.[36] His remarks on the restrictions in housing show not only the prejudice that existed against Jews, but the fact that they were condemned to a *de facto* ghettoization. Kayfetz, in fact, outlines his own cognitive map of the city:

> Housing was clearly restricted. I didn't realize this in my innocence. I knew that the area from Bloor to Queen and University to Ossington was predominantly Jewish. I vaguely knew that out beyond this area there was a vast *terra incognita* inhabited mainly by Gentiles. What happened when Jews tried to rent or buy in these areas I never knew because the idea had certainly not occurred to me. It was brought to my attention on contact with refugees from Germany and Czechoslovakia who came to Canada in the late 1930s and from whom I heard that Jews couldn't live there. On one occasion a phrase of theirs caught me up short and shook me when one of them referred to a section of the city as "*wo Juden*

nicht duerfen"—where Jews are not permitted. This had such a ring of repression in it that I wondered if we were living in the same city. The answer was that we were, but I had never ventured out of the area of my immediate environment—at least not to rent or buy. In 1941, the war was already on, and I overheard my employer's wife phoning hour after hour in reply to advertisements. Each time she called—she was looking for an apartment—she would ask as a matter of course "Is it restricted?" I was somewhat taken aback. She occasionally explained, "We're Jewish," but most of the time the code word "restricted" was fully understood on the other side of the phone. I realized then—and even more so in retrospect—that this was a degrading, humiliating procedure to go through but go through with it she did.[37]

Most significant, in contrast to earlier anti-Jewish sentiment, which was typically expressed in actions against individuals, by 1933 a blanket condemnation of Jews had emerged. More than ever, Jews now felt that antisemitism was firmly embedded in the very fabric of society.

Early in 1932, E. F. Singer, a Jewish member of the Ontario legislature, exposed the unfair practices of some insurance companies towards Jewish businessmen. As Jews they were considered bad risks and either were expected to pay higher premiums than Gentile clients or were refused insurance altogether. Support for such discriminatory treatment was readily forthcoming from various publications, one of which, *La semaine religieuse de Québec*, wrote:

> Who can count the multitude of usurers, crooks, defrauding merchants and bankrupts, incendiaries among the Jews of all nations? The attitude of certain insurance companies towards Jewish stores is instructive, conclusive. It is therefore reasonable and in keeping with the general good to tell citizens, "Do not borrow from Jews, have nothing to do with them, don't...."[38]

Not only were entire suburbs closed to Jews, but restrictive covenants prohibiting the sale of certain land or houses to Jewish buyers were upheld in the courts. In certain parts of Toronto, signs were posted stipulating that Jews were unwelcome. Summer resorts in the Muskoka region barred Jewish guests, and some hotels posted signs advertising, "Patronage exclusively Gentile." As Betcherman writes:

...the signs were like weeds. Eradicated in one area, they sprang up in another. Motorists driving into Toronto were greeted by a large "Gentiles Only" sign on a private beach just outside the city limits. Summer resorts displayed signs stating "No Jews or Dogs Allowed" and their owners distributed brochures assuring prospective guests that their clientele was restricted.[39]

As Rome put it: "The inflammatory agitation on the political and journalistic level could not but find translation on the social, professional level." In his examination of the Toronto professional scene, Speisman noted:

> Before the war and into the twenties, anti-Semitic sentiment, while usually veiled, appeared also when Jews attempted to seek employment outside the factory. Jews were seldom hired as sales staff at the major department stores or as clerks in local banks. Jewish university graduates who wished to become teachers found acceptance in Toronto schools impossible, and frequently sought careers in law or medicine as a result. Even independent professionals found Toronto rife with discrimination. Lawyers and engineers could not find employment with Gentile firms. Moreover, Jewish medical graduates were refused as interns in local hospitals, found it difficult to locate their offices in fashionable districts, and sometimes had to disguise the fact that they were Jews in order to secure desirable accommodation.[40]

Needless to say, the difficulties encountered by Jews in the professions were not confined to any particular region of Canada. In Regina in 1934, the General Hospital was informed by the superintendent that a Jewish radiologist was unacceptable to the staff and to the public, and that physicians with Anglo-Saxon sounding names were preferable, even at a higher salary, to Drs. Teitlebaum and Friedman.[41] And to quote Rome once again: "The library at the University of Toronto rejected a highly recommended application of a Jewish man frankly because, upon graduation, he would have difficulty in finding a position in the profession, and this would spoil the placement record of the school."[42]

The relative absence of Jews in other occupational groupings in Toronto is to be explained in part by the restrictions placed upon Jewish applicants, candidates, students, and professionals.

From the 1930s through the Second World War, Jews found it difficult to enter certain professions.... Jews could study law, medicine and dentistry only on a *numerus clausus* basis, and many a worthy Jewish student had to seek his livelihood in other pursuits. At the University of Toronto School of Dentistry, a dexterity requirement was a favourite ploy for keeping Jewish students out; the small number who made it into the program often found themselves subjected to open abuse by antisemitic professors. Graduates of the University of Toronto Medical School found that their prestigious diplomas could not obtain internships for them, so an entire generation of Jewish medical students emigrated to the United States seeking hospital posts to hone their craft. Canada did not want them.[43]

Rosenberg, writing in 1939, called attention to the fact that "Jewish professors, university lecturers and junior college principals in Canada numbered 11 (3 women), of which 5 were in Quebec, 4 in Ontario and 2 in British Columbia. The number of Jewish professors and teachers in Canadian universities is abnormally low, forming only three-tenths of one per cent of all university lecturers and college principals in Canada."[44]

It was practically impossible for a Jew to get a job as sales staff at any of the big department stores, and very few Jews were hired by the banks and financial institutions (it was standard practice in those days to ask for the applicant's religion on the employment form). Very few Jews worked for Ontario or Toronto Hydro or for government departments. One interviewee told us that a relative of his got a job in a company known for its discriminatory hiring practices by writing "Protestant" in the space reserved for religion on the application form. Her boss discovered that she was Jewish (she was absent on the major Jewish holidays), and she was summarily dismissed. Another recounted that, after applying for a job at one of the major department stores in Toronto, he saw the personnel manager crumple his application form and throw it in the waste bin only moments after assuring the applicant that his application would be given "careful consideration."

Another element of concern, and this emerged as a major theme in the interviews concerning the Christie Pits riot, was the antisemitism within the police force. One participant described his encounter with the police on the night of the riot as follows:

Now twice the police grabbed us and they were antisemitic. They were; they either didn't shove their nose in until somebody was getting the worst of it, to break it up, or they were strictly on their side. I remember twice they grabbed me, there was quite a few of them there and they grabbed me and they took me away and bawled me out…and told me not to go back there. And I went right back. And the third time they took me down to Markham and London and whacked me around a little bit. And that's the experience I had. That's exactly what happened with me.

He described another run-in with the police a few years prior to the riot, but at a time when Draper was already Chief of Police: "So I listened to the radio in around 1927. I was 13 years old. And a policeman walked behind me and I remember it was a rainy day and he kicked me in the behind and said, 'You little Jew bastard move on.' In them years it was a fact. I hit him. Sure I did. It happened more than once. They were very, very bad."

Another witness blamed police antisemitism for the tardy arrival of reinforcements at Willowvale Park after the riot had broken out:

The police department in general…they were police. But they did what the establishment wanted, OK? Jewish people had nothing to do with the establishment. Just as you have today, you have many orientals or people from Pakistan or India or whatever, there are immigrants now that the police almost ignore. And, but this is what used to take place with regard to Jews at that time. Jews were nothing. They were second-class citizens. Now, if something was going to happen, the general attitude of the police at the time was "let the Nazis get their licks in, we'll come in afterwards and separate them." 'Cause the Jews never fought back. So what took place was, hey, if we get there a little late, the attitude on the part of the police department wasn't in favour of Jews in general. Period.

Jocko Thomas, the *Star* reporter who covered the riot, confirmed that antisemitic attitudes were not uncommon among the Toronto police under Chief Draper: "I remember one senior reporter saying to me, 'If the Jews could only hear what the police say about them.' Some of the guys, you know, mostly had Jewish businessmen as friends and they were getting cuts on maybe something or another but they didn't have many good words to say about them."

Although antisemitism was a threat to all Jews in the city, young Jews in the public schools and leisure areas were more often subject to abuse than their parents, who ventured beyond the comforting confines of the ghetto far less frequently.

In talking about Jewish youth specifically, it is important that the Jewish population was relatively young compared with the total population (all origins) in Toronto. Of all Jews in the city, 55.09 per cent were between five and twenty-nine years of age compared with only 43.27 per cent of the total population (all origins) in this age range. (See Appendix B, Table 6.)

For the vast majority of young Jewish males, the poverty of their condition, a result of both their have-not immigrant status and the Depression, meant that they often had to find some way to supplement family income and that only through their own efforts could they acquire a few of life's small luxuries (such as candy and sports equipment). They would take any odd job they could get and consider themselves lucky to work for a pittance. Such employment would be undertaken in addition to going to school during the day and to *cheder* (afternoon Hebrew school), usually in the late afternoon and on Sunday. The seriousness of the economic situation for many Jewish families in the early thirties is indicated by the fact that many children were allowed or even encouraged to leave school before or at the age of sixteen, in spite of the high regard in which education was traditionally held by most Jewish families.

In addition to the secular and religious educational pressure, the need to find work when there wasn't much work to find, the material poverty of family life, and the conflict between "greenhorn" parents and children raised in Canada, Jewish boys had to face the problems of prejudice, discrimination, and antisemitically motivated physical violence. All this served to toughen them and make them street smart.

Some of these boys came from families who, in order to survive under Depression conditions, engaged in such *sub rosa* activities as bootlegging. "Bootlegging was perfect. Traditionally, it was a trade carried on from the person's house. You didn't go door to door peddling your product, your customers came to you. And as far as my ma's limited skills with English were concerned, there probably isn't a business in the world you can conduct with fewer words than bootlegging."[45] Involvement with bootleggers, gamblers, con men, and the like was a way of supplementing a family's or an individual's income. Sammy Luftspring, who grew up in this milieu, gives a vivid though perhaps slightly exaggerated account of how much this world was part of the Jewish community around Spadina and College.

> Thieves, hoods, gamblers, pimps and hookers and hustlers, bookies by the battalion, bootleggers in every third or fourth house, hard guys, con men, roustabouts, crazies, College and Spadina had them all. And they were part of the natural fabric of the neighbourhood, almost as if the straight guy who had no grift going for him was the exception. Except for the rabbis, of course, who certainly had no grift going for them but were very much a part of that natural fabric of the neighbourhood.... It was a separate country, that area, a whole world unto itself, situated right in the middle of a stuffy, straight-laced [sic] city of the dullest half million people the 1920s could produce, Toronto's *goyim* [sic] citizenry.[46]

Not unexpectedly, such an environment produced a number of youngsters who were good with their fists. A German Jew attributed the existence of Jewish boxers in Germany before Hitler's rise to power to the self-defence measures taken by Jewish boys in antisemitic attacks:

> Coming out of *cheder* was when we mostly faced the real struggle. We were already awaited by a young gang outside which fell upon the Jew-boys with the cry: HEP-HEP. [*Hierosilima est perdita*—Jerusalem is lost. A favourite antisemitic cry of German nationalist students from the time of the war of liberation against Napoleon.] We had to learn either to run more quickly than they or to defend ourselves. Out of the ranks of the *cheder*-pupils arose a line of well-known amateur boxers. Self-defence contributed to their sports training.[47]

In fact, there were many excellent amateur Jewish boxers in Toronto during the thirties, some of whom went on to become professional fighters and champions. Sammy Luftspring, Davey Yack (the mad Russian) and Norman (Baby) Yack (Yackubovitch),[48] Harry Katz, Spinney Weinreb (who fought under the name Marty Stone), Ossie Bodkin, "Pancho" (Saul) and Harry (Burke) Bergstein, and Nat and Max Kadin were but a few of the Jewish pugilists who were heroes to the Jewish boys in the district. There were others, perhaps greater in number, who were handy with their fists outside of the ring. In the twenties,

Solka and Harry Pancer (*di shtarke* Pancers) and the Ziegelsteins were known as tough guys. These were street fighters who learned their craft in the daily struggle to survive and threw punches that no referee would countenance. Among them in the thirties were boys like the "tough greenies"—the Starr (Starshevsky) brothers Nathan, Joey (Green), Victor, Eddie, and Shiah—and Morris Fishman who, even though he was small (he later went on to become a famous jockey), packed a mean wallop. There were boys like Irv "Spike" Tennenbaum, Maxie Mandel, Charlie "Butch" Harris, Lou Harris, Gordon "Cooky" Levinson, "Slow" (Sam) Stein, Harry Stein (known as "Suitcase"), the Longert boys, whose family had a hay store on Kensington, and the Yumceh (Abramowitz) brothers (including Abe, "Grasshopper" [Benny], "Pineapple" [Hymie], Davey, and "Punchy" [Joey] who were forces to be reckoned with. A possibly apocryphal story has it that they were called Yumceh on account of the way Benny once pronounced the letters "YMCA."

In short, the Spadina and College area included a large number of Damon Runyon-like characters. Sammy Luftspring describes some of them in his autobiography:

> ... the ghetto itself was a great place for spawning nicknames, too. Max Applebaum was known as Maxie Apples, and Max Appleby as Maxie Chicago. The Brodkin brothers were always known as the Daddy Brothers, Big Daddy and Little Daddy. There was Gimpy the Athlete (who was not gimpy but a fine athlete); Pork Chops (who wasn't all there, but who was loved for what was there); Cocksy (who was all there); and Joe the Goof (who goofed about as often as a computer).
>
> There was "Little Itch" Leiberman, who sold papers at Queen and Yonge for a hundred years, who today is supposed to have a bank balance into seven figures. And there was Squarehead, who was Jewish and not German, who was among those who might have made a million if he had survived the Dieppe raid of 1942.
>
> Squarehead ran a slophouse called the Taxi Grill, which was a favourite pre-war hangout of characters like Joe the Hobo and Danny the Indian. And what about Ya Punchick? He lived his whole life by that name without anyone ever knowing how he got it, or what it meant.[49]

The boxers and the fighters were looked up to by the other boys as protectors and guardian angels, especially when they were caught outside the Jewish areas of town and menaced by Gentile youths. The Jewish toughs had their hangouts in the Spadina Avenue and College Street area. They frequented pool rooms like Kanarick's (69 Brunswick Avenue, just north of College on the east side), the Garden (294 College above the Garden Theatre on the north side), the College Pool Room (355 College just west of Becker's Delicatessen), Lubastyik's (410 Spadina next door to Hyman's book store), Lindzon's (318 Spadina just north of Dundas), Wineberg's (318 Spadina at Cecil), the Hub or Barshtz's (305 Spadina next to the Balfour Restaurant), and the Standard (548 Dundas between Spadina and Kensington Avenue). They also used the local restaurants and delicatessens as their "headquarters." Different "gangs" of boys could be found at different times at different establishments.

Brunswick and College, where there were four eating places in close proximity, was one such centre. On the east corner of Brunswick and College was the famous Eppes Essen Delicatessen; two doors farther west was Peter Wellts' deli; on the west corner of Brunswick and College was Altman's deli. Across the road on the south side of College was Becker's deli. The Goblin restaurant at 470–72 Spadina was an important meeting place near the corner of Spadina and College next to the Royal Bank. Heading south on the same block one would have passed Louis' Restaurant (460 Spadina), the Red Star Café (448 Spadina), and the Heimish Winkle (Yiddish for "Cozy Corner") restaurant (440 Spadina). Between Baldwin and St. Andrew were the Main Lunch Room (374 Spadina) and Amalgamated Lunch (354 Spadina). A key gathering spot was Ladovsky's United Bakers Dairy Restaurant two doors south of the Toronto Labor Lyceum. Shopsowitz's was at 295 Spadina, but this was the pre-Shopsy's era. Sloteroff's on Dundas near Spadina was also an important meeting place. On occasion a call would come to one of these places asking for help where trouble was anticipated—often, for instance, at a dance hall—and whoever was there would be off to defend the honour (or persons) of their fellow Jews in trouble.

There was one such call for help on the evening of the riot at the Pits. A witness described the incident as follows:

> Now, well, we get a phone call at Sloteroff's, saying that some Jew was gettin' beat up on Brunswick and Bloor. Graham's Brothers was the name of the place they'd mentioned, it was a bookstore. I think it was a Jewish man, Graham's. I remember because I used to go out and get books from there. Now, we heard that they were gettin' beat up, now we didn't know who done the calling, but we

decided we're gonna go up there and help. So, I got five more guys, or six maybe, got into my car, it was a big huge car and we flew up to Bloor and Spadina, Bloor and Brunswick. Now, I didn't see anybody out, nowhere could you see anybody, I'd swung the car around to be in front of the Graham's Brothers and the boys got out, they were gonna go into Graham's Brothers....

A witness told us about meeting, years later, someone his brother— one of these guardian angels—had rescued:

Anyway, now, I walked into Syd Silver's one day about, oh just before he died about six or seven months before he died, the man's blind and I didn't know the man, I never met him, but evidently my voice must of sounded just like my brother's, Joey. Now, I wanted to buy a shirt, and I happened to know the salesman, he was a very good friend of mine, he used to work with me, and now I want to pick up the shirt and now I'm talking to the salesman, and the man who was blind, Syd Silver, says to me, "Can you come over here, please?" I walked over to him, he says, "Is your name Starr?" I says, "Ya." "Is your brother Joey Starr?" I says, "Ya." He says, "God Bless 'm." I said, "Why?" He said, "Well, when I was going out with my wife," he says, "we were at Sunnyside," and Sunnyside was a real walk away, everybody used to walk on Sunnyside Beach, like on the Board Walk. He says, "And while I was walkin', we got harassed by half a dozen *Shkootsem*" [non-Jews], and they were really givin' him a hard time, and just like God sent them, my brother came along with two or three of his boys. And they made a mess out of these guys, and before you knew it they were runnin', you know they really, really knew it, and when they made a mess, they made a mess, and they went. And he never forgot him, and just my voice, just happened to, you know, because my voice was like my brother's.

The situation of Jews in Toronto can also be described in terms of "territory" and ethnic identity. As Robert Harney has argued:

In the same way that the fracturing of information is a consequence of being a polyethnic city, so too each ethnic group or immigrant cohort had a different spatial definition of the city itself. Both in the geographical sense of an enclave and in the more

notional sense of ambience, the neighbourhood as a combination
of individual cognitive maps and psychic worlds for immigrants
and their children provided their focus and anchor in the city.[50]

The cognitive map of which Harney writes tells the individual where
the things that matter to him and the things to avoid are located.[51] Members of the same ethnic group would have more or less similar maps; the
more cohesive the ethnic group, the more similar the map. Of course,
different ethnic groups would have quite dissimilar maps. Harney argues that the immigrant possessed not only a cognitive map of the city,
but a virtual cognitive atlas of the world:

> Each sojourner or settler possessed, as well as a detailed cognitive
> map of his world, a sense of where his fellows were in Toronto
> and of what parts of the city mattered to him. The immigrant's
> alternative atlas, of course, could not be confined to Toronto. It
> included key points such as his town of origin, the routes and
> stops on his crossing, as well as locations where his extended kin
> were throughout the world. The historian who tries to fit the eth-
> nic group too neatly, geographically and psychically, into the city
> does damage both to urban history and to the study of immi-
> gration and ethnicity itself. For example, Toronto's Ward in the
> 1900s served both Italians and Jews throughout the province.
> From it men who went to work seasonally on the labour inten-
> sive northern frontiers of Ontario, or peddled through the lonely
> countryside, drew supplies and cultural sustenance. Through the
> neighbourhood passed cash remittances, ethnic goods—from to-
> mato paste to *talissim*—brides, returnees and intelligence reports
> about travel routes, work, housing and the reception newcomers
> could expect in other parts of the country. In this manner the
> neighbourhood as an ambience was always larger than the actual
> enclave. On the other hand, many of the immigrants who settled
> or sojourned in the Ward had very little knowledge or contact
> with other nearby Toronto neighbourhoods. Toronto was then an
> urban space which, in semiotic terms, spoke to each immigrant
> group differently and spoke to all of them. Since their settled Brit-
> ish and acculturated neighbours saw the city differently, they mis-
> understood the newcomers' behaviour.[52]

Jewish youths in the Toronto of 1933 possessed a cognitive map of the city that was highly uniform and consistent. It showed them which territories were their own—territories upon which they might venture forth in the secure knowledge that they were the uncontested masters of the turf. It also showed them the borderline areas, the no man's land between friendly and hostile neighbourhoods. Finally, it told them where the dangerous areas in the city were located and warned them not to go there unless in great numbers.

Harry Rasky conveys this sense of territory in his recollection of wandering into the enemy camp in search of "forbidden fruit":

> Expeditions were mounted into the dangerous Gentile world beyond the barriers of our fortress isolation…. Beaches in the east end of the city in far-off places beyond what was called the Danforth. The challenge was to get by the signs that spelled out the rule: "Restricted." To pass by without a look of guilt was like stealing green apples. How to look nonchalant when you know your nose might be just a little too long. A skilled observer might just cause that nose to be bloodied.[53]

Harney suggests that this sense of familiar and hostile territory was held by most immigrant groups, and

> for most groups, picnics and outings, even a visit to the graves of loved ones in Mount Hope Cemetery, required a trek across unfamiliar and threatening space. Leisure itself was a segregated activity for the immigrant generation, and the pattern followed them out of the city. Property owned by members of the ethnic group, by benevolent associations or parishes, usually on the outskirts of Toronto, were [sic] safe sites for planned leisure, picnics, or ethnic outings. Pontypool, east of the city, and Belle Ewart, near Lake Simcoe, were such locations for the Jews. Nearby farms served Italians, Macedonians, Chinese and Poles in the same way. In the neighbourhood, men and women built systems and networks that enabled them to survive as Torontonians and, in most instances, made it possible for their children to sally forth into the larger city to work, and to share public leisure places such as the CNE and Sunnyside.[54]

Associated with this notion of territory was the issue of defence. Neighbourhood gangs would have a primitive system of surveillance and response should foreign gang members cross into their territory. Part of the sense of youthful adventure included wilful incursions into enemy territory as a test of prowess and revenge for opposing incursions. Hugh Garner's book about Cabbagetown in the thirties suggests that this was standard fare in Toronto.[55] Most altercations between Jews and Gentiles took place in parts of the city where few Jews lived or, as in the Christie Pits riot, on the fringes of the Jewish areas. The Jewish boys' fights outside their territory, in the no man's land that separated the Jewish areas from the rest of the city or in public places like the beaches or parks, almost always involved antisemitism. The riot at Christie Pits was no exception to this; it stands out from other incidents only in the numbers involved and the degree of violence.

The demarcation of the city into friendly and hostile territories separated by areas of no man's land had a profound impact upon members of the Jewish community. Even though the community was not always agreed on how best to respond to provocations from the outside, it was, none the less, united in its perception of the underlying threat facing it. As we have seen, during this period of Canadian history, Jews encountered various forms of discrimination in their attempt to establish themselves in Canada and, more specifically, to carve out a secure economic footing to meet their everyday needs and future aspirations.

Surrounded by what they perceived as an unsympathetic, if not hostile, population, spokesmen for Toronto's Jews were quick to defend the community against unfair criticism stemming from antisemitic sentiments. When the *Evening Telegram* accused Jewish Communists of having incited the riot at Christie Pits, the Jewish community responded with its own account of the events of the evening. Although the report in *Der Yiddisher Zhurnal* was more subdued than those in the English-language papers, blame for the violence was placed squarely on the Gentiles:

> It was expected that the same gang that on the previous Monday incited the Jewish players by displaying a swastika along with shouts of "Hail Hitler" would once again attempt to cause trouble. And so it was. Although, this time, they made trouble for themselves....

It all began during the first inning when a few young Gentile low-lifes among the crowd began chanting "Hail Hitler" and other epithets aimed at the Jews. The Jewish boys nearby tried to quieten them and this almost resulted in violence. But order was successfully restored.

All was quiet until the end of the game, which the Gentile team won. As the crowd was dispersing, a group of Gentile boys celebrated the victory by yelling insults at the Jews, and they unfurled an old blanket on which was painted a swastika.[56]

The newspaper was flooded with inquiries about the number killed or dead through injuries. "Many Jews who telephoned the editorial office," it wrote, "were not simply seeking information but also advice on what to do. Based on their queries, it sounded as if they were experiencing a pogrom atmosphere."[57]

In a private conversation with one of the authors, a leading Toronto journalist and media personality described the riot at Christie Pits as "part of the mythology of Toronto's history." Fathers and grandfathers tell and retell their heroic exploits during the "battle of Christie Pits" to their children and grandchildren; the story has been passed across three generations. In a recent article in the *Canadian Jewish News*, for example, a report about a family reunion in Toronto indicates the significant position occupied by the riot in people's lives and memories:

> In the late 1920s Murray Krugel was a Canadian amateur middleweight wrestling contender and just missed winning a place on the Canadian Olympic team.
>
> But in August 1933, he found himself fighting in a different way against members from some so-called "Swastika clubs" during the Christie Pits riots. "He wound up with the Nazi flag after hammering some Nazi during the riot," Freeman says.[58]

At the end of a presentation by one of the authors to the Toronto Jewish Historical Society in the spring of 1985, a member of the audience recalled for us that within two hours of his crossing into Canada from the United States (he was a native of New Jersey) in 1947, he had heard a complete account of the Christie Pits riot. Since then, he assured us, not a week has gone by that did not contain at least one reference to this event.

In the Jewish community having been at the Pits during the riot is cause alone for pride. As we have been informed on more than one occasion, only a small proportion of those who claim to have been at the Pits that August evening in 1933 were actually there. But this fact, too, is interesting and we have to ask ourselves why people would want to misrepresent themselves in this way.

Certainly some of this "false witness" today has to be understood against the background of the Holocaust. Scholars such as Raul Hilberg have lamented the fact that millions of Jews went passively to their deaths in the ghettos, before the Einsatzgruppen, and in the extermination camps. At Christie Pits the Jews fought back; this time the Jews were fighters, heroes. As one of our respondents said:

> Well it was the first time for a period of time there where the Jewish community fought back.... You see, Jews were always known...as a peaceful people and they wouldn't fight back. They would take their licks.... And this is the first time they stood up....

It was, and still remains, a point of honour to have been part of the fighting contingent. In fact, "being there" at Christie Pits was more significant for some Jews than their combat experiences in the Canadian armed forces during the Second World War. According to another witness who had been at the Pits, "regardless of the fighting in France and Germany, they don't talk about that. They talk about Christie Pits. They never talk about what they did in the war. They always talked about Christie Pits." As so many put it in such a variety of ways, it was unforgettable:

> I think it left an indelible impression.... It may well have been the first appreciation that the Jewish community had had of what Nazism meant.

> You had to be there to see it, to realize how severe it was.... It was like leading up to something that you know is gonna happen, you know you're gonna have a Holocaust or something like that.

> Christie Pits has to be a highlight.... I can hardly remember any other riot of any kind that was comparable to that. It was really a riot. That was a really big one, you know.

The violence at the Pits was probably the most serious racially motivated example of its kind in twentieth-century Toronto. As one of our witnesses suggested: "this [Christie Pits riot] was a big event here. This was the biggest goddamn riot Toronto has ever seen, probably up to that time and I can't recall one that was as bad since."

CHAPTER 2 "Every Evil is Jewish"

...it is clear why Hitler upon coming into power did not make the pogrom in the same way that pogroms against Jews were made in other countries. On the contrary, the Hitler government took pains to make precisely bloodless pogroms, or as they are generally known, "cold pogroms." Such pogroms are in harmony with the extermination program which Hitler has always preached, and which he is preparing to carry out.
—Editorial in *Der Yiddisher Zhurnal*, 6 June 1933

It is a common assumption that the world knew very little of the Nazi atrocities perpetrated upon the Jews until about 1943; that we discovered the full extent of the "terrible secret" only in the closing months of World War II when the Allied armies smashed their way through the gates of hell and liberated the concentration camps. In fact, the events that transpired in Germany after Hitler's accession to power were reported in the mass media in great detail, and the beginnings of the great tragedy that was to befall the Jews of Europe were witnessed by the press of the free world. The stories emanating from Germany were not always believed by newspaper editors; after all, the stories of gassings of Belgian civilians by the German army during World War I had been, to a large extent, so much Allied war propaganda.[1] Nevertheless, the reports were so consistent and were confirmed by such unassailable sources that even those newspapers least sympathetic to the plight of the Jews treated them as accurate—if overstated—accounts of what was happening in Germany. Publishers who had some sympathy or admiration for Hitler took the position that atrocities were inevitable in the context of a national revolution and that it was in no way the fault of the political leadership. Overzealous supporters of Hitler were responsible for the excesses, many publishers and editors believed; they also believed that the hotheads would soon be subjected to the discipline of the party and that Germany would once again be brought entirely under the rule of law.

The violence provoked in Toronto by the public display of the swastika in connection with anti-Jewish sentiment was a product of both local conditions and perceptions about what was taking place in Germany at the time. With the appearance of the swastika emblem, local antisemitism seemed to merge with Hitlerism in the minds of most Jews. In order to appreciate why the swastika was chosen as a symbol by youth at the Beaches and Christie Pits, and why the young Jews of Toronto reacted to it in the way they did, it is necessary to review the press reports coming out of Nazi Germany that were carried in the Toronto newspapers.

Our purpose in presenting these newspaper reports in detail is not to prove a point about the Holocaust. We are not concerned with the question of whether Hitler and his henchmen plotted the murder of Europe's Jews in 1925, 1933, or 1941. Neither are we trying to establish that the world knew of the planned murder, even though such words as "extermination," "annihilation," and "extirpation" did appear again and again in the newspapers in 1933. We are not even trying to show that some leaders, journalists, and intellectuals were more perspicacious than others in recognizing the Nazi threat. We are concerned only with how the people of Toronto—Jewish and non-Jewish—reacted to the daily reports or denials of reports of atrocities, indignities, and expulsions suffered by the German Jews between January and August 1933. Walter Laqueur has issued a similar word of caution:

> Difficulties of research and organization quite apart, there is one main pitfall in a work of this kind: the temptations of hindsight. Nothing is easier than to apportion praise and blame, writing many years after the events: some historians find the temptation irresistible. But the "final solution" more perhaps than any other subject should be approached in a spirit of caution and even humility. It is very easy to claim that everyone should have known what would happen once Fascism came to power. But such an approach is ahistorical. Nazism was an unprecedented phenomenon.[2]

Toronto had four daily newspapers in 1933: two morning papers—the *Daily Mail and Empire* and the *Globe*—and two afternoon/evening papers—the *Toronto Daily Star* and the *Evening Telegram*. In addition to these mass circulation dailies, the Jewish community of Toronto was served by a Yiddish paper—*Der Yiddisher Zhurnal*—six days a week (there was no Saturday edition) with a daily circulation of between 4,000 and 5,000. The *Star* was the largest of the big four papers (with a circulation of about 215,000), and under the influence of its president, Joseph Atkinson, it was the most liberal in its views. It was the only paper of the four to defend freedom of speech and assembly in Toronto's parks,[3] and it was the most sympathetic to immigrants, minorities, and persecuted groups like the Jews, although by today's standards it was somewhat patronizing and, at times, mildly racist. These caveats notwithstanding, the *Star* could be described as Toronto's left-leaning populist newspaper.

The *Evening Telegram* was the second largest paper (circulation about 145,000) and the *Star's* chief rival. It was outspokenly anti-Communist, xenophobic, racist, and conservative, and cultivated what Michiel Horn refers to as "the British connection." It presented protectionist views and advocated fiscal restraint by governments, although it favoured public ownership of utilities. The *Evening Telegram* was closely associated with the social and political positions of the Orange Order and supported (most often successfully) Orange candidates in civic elections. Yet, the *Tely* was not a "bourgeois" paper; it was too suspicious of big business to speak for those interests and too sensationalist for the refined sensibilities of the upper class. The *Tely* might be described as Toronto's right-leaning populist newspaper.[4]

The *Globe* and the *Daily Mail and Empire* were both morning papers, much smaller in circulation than the *Star* and the *Tely* and not in serious competition with them. The *Globe*, originally a Grit paper brought to prominence by George Brown, had been read and respected by the Toronto elite. However, the then-current president, W. G. Jaffray, was a fundamentalist Presbyterian who had launched a pro-temperance and anti-Communist crusade through the newspaper.[5] The *Globe* had a large readership outside Toronto, as did the *Star*. The *Mail and Empire* had been a dull conservative newspaper until about 1930, when it brought in Vernon Knowles to reorganize its operation. It was read by the "man in the street" and covered local news in depth. In 1936 the *Globe* and the *Mail and Empire* joined forces to become the *Globe and Mail*.

Perhaps most important to the formation of the views of Toronto's Jewish community vis-à-vis Nazism and its swastika emblem were the stories and editorials carried in *Der Yiddisher Zhurnal*. This newspaper was founded in 1911 under circumstances that are now somewhat obscure.[6] By 1932, when Shmuel Meyer Shapiro was editor, the paper had become (as it remained throughout the 1930s) "the major disseminator of local news and the spokesman for the Jewish community."[7] Although sympathetic with the plight of the working man and warmly disposed to trade-union struggles, democratic socialism, and Labour Zionism, the *Zhurnal* nevertheless appealed to both the secular and the religious elements in the Jewish community.[8]

A large number of Toronto Jews in 1933 received a substantial amount of their information about the condition of Jewry locally, nationally, and internationally from the Yiddish press in general and the *Zhurnal* in particular.[9] According to our respondents, it was the *Star* that was read more regularly by Jews than any of the other English-language dailies at the time. Thus, a close analysis of the way in which the rise of Hitlerism was portrayed in the pages of the *Zhurnal* and the *Star* will tell us what symbolic value the swastika held for the Jews of Toronto in the summer of 1933.

If the appearance of the swastika had a catalytic effect upon Jewish youth, it also obviously had a meaning for the Gentile youngsters in Toronto who adopted the emblem as a club symbol or who used it to provoke a violent response. Analyzing the pages of the *Zhurnal* wouldn't shed a ray of light upon the meaning of the swastika emblem for Toronto's Gentile population. Reading the *Star* is of some help, but the *Tely's* presentation of the events in Germany during the first half of 1933 probably had the most influence of any of the dailies on the views of young people who were drawn to organizations like the Swastika Club.[10] The xenophobia of the *Telegram* struck a responsive chord in this segment of the Gentile population. One could note in this regard that the Swastika Club usually chose the *Telegram* as the vehicle to make its pronouncements public. If the *Star* and *Der Yiddisher Zhurnal* were bent on reporting the full horror of the Nazi persecution of Jews, the *Telegram* seemed to go out of its way to minimize the scope, intensity, and severity of the maltreatment.

In 1933, neither the *Star* nor the *Telegram* carried stories concerning the political situation in Germany until after von Hindenburg had appointed Hitler chancellor. *Der Yiddisher Zhurnal*, on the other hand, carried reports on various aspects of German politics involving the Nazis and brought home to the Jews of Canada the violence being practised upon the Jews even *before* Hitler's appointment as head of government and before the general population of Toronto was aware of what was occurring. In its edition of Thursday, 12 January, *Der Yiddisher Zhurnal* carried the following headline: "Hitler Seeks to Make a Million Dollars for the Nazi Party: Industry leaders have promised to make available to him through von Papen a million dollars to cover Nazi debts, if he forestalls general elections." A smaller notice on the same page tells of the ex-Kaiser's demand that his son leave the Nazi Party.

On the following day, 13 January, seventeen days before Hitler became chancellor, the *Zhurnal* reported the murder of Dr. Wolf at the hands of Nazi thugs. Dr. Wolf had been the president of several Jewish organizations. The paper also reported that Nazis had strongly protested the appointment of Professor Ernst Cohen as the director of examinations at the University of Breslau (today Wroclaw, Poland), an appointment that was to take effect at the end of January. On 25 January, the *Zhurnal* carried a description of the Nazi student protest against Professor Cohen in Breslau under the title: "Nazis Fight against Professor Cohen with Stink Bombs." National Socialist students joined together with NSDAP members from outside the university to disrupt Dr. Cohen's lectures.

On 26 January, in an editorial entitled "The 'Protector' of the Jews in Austria," the *Zhurnal* levelled an attack at Father Felner, Bishop of Linz, who, under the guise of wishing to protect the Jews from Nazi terror, accused them of being the driving spiritual force behind the evils of the world:

> Therefore, it is the duty of Christians to struggle against Jewish influence. In the middle ages this was done by isolating the Jews in Jewish ghettoes. Now this is unnecessary. This can now be achieved by legislative and administrative acts, which can turn aside Jewish spiritual influence, in order to prevent the world from being filled with Jewish demoralization.

Neither the *Star* nor the *Telegram* reported on Nazi antisemitism in the immediate aftermath of Hitler's accession to the chancellorship. In its front-page story of 30 January 1933, the *Star* reported the facts and emphasized the momentousness of the occasion for Germany in the following words: "After standing firmly against the Nazis for months, and repeatedly spurning Hitler's demands for power, von Hindenburg launched his fatherland on an entirely new course, in what may be one of the most decisive decisions in the nation's history."

In a short editorial note in the same issue it expressed some of the same sort of hope that the *Zhurnal* would try to generate in relation to the checks on Hitler's extremist policies. The comment was obviously written before the news of Hitler's appointment had reached the *Star*: "The public expects Hitler to become dictator of Germany. But Von Schleicher quit last week because President Hindenburg refused to allow him to exercise dictatorial powers. Hitler, therefore, may have to show some respect for democratic principles if he becomes chancellor."

Also on 30 January, the *Zhurnal* had speculated in a lead story: "Hitler May Be Appointed Chancellor Today...." But more ominously, another front-page story in the same issue foretold tragedy. Goebbels would make public a plan "...How Nazis Will Exterminate [*Oysrotten*] the Jews of Greater Germany: possibility that Hitler should become Chancellor throws a scare into German Jews—Nazis will carry out a bloodless pogrom, says Führer—Will expel Jews from public life and economy."

When Hitler was in fact appointed chancellor, the *Zhurnal* emphasized in its reporting the obstacles to Hitler's antisemitic plans, and the unity and confidence of German Jewry in facing the challenges presented by the new *Reichskanzler* and his government. On the one hand, a sub-headline told the worst: "German Jews look with mistrust upon cabinet of Nazi Chancellor—Believe president that he will not allow robbing of civil rights of Jews—Austrian Jews also in fear on account of Hitler government—London press holds that Hitler will not relinquish power from his hands—French politicians believe that Hitler has talked more than he will do." But the lead story announced that German Jews were united: "Prepared to Struggle for their Constitutional Rights." By this more optimistic scenario, Hitler would have to accept the cabinet that the president chose for him, and would have to promise to govern according to "recognized principles."

On 1 February, the picture painted of German politics by the *Zhurnal* was of a chaotic situation. The reports showed Hitler's grasp on the country to be unsure and faltering, challenged by violent opposition: "the worst Jew-devourer, a Nazi," had been named as Berlin's police chief; socialists and Communists had called a general strike; there were clashes in many German cities among police, Nazis, Communists, and socialists; and the Communist newspaper had been "confiscated." A further sub-heading highlighted that: "Nazi students and storm troopers have already started going on a spree—The Central Verein[11] consoles Jews that Nazis will be shamed in other countries—Vienna's Jewish quarter guarded against Nazi celebration of Hitler's victory"; however, the Central Verein was reportedly seeking to calm the Jewish population "by a statement that the fear of the Nazis is an exaggerated one. The

Nazis, says the Central Verein, will have to reckon with the impression that their actions against Jews will have outside Germany and in particular upon Mussolini, who doesn't hold with antisemitism."

In its first editorial after Hitler's accession, the *Zhurnal* called for a worldwide assistance effort by Jews. "It is useless to request justice from pogromists," the *Zhurnal* told the Diaspora. "For this particular gang the only argument is the weapons they use":

> Hitler will possibly be able to take away certain rights of Jews, he will limit Jewish possibilities. But one thing he cannot take away from Jews, the right to defend their lives and property.... The central Verein of German Jews has for a long time already been calling on the Jews of the country to join in a united front in appropriate self-defence organizations to fight each attack from the Nazis, to offer armed resistance to every attempted pogrom.

This editorial goes on to liken Nazis to the pogromists of Czarist Russia and Hitler to the Russian antisemite Pobedonostev. That this comparison was off the mark is easy to see now, and in fact, within a very short time, the editors of the *Zhurnal* had recognized that the Jews of Germany, indeed of Europe, were facing a foe the like of which they had not before encountered. In the face of this enemy, the Central Verein, and the *Zhurnal*, were ready to tell Jews to forget their ideological differences and come together to offer armed resistance to their attackers.

Now Jews comprised less than 1 per cent of the German population, and of this number, only a fraction had any military training and even fewer had access to arms and ammunition. This was bravado, designed to bolster sagging Jewish spirits and induce a needed sense of solidarity in a time of great peril. And yet there is much to be said for the real consequences of socially held myths.

The Toronto *Evening Telegram* came out with its editorial concerning Hitler's appointment on 1 February, and its expectation was that his government would be short-lived. *Tely* readers were told: "Up, Then Out, Likely Fate of Hitler as Chancellor."

The following brief survey dealing with the exclusion and humiliation of Jews in Germany is but a fraction of what appeared in the Toronto newspapers between January and August 1933. We contend that this constant stream of information available to the Jewish and non-Jewish communities of Toronto was crucial in determining both the selection of the swastika as an emblem by the Swastika Club and the Pit Gang and the effect that the sight of the swastika in Toronto had upon the Jews, especially the Jewish youth of the city.

On 12 March *Der Yiddisher Zhurnal* reported to Toronto Jews that Jewish kindergartens and music schools in the Prenzlauer Berg area of Berlin were closed. Furthermore, according to the story, Communists, socialists, and Jews were forbidden to enter civic clubhouses and sport areas. On 19 March the same paper carried the following story on its front page:

> Jews Thrown Out of Hospitals, Stock-Exchange, Theatre, Courts in Germany—All Jewish and Socialist Doctors Barred from Berlin Hospitals—Lawyers' Union Requested to Expel All Jews from Court and Legal Practice—No Jews on the German Stock Exchange, Hitler's Minister Demands—Former Jewish Conductor Not Allowed to Appear in Germany—Pogrom in Feuchtwanger's Apartment in Berlin.

On the following day, the *Toronto Daily Star* carried a brief report on page one: "Clearing Jews Out of Prussian Courts—All Jewish Prosecuting Attorneys to Be Discharged."

Within weeks of its electoral victory on 5 March, the Nazi government had made plans to set the Jews apart from the rest of the population, to exclude them from public life, to prevent them from practising their professions, to restrict their numbers severely at institutions of higher learning, to humiliate them. The *Star*, in a front-page story on 23 March, sketched for its readers Hitler's reform proposals. Among them were the exclusion of all Jews from official positions, a prohibition on Jewish immigration, and "the treatment of Jews as noxious foreigners." On the same day, *Der Yiddisher Zhurnal* carried a page-one story it had received from the Jewish Telegraphic Agency in Paris that included eye-witness accounts of Nazi indignities inflicted on Jews in Breslau:

> Hitlerites attacked a Jewish shoe dealer, Tennenboim, dragged him out of his store, ripped off his coat and the suspenders from his pants, and forced him to run half naked through the main streets of town. Into one of his hands they shoved a bust of Hitler, he had to hold up his pants with his other hand, and he ran and cried "Up with Hitler!" The Hitlerites followed him to ensure that he carried out their orders.

The race was now on among the German provinces to see which would be the first to be *Judenrein*, "cleansed of Jews." On 24 March the *Star* announced that the provincial government of the Palatinate (Pfalz) was planning to expel all Jews from its territory. The government of the Pfalz also ordered that no bank or postal funds be issued to eastern Jews until they had settled all debts. In a similar report that day, the *Zhurnal* informed its readers that all Jews who moved into the Palatinate after 1914 were to be expelled. Jews were leaving en masse, it reported, although they were not allowed to withdraw their money from banks.

Even before the March election, the Nazis had organized campaigns to boycott Jewish establishments. However, once they had taken power, the boycotts against businesses owned by Jews escalated. An American-owned chain store, Woolworth's, was a target of the Nazi boycott, since it was popularly, if erroneously, believed to be owned by a Jew. On 10 March the *Evening Telegram* gave front-page coverage in its second section to several incidents involving chain stores and other stores owned by Jews:

> A Wolff news agency report from Magdeburg said a number of women and children were trampled and injured in a panic when storm troops occupied a[nd] closed a big chain store. Several shoppers and employees were reported maltreated. Chain stores have become targets of demonstrations in a Nazi movement to decentralize big concerns.
>
> In Berlin, throngs of curious jammed the sidewalks in the fashionable Kurfuerstendamm to watch storm troops in front of several prominent shops urging buyers to boycott the Jewish owners. The resignation of a Jew who is executive committee chairman of the stock exchange was demanded by a Nazi crowd. All Jewish merchants in Annaberg were arrested.

On 27 March the *Evening Telegram* and the *Toronto Daily Star*, and on 28 March *Der Yiddisher Zhurnal*, carried essentially the same report on the expulsion of Jews from public life. The *Tely* quoted the statement of a Dr. Ernst Hanfstaengl, chief of the Nazi foreign press section, that this expulsion was not "by means of a pogrom." As Dr. Hanfstaengl then explained to his foreign audience, "The Jews who already have been ousted were put out because they were morally and politically unfit to safeguard German interests."

But unlike the *Star* and *Der Yiddisher Zhurnal*, the *Telegram* empha-

sized the ephemeral nature of antisemitic attacks, blaming them, as top
Nazi officials did, on a first-flush-of-victory fervour. "In their first burst
of ultra-nationalism in celebration of the victory of Hitlerites in the
election," the *Telegram* explained,

> individual storm troops admittedly harassed Jews against whom
> they held personal grievances. During that period of roughly ten
> days, humiliation of Jews unquestionably was widespread, and
> there were numerous instances of violence. The consequence was
> the frightened exodus of thousands of Jews who[se] stories led
> to the belief abroad that the Nazis were conducting a merciless
> pogrom.

A short note, entitled "Worst is Over," followed immediately. The
American Embassy in Berlin had reported "that physical mistreatment
of Jews in Germany has been 'virtually terminated.'"

On the next day, 28 March, the *Star* informed its readers that Jewish
employers were being compelled to pay their employees two months
in advance and that the executives of German medical societies had
recommended the dismissal of Jews from executive boards and com-
mittees. It continued: "At Bitterfeld, near Berlin, groups of Nazis forced
the closing of Jewish market stalls and ordered their proprietors out of
town. At Neumuenster a store which opened after having been closed
for two weeks by the police was invaded by a number of unidentified
men swinging clubs. Jewish stores were closed at Bata...."

Der Yiddisher Zhurnal informed its Toronto readership of further
measures taken against German Jews in a page-one story on 4 April:

> Jews May Not Leave Germany According to Latest Order of Min-
> ister of Interior—More Famous Personalities Relieved of Their Of-
> fices: Max Reinhardt Estranged from German Theatre—Famous
> Doctors and Lawyers Arrested—Only Germans Can Hold Office,
> Orders Law of Minister of Interior—Money of Jews Wanting to
> Leave Germany Is Confiscated—Jewish Factory Owner Commits
> Suicide.

The *Zhurnal* also reported that the German Federation of Amateur
Boxers had decided not to allow Jews to participate in fights. (We recall
that many of the Jewish boxers in Toronto were involved in the altera-
tions at the Beaches and the riot at Christie Pits.) The *Star* then reported

that Jews would be barred from the German civil service. Jews, Special Culture Commissar Hinkel had said, "will not obtain government jobs." And, meanwhile, the cabinet "passed a law prohibiting ritual slaughtering rites throughout Germany, and threatened to fine offenders or sentence them to six months in jail."[12]

Both the *Zhurnal* and the *Star* also reported that the Nazis had made deep inroads into the churches in Germany. "The Protestant Nazis," said the *Star*,

> ...were told equality for Jews was the promise of a future world, but was not to be expected in Germany. The Rev. Peter, one of the principal speakers, said St. Paul's epistle to the Romans about the equality of the Jew and the Greek applied to things spiritual and a world beyond, but not to this world, where "race purity" was ordained by God.
>
>   Iron Crosses were pinned on many of the clergymen....

Nazi Christians, the *Zhurnal* stated on 5 April, "have acted to wipe out all traces of Jewish religion in Christian teachings and a government 'culture tax' was seen today as a further move toward nationalization of the Protestant church."

On 7 April the *Zhurnal* reported that Jews had been almost entirely purged from public life in Germany. Doctors, dentists, judges, lawyers, professors, and teachers had been dismissed in droves. In its toughest report to date, the *Star* confirmed the story on the front page of its 8 April edition. "Germany to Degrade Jews to Second Class Citizenry: Thousands to be Banished from Civil Service Under New Decree: Drastic Upheaval," was the headline.

> All civil servants of Jewish descent will be retired except those in the service before August 1, 1914, and those who actually served in the trenches during the war....
>
>   Twenty-five hundred Jewish lawyers in Berlin, disqualified by the Nazi order which barred them from the courts, are waiting to hear which of them will be chosen as the 35 to whom permission to practice will be granted....
>
>   At Munich an order was issued to-day forbidding Jews to matriculate as medical students in Bavarian universities. At Leipzig Jews will be barred from the university for ten semesters.

The *Star* went on to explain the Nazi rule of exclusion: "The exact amount of Jewish blood which henceforth will serve to exclude persons from official posts was clearly defined today in a decree. Twenty-five per cent Jewish blood will be sufficient to classify the possessor as a member of the Jewish race."

The reports of degradation, humiliation, and suffering of Jews under the Nazi thumb were often challenged by other reports carried in the *Telegram* and occasionally in the *Star*. For example, on 12 April, the *Evening Telegram* (on the front page) and the *Toronto Daily Star* (on page 3) carried a story written by George Hambleton, a Canadian Press staff writer, which provided an assessment of the situation of the Jews in Germany. Although it pointed to the trials and tribulations of German Jews, it blunted the sharp attacks on the Nazi government launched by both the *Star* and the *Zhurnal*. Hambleton wrote of the eyewitness reports of physical ill-treatment as allegations, arguing that both sides were guilty of "wild propaganda." His interpretation of the new decrees concerning the practice of law differed from that of the *Zhurnal*'s and the *Star*'s reports of 8 April, both of which claimed that only 35 Jews would be allowed to practise law in Berlin, not the 900 suggested by Hambleton. The headline said it all: "New Germany All-German Under Hitler's Iron Hand: Investigation Fails to Disclose 'Atrocities'—Jewish Lawyers on Same Basis as Gentiles."

On the very next day an ominous front-page report appeared in the *Star* describing plans by German students to collect so-called un-German books and to burn them publicly. The story spoke of the torching of the books as a "Holocaust." The *Star* reproduced for its readers the principal points on which the "campaign against the un-German spirit" was to be based:

> The purity of our language is our precious treasure.
> The Jew is our most dangerous opponent.
> The Jew can only think Jewishly. If he writes German, he lies.
> We demand that all German students despise the Jew as an alien.
> We demand that the censor compel all Jewish works to appear only in Hebrew. If they appear in German, they must be clearly marked as translations....

In the 13 April issue of the *Star*, Pierre van Paassen reported on the flight of Jews from Germany. Pierre (Pieter Anthonie Laurusse) van Paassen

(1895–1968) grew up in Gorcum, Holland, and emigrated to Canada in 1911. Before World War I he became a pastor's assistant in a Methodist mission to Ruthenians in Alberta. During the war he served in France with the Canadian forces. He worked for the Toronto *Globe*, the *Constitution* in Atlanta, Georgia, and the New York *Evening World* before joining the staff of the *Toronto Daily Star* in 1932. He was an ardent supporter of Zionism and defender of the Jewish people. It was van Paassen who wrote a moving eulogy for Vladimir Jabotinsky. The *Star* dismissed van Paassen over a disputed irregularity in his coverage of the Spanish Civil War, and he turned his talents to writing books. His titles include: *The Deep-Red Banner of the Cross* (1937); *Days of Our Years* (1939); *The Time Is Now!* (1941); and *Who's on the Lord's Side, Who?* (1942). In 1946 van Paassen became a minister in the Unitarian Church.

During March and April of 1933, van Paassen was in Germany as the *Star's* foreign correspondent. More than any other single individual, van Paassen, at great personal risk—he was arrested by the Gestapo and briefly held—sounded the alarm by exposing the atrocities of the Nazis in his almost daily reports. The picture he painted was a bleak one and it conveyed the fear gripping Germany's Jewish population in the wake of the Nazi terror.

> In the big German cities [van Paassen wrote] Jews are closing up shops, warehouses and factories. Practically all Jews are trying to liquidate their business before getting out.
>
> The governments of the Rhineland provinces have decreed that all Jews who have entered the country as immigrants since 1914 must leave within three months. The other Jews, who are descendants of merchant families who have settled in the Rhenish cities in the wake of the Roman armies, that is to say, a thousand years before Berlin existed and at a time when the Prussians were but a savage tribe of swine-herds who hunted aurochs in the swamps of Brandenburg, these families are sitting behind shuttered windows, fearing eruptions of Nazi terrorists.
>
> Dare Not Leave Home
>
> Berlin's "Westen", where a large percentage of the population is Jewish and which a month ago was one of the liveliest quarters of the Prussian capital, with life intense and colourful, is like a silent tomb. Terrorized, the Jews dare not show themselves in the street.

This does not save them, however. The Nazi newspapers warn the stormtroops to watch those people "whose guilty conscience" keeps them from emerging into the light of day. The "Westen" is a deserted district. Rich and poor feel themselves menaced. It is definitely known that the wealthy Jews of Cologne, Frankfurt-on-the-Main and East Prussia have no other thought but to leave Germany. Representatives of German Jewish bankers and industrialists in Paris are making preparations to find places of lodging for their chiefs and their families as it is felt that "not a single Jew will ultimately be safe in Germany."

In the same article, van Paassen considers the fate of Jews in his own line of work, journalism and newspaper publishing.

The Socialist and Communist papers being proscribed, the Nazi government is now occupying itself with purging the liberal press. The great *Berliner Tageblatt*, owned by Herr Rudolph Mosse, has a staff of Nazi censors night and day in its editorial rooms. All Jewish editors and reporters have been discharged on the order of the censors. A Jewish boy may not even report a fire or a hockey match, for fear that "his Semitic mentality poison German morality." Among those discharged by the *Berliner Tageblatt* is Herr Theodore Wolff, for years one of the most brilliant commentators on European affairs whose daily critical essay on the front page of the *Tageblatt* was as eagerly studied in London as it was in Moscow, Paris, Rome and Washington. Like its great fellow-liberal journal, the *Vossische Zeitung*, the *Tageblatt* is allowed to print nothing but government communiqués and news items without commentary. But even the news must first be approved by Nazi censors....

The Nazi papers offer a curious spectacle—but a very significant one. Hitler is calling his storm troops to moderation quite frequently now. But his appeals are printed in small letters on the third or fourth pages, while the excitations of Goering to keep on "hitting the Jew and exterminating the Marxists" are placed on the front page in big fat letters under the heading: "To hell with the Jews!" (*Juda Verrecke!*)

In the coming months, the Toronto English and Yiddish newspapers would report ceaselessly on exclusions, quotas, expulsions, book-bannings, and book-burnings. "The 'cleansing,' meaning excluding Jews from all branches of German life, yielded new results today," the *Zhurnal* reported about exclusionary decisions by sports associations, press groups, and universities. In the same vein, the *Evening Telegram* carried a story on 19 April concerning quotas on Jews at German universities. "The Aryan law, which bars nearly all Jews from civil service and degrades them to second class citizenship, is being invoked in all German universities by Chancellor Hitler's Cabinet." The *Tely* went on to explain the matter exactly:

> The Aryan clause defines any person having one Jewish grandparent as a Jew. The only exceptions made under the civil service ban were Jews in State service before August 1, 1914, or those who served in the trenches or whose fathers or sons were killed in the war.

On Hitler's birthday, 20 April, Toronto Jews read in *Der Yiddisher Zhurnal* that students at Munich's university had adopted a resolution according to which Jewish medical students would only be able to dissect Jewish, not Christian, cadavers. Henceforth, the paper wrote, Jewish students "will be allowed to practise only on Jewish cadavers." On the same day, the *Star* reported that a general amnesty was issued for those who had committed crimes out of patriotic motives, meaning that those tormenters of Jews who had been brought to "justice" would be set free.

Der Yiddisher Zhurnal also examined the situation of Jewish jurists in Germany for Yiddish readers in Toronto. Statements by government officials had given Jews some hope that the massive expulsion of Jews from the courts of Germany would be tempered. Such hope, according to the Yiddish paper, was without foundation. The appeal of Bavarian Justice Minister Frank, in supporting the removal of all Jewish lawyers from German courts, was quoted: "We won't tolerate judges of foreign races, because Judah is aiming in this way to secure its domination again in Germany."

There was also bad news for Jewish authors and prospective Jewish university students. On 24 April *Der Yiddisher Zhurnal* reported that in Breslau, "All Works by Jewish-German Authors Are Confiscated by the Nazis." In Kiel, agents of the Military Committee to Fight the Un-Germanic Spirit confiscated the works of Jewish authors in the university bookstore. In another story entitled "No Jews Are Now Accepted in

German Universities," the *Zhurnal* painted a bleak picture for Jewish students:

> "The execution of the law concerning the percentual norm for Jews in universities and other institutes of learning has proved to be bound up with difficulties for the German government," reported the *Frankfurter Zeitung*. It points out that since, according to the government's interpretation, Germans born of mixed marriages and simply Germans of Jewish background are considered as Jews, it is very difficult to determine how many Jews are in German universities.
>
> The university administrations are awaiting instructions from the government which is supposed to explain to them how they are to act vis-à-vis the students who are already in the universities. It is expected that Jews will not be admitted at all to the universities for a number of years until the number of Jews who are studying is reduced to the desired quota.
>
> The newspaper reports that many institutions of learning are already not accepting Jewish pupils because they are waiting for such a law to be passed.

Also on 24 April, the *Star* reviewed Hitler's *Mein Kampf*. If there was any doubt in its readers' minds about the "philosophical" basis for the murder, torture, exclusion, and indignity suffered by German Jews, it was now dispelled.

> A reading of this book will make it clear why outrages were committed against Jews and why the campaign of anti-Jewish discrimination goes on without slackening. In this volume Hitler tells that he has been an anti-semite practically all his life. Early in life he discovered "the moral filthiness of the Jew," and he asked: "Is there any dirty, any shameless business anywhere of any kind in which there isn't at least one Jew mixed up?" The manifold activity of the Jew sent shudders through his adolescent brain full of propaganda pamphlets, and at last he recognized in Jewry "this pestilence, this spiritual pestilence, worse than the Black Death of old, with which the nation is being infected: there was no denying the fact that nine-tenths of the literary filth, the artistic pruriency and the imbecility of the stage could be laid at the door of a race that was less than 1 per cent of the population of Austria.

...This section of "Mein Kampf" is headed "Conversion to Anti-Semitism," and it concludes: "If the Jew wins...his crown of victory is the death-wreath of humanity, and this planet will once
again, as it did ages ago, float through the ether bereft of men.
Eternal Nature inexorably avenges the breaking of her law. And
to-day I believe I strive in the way of the Almighty Creator. When
I defend myself against the Jews I fight in the work of the Lord."
    Every Evil is Jewish....

In a front-page story on 26 April the *Star* wrote of those books by
Wells, Einstein, and Marx, among many others, that were on the Nazi
black list and doomed to fire. The following day *Der Yiddisher Zhurnal* carried the report that "the anti-semite Hitler and the soldier Seldte
will take the place of Einstein, Barbusse, Feuchtwanger, Remarque, and
other famous persons in the literature of the new Germany." The works
recommended to the new Germans, Canadian papers like the *Star* told
their readers, included "Chancellor Adolf Hitler's autobiography, 'My
Struggle'; books by Gregor Strasser and Gottfried Feder, Nazi leaders;
war novels by Franz Seldte, leader of the Steelhelmets, and other war
books by nationalist authors." In the next sentence, the *Star* went on to
report that, "the dye trust, the greatest firm in Germany, dropped 21 of
its 60 directors because they bore Jewish names." The article concluded
with reports of a number of resignations in the world of science and
scholarship.
    Quotas imposed upon Jewish students were also outlined in the *Star*:

> The cabinet has adopted a law fixing the admittance of Jewish stu-
> dents in German universities and state schools, according to their
> ratio of the entire population.
>   Jewish children whose fathers fought in German trenches dur-
> ing the great war, or one of whose parents is Aryan, are exempted.
> Children of Jews who emigrated from the east after August 1, 1914,
> are completely barred.

Der Yiddisher Zhurnal carried the same story and, as well, reported
the news that the Association of Jewish Youth Organizations had been
excluded from the Reich Committee of Youth Organizations and was
thus cut off from government financial support, youth programs, and
so on.
    On 4 May *Der Yiddisher Zhurnal* added to a story about continuing

purges in universities a report that Nazi religious leaders had asked for a ban on mixed marriages and on the attempted conversion of Jews to Christianity. On 9 May, the *Star* noted that further restrictions were to be imposed upon those Jews remaining in the civil service: "Jews maintaining offices because of war service must now show they underwent fire in the war and those who were ever identified with Communists or the Republican War Veterans Association are barred."

In his column in *Der Yiddisher Zhurnal* of 7 May, M. A. Tenenblatt summed up the precarious situation of the German Jews. He could not have known at the time just what the "final" solution to the Jewish question in Europe was to be; his forebodings were based on the facts at hand when he wrote:

> The entire apparatus of such a powerful government works against the remaining Jewish existence in Germany at a galloping pace. With some sort of solution the Jewish question will be ended in Hitler's Germany too. But before the "solution" is found, nothing will remain of German Jewry. Today all German Jews know this already and thus they are bringing their lives there to an end and seek to flee, the sooner the better.

On 12 May the *Star* reported that "Employees of Germany's largest chain store company, Epa, went on strike...demanding removal of the company's Jewish directors." On the same day the Yiddish paper carried the news that Jews were to be expelled from Germany for not paying their taxes on time, that the Nazis were considering a ban on the Order of the B'nai Brith, and that stateless persons, most of whom were Jews, would be interned in concentration camps. The new slogan of the Nazi press, the Yiddish paper claimed, was "Germany Lives When the Jew Dies."

On 16 May the *Zhurnal* reported on a plan to throw Jewish bankers and tobacco workers out of business. In the same story it told of a strike by workers at Ullstein publishers on account of the return of some of the Jewish staff. On 18 May the paper carried the story of a Nazi order according to which all Jewish white-collar workers in Germany were fired as of 1 October. It also noted that Jewish grocers could no longer buy or sell goods and that Jews in the provinces, unable to buy food, were flooding into Berlin. A further five thousand Jews had fled the country, the report said.

In its 2 June edition, the *Toronto Daily Star* reported that German telephone operators would no longer be allowed to use Jewish names when checking the spelling in telephone listings:

> The Nazis, in their determination to rid Germany of anything savoring of Semitism, are nothing if not thorough. Their activities have even entered the field of the German telephone service. German "hello girls" have now been ordered to stop using old Jewish names to facilitate the work of transmitting messages.
>
> The girls have been in the habit of saying "D" for David, "J" for Jacob, "N" for Nathan, "S" for Samuel, and "Z" for Zacharias. In future they are to say "D" for Deutschland, "N" for national, "S" for Siegfried, "J" for Joachim, and "Z" for Zeppelin.

On 7 June the Yiddish paper reported further exclusionary and discriminatory practices against Jews in Germany. One sub-headline read in part: "Jews Are Still Being Tossed Out of Their Positions—Their Places Are Being Taken by Nazis, Reports Minister—Company Advertises It Is *Judenrein* [cleansed of Jews]." The story also contained the news that sixty-seven Jewish lawyers in Frankfurt had received letters from the Minister of Justice stating that they would no longer be allowed to enter courtrooms, and that one hundred and thirty-six persons, most of them Jews, had been purged from the government radio system. The German Dunlop Rubber Company had also announced that it was "free of Jewish influence" (in other words, it had fired the Jews on its staff). Finally, the *Zhurnal* reported that the director of the Berlin Opera, Otto Klemperer, a Jew, had been fired.

Two days later the Yiddish paper wrote that Jewish lawyers in Germany would no longer be retained by municipalities to represent them and their interests. On 11 June the *Star* carried a bizarre page-one report with the heading: "Extend Jew Ban to Ashes of Dead." The item that followed read:

> Extension of the Nazification campaign to the ashes of the dead was proposed to-day in a resolution introduced in the city council by a Nazi faction.
>
> It would provide that ashes of Jews could not be deposited in Christian cemeteries or columbariums.
>
> Because the orthodox Jews prohibit cremation, many Jews deposit the ashes of their dead in Gentile cemeteries.

On 12 June the *Star* reported, on page one, that all persons of non-Aryan descent (the code word for Jews) would be barred from the German movie industry. "All producers, directors, authors, composers, cameramen, stagehands, sound men and cutters must declare themselves of Aryan descent and must submit either passports or birth documents showing the religion of their grandparents."[13] And the next day, 13 June, it expressed the belief that Germany was planning to fire all Jewish workers.

Der Yiddisher Zhurnal noted on 14 June that drugstores were not filling prescriptions issued by Jewish doctors and that schools would not accept notes written by Jewish doctors. Citing the Jewish-German Zionist newspaper *Die Jüdische Rundschau,* the Toronto Yiddish paper reported that yellow armbands for Jews were about to be introduced. An editorial in the same issue of the *Zhurnal* referred again to the "extermination program with respect to the Jews."

The main headline in the *Zhurnal* of 27 June read: "Jewish Merchants and Manufacturers Locked in Concentration Camps in Germany: Jewish merchants accused of economic sabotage. More than 100 Jewish doctors fired in Frankfurt. Nazi commissar of religion will decide if converts are Jews." The following day the Yiddish paper announced that the Nazis were beginning to take over Jewish organizations in Germany. It was expected, said the *Zhurnal,* that the Central Verein and leading Zionist organizations would be declared illegal. Furthermore, Jewish doctors were prevented from having their own private clinics or convalescent homes, seventy Jewish notaries had been expelled from office, and police were conducting raids on local establishments frequented by east-European Jews.

On 29 June the *Zhurnal* reported that foreign Jews with little income would be driven out of Germany. There was, it also warned, a plan to sterilize Jews, the mentally ill, and the physically handicapped. Part of the main headline reporting the proposed sterilization read: "New Nazi Plan to Exterminate Jews Adopted." Another article told of the arrest of more than two hundred Jewish children in Berlin, members of Zionist youth groups attending a memorial for Chaim Arlosoroff, a leader of the Mapai Party in Palestine who had been gunned down by unknown assassins on the streets of Tel Aviv a few days earlier.

On Monday, 3 July, the *Zhurnal* contained reports that Jews could no longer belong to trade unions, that in Tilsit a 10:00 p.m. curfew had been placed on the Jews, and that Jewish patients were no longer allowed to sit in waiting rooms while seeking medical attention. Items on 7 July noted that six thousand Jewish doctors had already been fired and that the infamous pamphlet the *Protocols of the Elders of Zion* had been adopted as a school text in Germany. The paper of 10 July carried the story of a Nazi raid on a self-help meeting organized by Jewish doctors. Nazi doctors who had learned of the meeting led the police to it. The Jewish doctors were arrested. Another story in the same issue, entitled "Germany's Goodheartedness Won't Allow It to Do What It Must with the Jews, Says Nazi," reported the ominous comment of the Reich's Commissar of Justice, Frank:

> "What German Jews are now experiencing is not yet in fact the full measure of that which Germany is justified in doing to the Jews.... Germany can do what it wants, including even exterminating the Jews," he proclaimed.

On 12 July the Yiddish paper noted that the German Chess Association was officially *Judenrein,* and quoted a Nazi judge as saying that ritual murders by Jews were a fact. Another report told of Jews being expelled from the executive of metallurgical industries. However, the report continued, the lack of expertise among its remaining employees had forced the company to hire some of the Jews back on a contractual basis.

On 21 July both the *Star* and the *Zhurnal* carried news of the closing of the Jewish Telegraphic Agency in Berlin. According to the *Star* report:

> The government to-day ordered the Jewish Telegraph [*sic*] Agency, a Jewish news agency, to close its offices and cease serving German papers. The order was "for the protection of public security." It was believed the agency would be permitted to continue to send German news abroad.
>
> A Jewish telegraphic agency dispatch from Berlin said the secret police confiscated all furniture and equipment in the bureau.

The atmosphere in Germany by mid-summer was eloquently portrayed in the following front-page *Zhurnal* headline of 1 August: "God Calls Kill Off the Jews, Nazis Openly Call to Pogrom: Berlin is suddenly covered with bloody pogrom agitation. Jews are not humans, it is proclaimed, but poisonous snakes..." A leaflet distributed in the capital linked the hysterical outbreak of antisemitism to the swastika and to what was to become the "final solution"—extermination.

CHAPTER 3   "Keep the Beaches Clean"

At various beaches in the Toronto vicinity swastikas were displayed. In particular, swastikas were put up on the building and in the area of a canoe club and what is more with the words "Hail Hitler." In addition, many persons on the beach wore swastikas on their leather windbreakers, oil coats and sweaters or they wore a button with a swastika. Furthermore, notices were posted on the beach to the effect that undesirables should stay away. These demonstrations originated with the so-called Swastika Club. This was a voluntary association which had no organs—no president and no secretary—and raised no membership dues. The members only wore a swastika as an emblem. No speeches were to be held and no parades were to take place. The wearing of the emblem was to have the desired effect. It was assumed that this was within the law and that nothing could be undertaken against it.

The appearance of the swastika excited the Jewish population exceedingly and repeated clashes occurred.... The mayor of Toronto, Stewart, sought expert opinion from his legal counsel as to whether the police should order those wearing the swastika to take it off. The legal counsel concluded in this regard that the police would be justified in intervening if, in their view, peace were to be threatened by some demonstration.

—L. Kempff, German Consul-General, in a dispatch to Berlin, August 1933

Kempff proceeded to inform his superiors that the mayor of Toronto, fearful that public displays of the swastika could result in a serious demonstration, objected to the presence of the Swastika Club. At the mayor's request, continued Kempff, the Swastika Club was dissolved and replaced by a new society.

The second event the Consul-General reported was the actual riot itself. The incident sparking the riot was described objectively and was based on accounts which appeared in the Toronto papers. What little editorializing done by the German Consul was obviously undertaken to please his new political masters in Berlin. According to Kempff, "a large number of citizens" objected to the mayor's warning that displays of the swastika were liable to prosecution. Dissatisfied with the decision to abandon the Swastika Club, Kempff said, "numerous members of the Swastika Club...were supposed to have joined a new Swastika organization."

The report also referred to events occurring around this period in two other cities near Toronto—Kitchener and Orillia. In the former, wrote Kempff, "there were signs, albeit weak ones, of Fascist activity," culminating in a meeting chaired "by one of those persons who had particularly distinguished himself in the Swastika Club in Toronto." As for Orillia, all of the Jews were in receipt of a letter warning them not to appear on the beach on a particular Saturday. "The letter was signed 'O.S.C.' (Ontario Swastika Club). The result was that on Saturday not a single Jew was at the beach. Of course, there were no swastikas to be seen either," signed off Kempff.

On 1 and 2 August, headlines in the Toronto English-language newspapers introduced readers to the formation of a Swastika Club in the city. They reported that members of the newly formed club had organized their first march up and down the boardwalk from Balmy Beach to Woodbine Avenue. As far as the Jews were concerned, the headlines called attention to the potential spread of Nazi horrors in their own backyard. "Nazi Organization Seeking to Oust Non-Gentiles Off Beach," wrote the *Star,* while the *Telegram* announced that "Toronto 'Swastikas' Arouse Jews: Hundreds Don Swastikas in Drive to Rid Beaches of 'Undesirable Persons.'" On 2 August the *Globe* informed its readers that the police would halt a possible " 'Swastika' Clash," while the *Mail and Empire* captured the public's attention with the following bold headline: "Balmy Beach Dance Hall Closed to Avert Swastika Row: Nazi Parade Tours Boardwalk Singing Anti-Jewish Doggerel." Amplifying its previous day's account, the *Star's* lead front-page story of 2 August stated that the swastika emblems had vanished from the Beaches as Jews paraded there. Mistakenly, however, it announced that the Swastika Club would disband. *Der Yiddisher Zhurnal,* in its 2 August coverage of the story, simply offered further evidence that Jews were targets for abuse. In comparison to the horrors facing German Jewry, the sudden appearance of the Swastika Club in Toronto was hardly cause for alarm. Enormous anxiety and suspicion were nevertheless aroused in the Jewish community: would the hatred against Jews spewed out by Nazi propaganda attract support in Toronto?

Intent on demonstrating its disapproval of the "recent influx of obnoxious visitors" to the Beaches area of Toronto, the organization known as the Swastika Club was first formed in Ward 8. According to the *Telegram,* it was based "on the line of the famous Hitler brown shirts in Germany." To date, reported the press, six local branches, with a membership of over four hundred, existed in the east end.

Tensions around the Beaches area originated in the south-eastern part of the city, a section miles from the Jewish residential area. Toronto's eastern beaches and parks were a favourite picnic area for thousands of Jewish immigrants who could not afford to buy or rent summer cottages and who did not have the means to travel to summer resorts (many of which, in any event, did not welcome Jews). The customs, cuisine, and language of the weekend visitors were different from the prevailing norms in that area of the city.

Residents of the Beaches were disturbed at the increasing presence of outsiders and their seeming disregard for "proper" behaviour. "You couldn't find a place to sit down on the beach or on the park land," one Beach resident recalled. "And there were branches torn off these young trees...and half-eaten food, peels, candy wrappers strewn all over the place. And this was your area where you were living and you would come down and see all that every Monday morning. No wonder people were annoyed."

A resident of Balmy Beach since 1920 provided us with interesting background material concerning the nature of the area and the underlying causes of local hostility to weekend visitors:

> Balmy Beach was a little district about two blocks from north to south and about maybe five blocks from east to west. And it was like a very small town. Everybody knew everybody.... I don't recall more than two families moving out of the district the whole time I lived there. And it was a very small close-knit community. No one would have dreamed of locking their doors. In fact, you never closed your door in the summer.... And the men all came home around the same time around six-thirty at night and had supper and then your mother shoved all the kids in bed. I was still getting put to bed at seven when I was about fourteen. Then everybody went down to the Beach.

...There is a boardwalk and there is a park behind it.... There were houses all along the front there. And each one had a boat-house built into the bank, you see. Every family had at least one canoe...and you would sit on the sand at night and then build a bonfire and cook wieners or corn and whatever is in season.... A couple of the men, one of them had a banjo and ukulele and they had a singsong and all the canoes would be out on the water.... But then on Saturday nights there was a dance at the Balmy Beach Canoe Club but it was just for residents. And they contributed money, but it wasn't really a thing you could pay to get into. And the women all wore evening dresses, quite a nice thing to see.

But then politics disturbed the serenity of this Beaches idyll. "Well, when Sam McBride was the mayor...it [the city of Toronto] came along to buy these lakefront properties, and people didn't want to sell so they expropriated them. Well this made everybody mad as heck if you must know." The expropriations did indeed lead to a growing anger among the local residents directed against both the city administration and the exotic visitors who were drawn to the new facilities.

Another long-time resident of the Beaches remembered the summer of 1933 vividly:

After the parkland and boardwalk were completed and young trees planted, people from the inner city and the west end came to the beach literally by the truckload. Benches were improvised from planks and small barrels and used as seating in stake trucks with tall removable sides. Those with private cars sometimes changed into bathing suits in the cars. The streets leading to the beach from Queen Street were lined with cars and trucks on both sides all the way down. Sand and parkland were so crowded that local residents were unable to use the facilities on Sundays. A walk in the area on Monday morning was *not* a sight to behold. The re-fuse cans were filled to overflowing and fruit peelings, half-eaten sandwiches, candy wrappers, etc., and small branches from the young trees were strewn everywhere.

Each of the English-language daily newspapers quoted from conver-sations with area residents who repeated that the beach and park were being transformed every weekend into a picnic ground. The local res-idents, they claimed, had difficulty keeping their lawns clear of these strangers and were inconvenienced by parked cars that blocked their driveways. They also felt that using parked automobiles as dressing rooms for bathers was indecent and intolerable. As the *Mail and Empire* put it:

> Every Monday morning it takes 13 men half a day to clean up the beaches. They start at one end and go to the other. The beach is strewn with sandwiches, bad fruit, newspapers, all kinds of garbage. The result is that the district has become a fly-infested area. The beach swarms with flies, a fact which any person swimming here will attest. Flies never plagued the district up till the beaches were littered with junk. Cars and trucks are jammed in there so tightly that residents can't get in and out. We are happy to have visitors here because we are darned proud of the district. All we ask is that they observe some rules of decency. It is a regular thing for us to look out a window into a car in which two or three persons are changing their clothing. And on Sundays trucks bring loads of men and women who stay all day and take no care about how they dress nor where they strew the remains of their lunches.[1]

Though "outsiders" visiting the beaches included members of the city's various ethnic minorities, attention focused entirely on the presence of Jews. An unsigned letter received by the Parks Department on 29 June 1933 reflected the concerns of a Beach resident:

> Do you think it would be possible to place a few picnic tables under the trees in Kew Beach Park, this side of the tennis court...and also to place a sign upon the trees—The area for Gentiles only. At the present it is quite impossible to get a table in the Park, at all on Sunday: for the Jewish people seem to get every table in the Park and even if there were room for others to sit at the same table, one would hardly like to share the same table with them as our ways are so entirely different. Last week while hunting for a table so that we could spread a cloth and have a nice cool outdoor lunch, we came across 2 or 3 tables but they were allready [*sic*] occupied by Jewish people sleeping on them, so we had to be contented with eating on the grass and then our picnic was spoiled with ants crawling on the food.
>
> I have seen the Jewish people stand their children, (and rather big children at that) on the tables and strip them, then dry them

after being in the lake and then dress them. Now who could sit and eat at that table with them?[2]

Referring to the Jewish presence, a former Beach resident remarked: "There probably were other ethnic groups too. You couldn't pick out whether this person was Polish or that person was Jewish or what they were. But somehow or other the anger seemed to be aimed at the Jews."

On the evening of 1 August, the first Swastika party route march was co-ordinated along the boardwalk from the Balmy Beach Canoe Club to Woodbine Avenue. A group of nearly one hundred youths, acting in support of the newly formed swastika-flaunting organization, paraded down the eastern beaches' boardwalk singing an anti-Jewish song to the tune of "Home on the Range":

> O give me a home, where the Gentiles may roam,
> Where the Jews are not rampant all day;
> Where seldom is heard a loud Yiddish word
> And the Gentiles are free all the day.[3]

Adherents of the Swastika Club declared that same evening that they intended to stage a similar parade and sing the same or similar songs along the boardwalk at three o'clock next Sunday afternoon. While the name "Jew" was nowhere specifically mentioned in any of the organization's announcements or literature, Toronto Jewry was immediately convinced that the Swastika Club's objectives were antisemitic in character. Certain that the epithet "obnoxious visitors" applied to them, some sixty to seventy "sturdy Jews," as the *Star* described them, arrived at the beach *en masse* around nine-thirty in the evening. They marched down Kew Beach Avenue and paced the boardwalk to the Balmy Beach clubhouse, where the swastika sign had been posted. But the signs had all been removed before they arrived.

These Jews were part of the "up-town gang," led by Al Kaufman, self-styled "king of the hoboes." Five and six abreast, they walked along the boardwalk without interference. "Kaufman," the *Star* reported, "with a large dog on a leash,"

> ...walked ahead of the party down the steps and on the narrow boardwalk along the lake front of the clubhouse. No one said a word to him. He walked past the members of the club who were

at the refreshment counter, and his gang followed. They followed him up the steps at the eastern side of the club and on to the lawn. "As soon as we got on the club grounds we mingled with those who appeared to be members of the club and at the same time looked for emblems of the Nazi organization," Kaufman told the *Star*. "We couldn't find any. If we had we would have torn them off and if there had been any trouble I think we could have taken care of ourselves." Kaufman and his "gang" paraded in small groups up and down five streets close to the clubhouse property, looking for Nazi emblems, but reported that they couldn't find any trace of one.[4]

Members of the Balmy Beach Canoe Club had learned of the proposed invasion of their clubhouse grounds and had prepared accordingly. Reported the *Star*: "Younger Beachites had broom handles and some of the more athletic had lacrosse sticks, having gone straight to the club after the game at the Beach Stadium."[5] The appearance of the young Jewish men caused alarm among club officials. The police officer on the beat notified No. 10 police station and Inspector Majury, accompanied by a sergeant and several officers, appeared shortly afterwards and cleared the ground. The protesting group reportedly showed no resistance and dispersed in a more-or-less orderly manner. On the advice of Inspector Majury, Commodore Gordon O. "Curly" Thorne of the club halted the dance in progress in the ballroom and called upon those present to disperse and leave the clubhouse to avoid trouble. About four hundred persons were present in the dance hall at the time. The orchestra played "God Save the King," and those present were gradually ordered out. On his return to the Main Street police station shortly before midnight, Inspector Majury was reported as saying: "We have large crowds out here every night during the summer. So far we have had good feeling among all our citizens and we intend that nothing shall be done to spoil it. There was nothing to-night to cause any friction among any sections of our population. We only took precautions."[6]

The inspector's attempt to minimize the potential for violence was probably overly-optimistic if one can believe the *Globe*'s version of the incident. Although the Swastika organization had been warned that Jews were on their way to tear down the signs, they had not yet mobilized their members by the time the crowd reached the clubhouse. A sign that had been on the post in front of the building had been taken down earlier in the day. It was not long, however, until the Swastikas assembled. About two hundred strong, they marched from one end of the boardwalk to the other.

"They marched in files of about ten deep, with a number of the more husky members in the front ranks."[7] Many of them wore the shining swastika emblem. In the rear, the throng of followers intermittently shouted "*Heil*," while strains of "God Save the King" were also heard. As they neared the western extremity of the boardwalk, the leader ordered an about-turn and the Swastikas walked back to the Balmy Beach clubhouse where they gathered and stood about in a circle for some time. At close to midnight they had not yet dispersed. The *Globe* reported:

> The Jews arrived on the scene in a large transport truck, and left by the same medium. Although police were on the job prepared for trouble, there was none, the Jews going in an orderly manner when requested to do so by the police. And the police did not interfere with the Swastikas as they marched up and down the boardwalk. Had the Swastikas been organized when the Jews arrived, there would have been an opportunity for the two parties to start trouble. As it was, they did not actually meet. But that there is considerable feeling in the matter was evidenced by the numbers in the Swastika parade.[8]

Though Kaufman and his associates were unable to find evidence of the swastika, the emblem was certainly being displayed in the area. The "storm centre of the campaign," to quote the *Star*, was Balmy Beach where, until the previous evening, large signs bearing the symbol together with the words "Hail Hitler" were exposed in full view of the clubhouse. It was only after news of the campaign became public that the signs were removed by club officials. Youths wearing swastika badges, which were made of nickel with a red swastika cross impressed on them, paraded up and down the boardwalk from Kew Beach to Balmy Beach early in the evening. There were also several young men in white sweatshirts stencilled with a black swastika emblem. Despite official claims that the Balmy Beach Canoe Club was not involved with the newly formed Swastika organization, much of the evidence suggested otherwise. To begin with, an "Open letter to all members of the Balmy Beach Canoe Club," from Swastika Club Local No. 5, was posted on the club's bulletin board.

Recently, as you no doubt know [the letter began] conditions have become unbearable, and Beach people are gradually being forced to go elsewhere to avoid the presence of undesirables. Local No. 5 of the Swastika Clubs has been formed in Kew Beach, and now has a membership of forty. Commencing Monday, July 31st, our members will appear on the beaches, boardwalk, and in Kew Gardens and adjacent parks wearing a nickel-plated badge with a swastika thereon. They will simply wear the emblem. There will be no parades or demonstrations. No speeches will be made. We feel that the emblem will have a desired effect. This is quite legal, and no interference can take place.[9]

"There is no membership fee," the letter continued, "no president or secretary-treasurer. All you are asked to do is buy an emblem and WEAR it." The letter added that the badges were attractive, were being sold at absolute cost, and were being distributed as a labour of love, not a racket. Another notice posted on the bulletin board, headed "Join the Swastika Club," followed the same line:

Residents, both young and old, of the Beaches, are not a little per-turbed at the recent influx of obnoxious visitors to Kew Gardens and surrounding territory on Saturdays and Sundays. Have you the courage to outwardly indicate your disapproval? If so, join the Swastika Club. It has no president, secretary, etc.[and] its sole object is to maintain the beauty of the neighbourhood in which its members are residents and taxpayers, and to enable those residents to enjoy, in comfort, the beautiful parks and beaches of the area. If you wish to join sign the sheet with your name, address and phone number. There are no fees. The club badge may be obtained on payment of twenty-five cents (actual cost). Please give your orders to the man in charge where this notice is posted. PLEASE WEAR YOUR BADGE WHENEVER YOU ARE ON THE BOARDWALK, IN KEW GARDENS OR ANY OTHER AFFECTED AREA. Have the COURAGE OF YOUR CONVICTIONS. Join the Club AND WEAR THE BADGE. A sample badge may be seen on the premises. Let your slogan be THE BEACHES FOR THE BEACHES.

Gordon Thorne, commodore of the Balmy Beach Canoe Club, re-fused to comment on the Swastika organization or the fact that signs had been posted on the beach in front of the club: "No one had any permission to erect the signs; other than that I have nothing to say." As for the notices on the bulletin board, John Fitzgerald, a club member, remarked to the *Mail and Empire*:

> Somebody asked if they could stick the letter up and I said it was o.k. without reading it. Then I noticed that my name was signed to it. Even then I didn't read it and I can't say actually what it had in it because it was taken down and thrown away before I had a chance to read it.[10]

According to the written notice, Balmy Beach members who wished to join the Swastika Club were asked to pay twenty-five cents for their emblems to Mr. Fitzgerald. When asked by the *Telegram* for the names of the organizers of the movement, he described the Swastika organization as a "mystery club." "To whom do you give the money for the badges?" he was asked. "A man I know to see delivers the badges and I pay him for them. I can't tell you his name," was the reply.[11]

A resident who was close to leading members of the Balmy Beach Canoe Club in 1933 claimed that the newspapers were misled by Fitzgerald:

> To begin with, the Swastika Club had nothing to do with the Balmy Beach Canoe Club and they didn't even know who put the notice up. What I liked was Johnny Fitzgerald being the semi-official spokesman for the club. Johnny Fitzgerald was a kid who hung around the club and he was a few bricks short of a load and he had nothing to do with the club whatsoever. But he gave this interview to the reporters. So you can forget anything John said.

According to this commentator there had been trouble at the canoe club independently of the activities of the Swastika Club, with a "rumble" at a dance between groups of boys, some of them Jewish. When asked who belonged to the Swastika Club, she replied: "Oh nobody knows. We never found out who belonged to it. It wasn't the kids at the club. None of them belonged to it." And her comment on the suggestion that there were boys walking around the Beaches wearing swastikas was simply, "Yeah, I remember reading that in an article, and I remember my husband saying 'well funny we never saw anything like that.'" However, a resident of the Beaches for more than sixty years recalled that members of the Balmy Beach Canoe Club played a key role in the formation of the Swastika Club. According to her written account:

> While nothing could be done about the situation in the public area, members of the Balmy Beach [Canoe] Club decided to take matters into their own hands, as an area around their clubhouse was private property. They improvised a black flag bearing a white Swastika and "Heil Hitler" also in white, and flew it above their clubhouse. The young people in the area wanted to join with the Balmy Beach members and the "Swastika Club" was born.
>
> One had to be eighteen years of age, and a membership badge could be purchased at a variety store at the corner of Queen and Wineva. The Badge was chrome and bore a red Swastika.

A prominent member of the Swastika Club described for the *Telegram* how his branch came into existence, but refused to allow his name to be published. According to his account, a number of members of the club had erected the swastika sign on a post in front of the clubhouse in order to warn "these persons" that they were not wanted in that territory. Then the unknown stranger appeared, representing the Kew Beach local, and posted the sign on the bulletin board. Within a few days, thirty-five members had been enrolled in the club. The first badges, showing a black swastika on a metal background, were similar to a sheriff's badge. Later the scarlet emblem was adopted, to distinguish it from the German swastika. Still another member of the Club, "well known in sporting circles," according to the *Telegram,* admitted to being an organizer of the Balmy Beach local on condition that his name not be disclosed. He informed the *Telegram*'s reporter that there had been several small disturbances at the beach of late. More specifically, the "obnoxious visitors" had attempted to use the clubhouse dressing room and had been greeted with a pail of cold water.[12]

The discrepancies in these accounts probably arise because at least some members of the canoe club may have been sympathetic enough with the aims and objectives of the Swastika organization to join it. However, according to canoe club officials, attempts to link the club with the Swastikas were misplaced and deflected attention from the realities of friendship and goodwill between the canoe club and the Jews. As John Fitzgerald explained:

Why, we have no quarrel with Jews. There are some Jewish members of the club whom we all cherish as friends and good fellows and girls. There are just as many Gentiles who create nuisances and indecent exposures. So far as I know, the Swastikas are opposed to them as much as anyone else. But, understand that I am not a member of the club [Swastika]; I know nothing about it except what I hear and I don't even know who its members are. Naturally, we regret that the incident of the sign occurred and we apologize sincerely if any embarrassment has been caused anyone.[13]

The same commentator who questioned Fitzgerald's credibility nevertheless agreed that antisemitism had little to do with the agitation on the beach:

But as far as anti-Jewish feeling, antisemitism goes, I think it was strictly xenophobia. We don't want anybody in our beach and the thing is at that time the Jews were the only visible minority there was because the Chinese never left Elizabeth Street.

Another resident of the Beaches area at the time agreed that antisemitism had little to do with the trouble there, although, according to her recollection, several Jewish families moved out of the area on account of the ferment.

Efforts by canoe club members to deny Swastika affiliation lacked conviction, as far as *Der Yiddisher Zhurnal* was concerned. For this newspaper, the link between the clubs was obvious, not merely alleged, as it was for the English-language press. The *Zhurnal*'s 2 August headline proclaimed that a Nazi organization had been established in Ward 8 to rid the Beaches of Jewish visitors. The *Zhurnal*'s report of the Swastika Club's formation was brief compared to the accounts in the English-language press; but the report set the tone for what followed over the next few days. It was clear, the *Zhurnal* felt, that Jews were the central targets of the Swastika Club. Moreover, it was hypocritical for the organization to present itself as a peaceful one. *Der Yiddisher Zhurnal* wrote:

A "Swastika Club" which considers Hitler as its patron saint, and is not yet intelligent enough to understand the entire Nazi program, was established in Ward 8 and has meanwhile established one holy and "patriotic" goal: to drive the Jews from the beaches areas.... The arrogant lads who are appealing to all residents of Ward 8 to join their organization are not yet sufficiently arrogant to say who they are. But only the leaders are hiding....[14]

A theme emphasized by the *Zhurnal* from the beginning was the veil of secrecy around the club's newly formed leadership and the warranted suspicion of ulterior motives.

Unlike the English-language press, which only reported these events, the *Zhurnal* also editorialized on the developing situation from the very outset. Its 2 August editorial, "It is 'Made in Germany,'" read:

> It is very possible that the organizers of the "Swastika Club" in Toronto only intended to drive the Jews from the city parks and beaches, where Jews from various areas of the city come after work on Saturdays and Sundays to cool themselves off and enjoy themselves. But it is also possible that the Hitlerite idea has sunk roots in Toronto....
>
> It is truly not necessary to become hysterical, but the situation is very serious and ought to be so regarded by Toronto Jewry. One must not allow this "Hitler bastard" to grow. It is "made in Germany" and must not be permitted to enter Canada.[15]

If *Der Yiddisher Zhurnal* and spokesmen in the Jewish community attempted to maximize the potential threat of the Swastika Club for Jews in the city, spokesmen for the Swastika organization attempted to allay such fears. In fact, argued Swastika adherents, the club's objectives were noble and indeed worthy of emulation by other civic-minded groups and organizations. "Keep the beaches clean" was the Swastika organization's adopted slogan. As the *Mail and Empire* reported: "Up and down the boardwalk along the Eastern Beaches, in the locker-rooms and on the dance floor of the Balmy Beach Canoe Club, on the Lake Front, Hubbard Boulevard and Kew Gardens verandahs, everywhere in the Beaches section of Toronto, this slogan of the recently-formed Swastika Club was subject of discussion last night."[16]

According to members of the Swastika Club, the new organization was directed not primarily against Jews as a race, but against indecent conduct on the beaches. The *Star* quoted one member as follows: "It [the Swastika Club] is comprised of Beach residents who want to keep the Beaches clean and nice, and have adopted this way of doing it. It is not a gang of hoodlums or an anti-Jewish organization."[17] Another member interviewed by the *Globe* "intimated that Jews who were residents of the section might join if they wished."[18] In response to the *Star* reporter's question, "Could a Jew join your club, if he expressed his sincere wish to cooperate in keeping the beaches nice?" a club member replied, "Absolutely. There are many Jews, residents of the Beaches district, who are absolutely in accord with our campaign."[19] Refusing to name any such Jews, this member insisted that any person could join and buy a badge. A *Mail and Empire* reporter, meeting with several members of the Swastika Club the previous evening at a confectionery shop at 2209 Queen Street, described the encounter as follows:

> Each was wearing the silver-plated disc enscrolled with the red swastika emblem. They denied that their organization had any association politically, racially or religiously with any other organization, that it was formed for the intention of preventing indescent [*sic*] conduct along the beaches by its members notifying police of improper actions and that Jews were welcome to join if they were Beach area residents.[20]

In the same report, the newspaper quoted a man who, declining to give his name, had telephoned the previous night with what he claimed was an official communiqué from the Swastika Club's inner sanctum:

> The Swastika Club. The club for Beach residents of all creeds. We are in no way connected with any political, foreign, or religious organizations. We are not a military organized body. We have absolutely no affiliations with any Nazi, Fascist, or similar organization. Our badge is a token of good luck in our endeavour. Our aim is the maintenance of our Beaches and parks in a manner befitting their beauty.[21]

Announcing that the statement expressed the feelings of Swastika Club locals 5 and 6—representing Kew Beach and Balmy Beach respectively—he refused to divulge whether other locals had been formed at the other beaches. Moreover, he denied that the original Swastika Club had any affiliation with the group of about one hundred youths who paraded along the boardwalk to the Balmy Beach Canoe Club singing an anti-Jewish song. He added: "We have no organized parades. We sing no songs. We are simply a silent protest against disfiguring our beaches and parks."

Throughout the city, prominent civic leaders, clergymen, and Jewish citizens deplored the organization's tendency to incite racial ill-feeling. At the same time many felt that Torontonians would not stand for such a movement, and were inclined to minimize the affair as the sporadic outburst of a few young people on the eastern beaches. By contrast, residents of the Beaches predicted that outbreaks of violence could be expected if the organization continued to exist. On 1 August the *Evening Telegram* reported that on Sunday, 30 July, at least three fights had broken out in the Beaches area between residents and visitors and suggested that further trouble could be expected. "Just wait another two weeks until our organization is completed," the *Telegram* quoted one member of the Swastika Club as saying.

Reaction to the sudden appearance of the Swastika Club, and to its adoption of the Nazi emblem, ranged from outright disgust to harsh disapproval. To the Jews, the Swastikas were blatantly antisemitic and represented a deviation from the British standards and ideals held in high esteem by the citizenry of Toronto. "It is beneath contempt," commented Rabbi Samuel Sachs, Chairman of the League for the Defence of Jewish Rights, the day before the League issued a statement condemning the tactics of the Swastika Club. "There always are people like that," he continued, "and it should not perturb anyone, except that I do not like to see the Swastika displayed anywhere in Toronto where the government is based on real democracy. It smacks too much of Hitlerism and Fascism."[22] For Meyer Steinglass, managing editor of the *Jewish Standard*, the Swastika Club was the nucleus of a Hitler organization. "It is not merely a manifestation of anti-Semitism," he said, "but it is a contradiction of the principles of political and social equality as championed by our form of government in Canada." He continued: "We must remember that Fascism is as much opposed to our democracy as it is to Jews. The Jews are not the only ones in danger from such a movement, for Fascism is as much a threat to Canadian liberty as Communism; it is just as ruthless in the suppression of individual rights and liberties."[23]

Attempting to rouse the ire of Toronto's citizenry, he encouraged people not to define this newly formed swastika organization as a Jewish problem only: "If public opinion generally does not speak up in denunciation of such a movement, by its acquiescence the public is supporting it and guilty of allowing it to spread."[24]

Some Jewish philanthropic community leaders saw the formation of the Swastika Club in Toronto as a continuation of a Fascist-inspired movement against the Jews in Montreal. This story received prominent attention in the *Star*'s 2 August edition—"Hint Beach Ban on Jews Part of Vast Propaganda"—and also served as headlines for both the *Zhurnal* and the *Jewish Standard* of 3 August. Jews were not alone in condemning the activities of the Swastikas: Christian clergymen, too, denounced the antisemitic movement that was sweeping the east-end beaches. "Absolutely unchristian," stated Rev. W. L. Baynes Reed, rector of St. John's Norway, a Protestant church in the Beaches area. He added: "You may be sure the Christian clergymen of the city will denounce, in the strongest terms, such a narrow attitude. All races pay taxes and have equal rights on the city beaches... This sort of thing only leads to needless cruelty and suffering."[25] The Rev. D. N. McLachlin, secretary of the board of evangelism and social service of the United Church, agreed with Jewish community leaders' perception that the Swastika Club was an attempt to assist Hitlerism in gaining support in Canada:

> It is very unfortunate that the influence of Hitler should have gained a foothold in Canada. There is no room in this country for such pernicious doctrines as the Nazis are preaching. Unless this Swastika Club, so-called, is nipped in the bud, I have grave fears that we may have a serious situation on our hands.[26]

Reactions from Toronto city aldermen were equally critical of the newly formed Swastika Club. Some believed that it was best ignored, while others publicly opposed it, though they were not opposed to the legitimate grievances of Beaches residents. "The whole principle is all wrong," said Alderman Nathan Phillips, "and I don't think it will gain any prominence in an enlightened city like Toronto." He added:

> Our institutions are on a sound foundation and this sort of rot simply won't go. Any organization that is afraid to come out in the open and refuses to give the names of its officials won't make much headway. The same thing will happen to it as has happened to similar organizations in other places. Its objectives could not be condoned on political or moral grounds. At best, the grievances of the Beach residents could be acknowledged sympathetically.[27]

"Needless to say I think that this movement to oust the Jews from the waterfront is an insult to our Canadian institutions and that it is inconceivable for anyone who calls himself a Canadian to emulate Hitler," declared Alderman J. J. Glass.[28] Alderman F. M. Baker, of Ward 8, concurred in condemning the Swastika Club, but requested an increased police presence in the Beaches. "There are a certain class of visitors," he said, "who undress and change into their bathing suits right on the open beach. Some of them go around practically stark naked. It is a terrible condition and there is certainly a need for more police supervision between Woodbine Avenue and Kew Beach." Aldermen F. M. Johnson and Robert A. Allen of Ward 1 and Alderman G. C. Elgie of Ward 8 were among those who went on record as officially opposed to the Swastika Club's campaign.

In a statement issued 1 August, at midnight, Mayor Stewart declared that alleged Hitlerism and reported demonstrations at the eastern beaches would be thoroughly investigated by the police. Toronto, the mayor insisted, would never tolerate any group that attempted to take the law into its own hands. His statement read in part:

> Let it be understood with the utmost clearness that we administer our laws through police courts, and not through private groups, clubs or demonstrations. We have an abundance of British ideals which our people might emulate and follow: we need no inspiration from foreign sources and foreign isms, but simply a proper respect for laws and order and British traditions.... This matter will be investigated right to its rest and will be dealt with firmly and fearlessly. We must follow British tradition, the British idea, in Toronto: the organizations or the political organisms of foreign lands do not need to be adopted, used, nor aped in this country.[29]

In a report to Mayor Stewart on what he described as "the altercation which occurred last night between the Beaches Club members and some of the Hebrews of the city," Chief Constable Draper stated:

> Some of the members of the Canoe Club placed signs bearing Hitler emblems on the lawn, which caused Hebrew protests. A call came to No. 10 station between 9 and 10 o'clock p.m. that a number of Hebrew people were there trying to cause a disturbance.
>
> In company with P. S. Robertson, P. S. Milton and four police constables, Inspector Majury visited the hall in question and, as a means of averting any further disturbance, advised those in charge to close same. This was done and the grounds cleared. There was nothing of a serious character transpired.

An effort is being made to obtain one of the emblems, referred to, which apparently caused the disturbance.[30]

By the afternoon of the same day, a number of conflicting rumours were spreading concerning possible dissolution of the Swastika Club. In two well-set-off headlines, the *Star* announced: "Swastika Clubs Disband/Say Aims Misunderstood" and "Swastika Clubs are Short-lived." According to this latter report, the Swastika clubs of Kew Beach and Balmy Beach had, in fact, already disbanded. Both the *Toronto Daily Star* and the *Evening Telegram* received anonymous telephone calls from a man who read what appeared to be a prepared statement. In line with the announcement issued by Mayor Stewart, the caller said, the Swastika clubs were no longer in existence. "The desire of ex-members of the clubs," the caller informed the *Telegram,* "is only to co-operate to the fullest extent with the civic administration."[31]

Two further anonymous calls were received by the *Telegram.* In each case the caller insisted that the Swastika clubs fully intended to pursue their objectives. Moreover, the newspaper was informed that Local No. 7 had been established at Lake Wilcox the previous day. The second caller's statement was even more defiant:

We deny the disbanding of the Swastika club. As long as this is legal we will stick to our guns. We will cause no trouble whatsoever, no pranks or demonstrations. We hope in the future to form many more locals in Toronto. We believe that the residents of the Beach will back our movement and if necessary we will have a petition signed by as many Beach residents as care to do so.[32]

The *Telegram* headlined its story "Anonymous Speakers Say Swastikas Won't Disband Despite Mayor's Request"; the *Globe's* headline read: "Swastikas Continue in Beach Campaign 'Within the Law,'" and the premature report of the dissolution of the clubs was attributed to a dissatisfied former member.

CHAPTER 4 "Jews Flee in Terror from Nazi Torture"

They were chained together. All clothes were taken from them. They were naked. They were given food once a day. Every night they were visited by Nazis and their ladies when they were made to run around the cellar under the whiplash of their tormentors. They were made to sing the Nazi campaign song: "In Jewish blood we'll bathe." Nazi boys extinguished their cigarette butts on their bodies. They were beaten with metal rods.
—"Naked and Chained Distinguished Jews Murdered by Nazis," *Toronto Daily Star*, 1 April 1933

Sporadic violence along Toronto's eastern beaches, of an antisemitic cast and involving Jewish and Gentile youth, was common fare in the early 1930s; but conflict intensified during the summer of 1933 following the Nazi accession to power in Germany. The sudden appearance of the swastika symbol freely flaunted by members of the newly established Swastika Club provided a qualitatively different dimension to the anti-Jewish sentiments heretofore expressed by Gentile youths. The swastika was identified with the Nazi regime and symbolized the murders, tortures, and beatings suffered by German Jewry. Unable to direct their anger and frustration against the actual perpetrators of this violence, Jewish youth could at least strike out at those who symbolically aligned themselves with the perpetrators.

As Chapter 2 made clear, the Toronto newspapers chronicled the exclusion and humiliation of Jews in Germany during the spring of 1933. There were also numerous horrifying page-one reports of physical violence directed at Germany's Jews-murder, kidnapping, beatings, and torture. The violence that erupted at the Beaches and Christie Pits has to be understood in light of the tensions such accounts generated in Toronto.

More than anything, the swastika represented physical violence and degradation to Jews. The violent responses to appearances of the swasti-ka in Toronto were a product of outrage at Nazi atrocities, helplessness to act in defence of German Jewry, and anger at those who, for whatever reason, adopted and displayed the hated emblem. The Swastika Club's denial of a connection to Nazism rings hollow when we consider the extensive reporting of violence occurring against Jews in Nazi Germany.

One of the first mentions of Nazi antisemitism in the *Star* was a front-page item on 7 February 1933 describing the stormy end of a Reichstag committee meeting during which Hans Frank, a Nazi cabinet minis-ter, delivered a tirade against the Jews in the SPD (Sozialdemokratische Partei Deutschlands). The *Tely* first hinted at Nazi violence against the Jews on 25 February in an op-ed page column by Jim Hunter: "Little Hitler is making a lot of noise. He has no use for the Jews, and they are leaving the country, so we hear, in droves. It's a bit pathetic when we stop to remember that these same Jews served the Fatherland well in the Great War. There are only six hundred thousand of them in Germany, and yet one hundred thousand fought for Germany and twelve thou-sand paid the supreme price." In the month preceding the last demo-cratic elections in Germany, on March 5—elections that gave the Nazis the largest number of seats in the Reichstag—all three Toronto newspa-pers emphasized the political violence occurring in Germany between Nazis, Communists, and Socialists. However, only *Der Yiddisher Zhur-nal* reported on the violence directed at the Jews of Germany in a con-sistent way throughout the month. The *Star* began to make a major issue of Jewish persecutions only at the very end of February.

The Jews were to learn soon enough that the enemy they faced in Nazism was quite different from their traditional religious and political foes. The object of Catholic antisemitism had been the conversion of the Jews; while the eastern-European princes, kings, and czars traditionally used the Jewish population as a political safety-valve or scapegoat. The goal of Nazism was different—to rid the world of the "Jewish bacillus," to destroy the *genetic* basis of Jewry. Religious, class, or political affilia-tions were irrelevant; the Jew would spread his spiritual poison because it was his biological destiny to do so. According to the Nazi rhyme, "Was der Jude glaubt ist einerlei/In der Rasse liegt die Schweinerei." (What the Jew believes isn't important/The dirtiness lies in the race.) The im-plications of this racist bastard child of Darwinism were not spelled out at the time of Hitler's accession to power, but the terrible secret would not remain buried for long.

In a lead story of its 13 February edition, the *Zhurnal* accurately caught the language of the new socio-biological form of racism that was Nazism in a speech given by a Nazi deputy: "Nazi Leader Pledges to Revive Anti-Semitism in Germany: Kube, deputy in Prussian parliament says that Jews have polluted Germany like bedbugs. The only way to smoke them out is to drive them out," read the headline. No great imaginative leap is required to see that extermination was the likely "remedy" for a "problem" described in such terms.

The Toronto *Star* first called attention to antisemitic violence in a front-page story on 27 February by Pierre van Paassen. Van Paassen described a terrifying scene in which a Jew was beaten to death in Wedding, a working-class area of Berlin and a Communist stronghold:

> I walked over to a newspaper kiosk to buy a theatrical paper. I had just turned up the column of the ads in the paper and was mentally comparing the merits of the various theatre announcements when another customer whom I vaguely noticed walking away from the kiosk cried out with all his might. I whirled around. Four men had pounced upon him. They were beating him in the face. Every blow brought blood. As he collapsed to the ground they kicked him in the stomach and in the mouth. Then his attackers fled—four brown shirts, Nazis!
> JEW BEATEN TO DEATH
> A crowd was gathering. The unconscious man's face was unrecognizable. A policeman walked up. "Who is this?" he asked. "Ein Jude!" (a Jew) somebody said in the crowd. There was a moment's silence.
> "So soll man alle [*sic*] Juden tun," somebody shouted. "That's the way all Jews should be treated."
> The policeman smiled. He knew enough. He looked down at the bloody mass at his feet and took a notebook out of his pocket. There seemed to be no hurry in getting the injured man away.
> And then something happened, which made that crowd stand dumbfounded. A tall well-dressed negro pushed his way to the prostrate man. He turned him over on his back. "Dis here man is gonna die if you don't get him to the hospital," said the negro in English.
> "You folks gonna help or not?" the black man asked.
> A taxi cab came up. The driver refused to take the charge. "Zu schmutzig!" Too dirty, he said. The negro threw off his overcoat and wrapped the wounded man in it. "Ah will take him on ma

lap," he offered. Together we pushed him into the taxi after promising the driver double fare.

The crowd stood by stolid, grim, without the slightest show of emotion or indignation, impassive, dull-witted you would have almost said. As we drove to the hospital the negro said to me: "Dis am a civilized country, bo! Watch yo step!" When we arrived we were told that we had been carrying a dead man.

The *Evening Telegram* tended to play down the extent of anti-Jewish violence in Germany and cautioned that the reports coming in from Jewish refugees and other sources were to be taken with a grain of salt. As we shall see, the editors of the *Tely* seemed to approve of Hitler's terror against the Communists in Germany and were reluctant to portray Hitler as a Jew killer. However, even the *Telegram* could not countenance pogroms. Finally, on 21 March, the *Tely* carried a story written by the famous German-Jewish novelist Lion Feuchtwanger, in which the seriousness of the situation of Germany's Jews was portrayed in no uncertain terms. Feuchtwanger, at first disbelieving of accounts of terror against Jews, came to believe, and to ask:

> What has in fact happened in Germany? Six hundred thousand very young men to whom every characteristic can be acknowledged except moderation have been stirred up by every means against the workmen and the Jews. These young men have been supplied with arms and have been granted power such as has never been granted to a policeman in Germany.
>
> Thus equipped, they have been turned loose upon the people and the life and property of the greater part of the people has been subordinated to them.
>
> It is not contradicted that these storm troopers, in a spirit of levity "rubbed down," as the saying goes, a large number of Jews who probably will never get over the rubbing down for the rest of their lives.

But even Feuchtwanger had to attribute the violence against the Jews to the excesses of Hitler's followers and not to the Nazi government itself. In fact, he believed that the government had lost control over its police agencies.

The *Star*, in the meantime, had been carrying atrocity stories as front-page news. On 14 March the brutalities heaped upon hapless German Jews attempting to flee the country were heralded in the headline: "Jews

Flee from Germany Badly Beaten, They State: One Hundred and Fifty Reach Poland—Some Head for France: Many Penniless." On the following day the newspaper's banner read: "German Jews Live in Dread/ Many Flee Nazis' Wrath/Refugees Pour into France and Poland/Many Report Beatings/Border Is Guarded." In its edition of 20 March the *Star* carried a report of a riot in Vienna caused by antisemitic students rampaging in the streets of the city. Further horrors were reported on 22 March, echoing similar items in *Der Yiddisher Zhurnal*. A *Star* article from London read in part:

JEWS ARE MURDERED
...Vivid details of the anti-semitic activities in Germany, including the revelation that for the last three nights the body of a murdered Jewish citizen has been deposited at the entrance to the Weissensee cemetery in Berlin, were received here from unimpeachable sources to-day. The Weissensee cemetery is the largest Jewish burial ground in the German capital.

On the first night of the apparently systematic campaign, the keeper at the caretaker's lodge of the cemetery was awakened by the honking of an automobile horn. He stepped out of the house and stumbled over a corpse lying in the glare of an automobile's headlights.

In the car, he said, were men in the uniform of Nazi storm troopers. "Bury him," they commanded, according to the caretaker. "We've given him a free funeral so far." The body was mutilated beyond recognition.

The next night the caretaker heard no noise, but on the following morning he found the body of another murdered Jew in the same place. The third night, the caretaker said, he waited up, feeling that the gruesome scene would be reenacted. He was rewarded by the arrival of an automobile containing four men in Nazi uniforms who, he declared, dragged out the body of a third Jewish victim and deposited it before the cemetery gates.

The reports of violence achieved still greater prominence the following day with the *Star's* bold page-one headline: JEWS FLEE IN TERROR FROM NAZI TORTURE. The story bore the title, "Two Jews Are Lashed with Thongs of Steel by German Terrorists: Communists, Socialists and Catholics Objects of Nazis Scourging: U.S. is Inflamed: Indignation Meetings Planned in 300 Cities of Republic—New York Leads," and supplied gruesome details: "It is reported that 'thousands of captives in German cities and towns have been herded into barracks and rooms, lined up against walls, beaten with fists, truncheons, whips or wire rods until bleeding, and then forced to swallow from a pint to a quart of castor oil at one time...."

On the last day of March the *Star* addressed the scale of the violence in a story headed: "Nazis Reign of Blood Eclipses Massacres of Medieval Times: Total of 115,000 Arrested, Held Without Trial—Hundreds Slain: Others Tortured: Many Driven Insane—Jewish Judge Beaten, Mangled in Public":

> There is no precedent in modern history for the terror that rages in Germany to-day. The frightful blood-baths of medieval St. Bartholomew and the Sicilian Vespers pale in comparison with the horrors that are being perpetrated to-day on defenceless human beings by the fiendish bands of Naziism.... I have interviewed scores of refugees. I have seen wounds that would nauseate stout-hearted surgeons. I have listened to accounts that froze my blood. I have read secret reports that took my breath away....

In the same issue, the *Star* printed the contents of a letter received by a Toronto girl from her sister who was visiting Switzerland. Under the headline: "Bodies Found Minus Eyes in Germany, Says Letter...." the story told of a writer,

> ...a cultured girl and a Gentile, who said: "The people have become like animals, from what I can see. How they go after Socialists, Communists and Jews! They force them to drink bottles of castor oil until they are half dead. Some they give vinegar to drink and they beat them until unconscious. One man who was through the whole war was taken from his wife and two children and beaten until dead. Hundreds are taken from the river drowned. Even bodies without eyes were found. They looked so gruesome that even the police were revolted at the sight. First, these people have their papers taken away and then they are tortured. It is impossible that you in Canada can be informed of the actual truth.
>
> "I can hardly believe the above," remarked the recipient of the letter, "but my sister is a quiet girl and not given to exaggeration. Besides, we are Gentiles and she has no reason to enlarge the facts."

The *Telegram* rarely carried atrocity stories, and on the few occasions when the Nazi terror was covered, it was done in the second section

or on back pages. Furthermore, the stories were generally not presented as a true description of events but as distortions, exaggerations, or
partial fabrications. In an item of 23 March bearing the headline, "Berlin Threatens Reporters if Atrocity Stories Sent Out—Mad Torture of
Jews Is Related by Refugees—Fancied Slight to Nazi Is Enough to Bring
Whipping with Wire, Say Fugitives," the reports are not accepted at face
value, but are viewed only as an indication of the "atmosphere":

> While the reports cannot be specifically confirmed their broad
> outlines agree, and indicate an atmosphere of fear among those
> who have come under the Nazi ban.[1]

Even the cautious *Tely* had to admit that these reports were disturb-
ing and cause for concern.

The *Toronto Daily Star* began the month of April with no fewer than
six separate stories about events in Nazi Germany. Its front-page lead
story, which described the torture of four famous prisoners of the Reich—Egon Erwin Kisch, Otto Heller, Dr. Alsberg, and (possibly) Carl
von Ossietsky—was headed: "Naked and Chained Distinguished Jews
Murdered by Nazis: Beaten to Death by Steel Rods and Burned with
Cigarette Butts: Torture Reported: Official Decree Allows Nazis to Beat
Jew Communists, Pacifist Liberals."

The *Star* reports increased in frequency and intensity. On 4 April the
paper ran a story headed: "Nazis Cut Out Eyes of Berlin Lawyer Before
Killing Him: Daughter Flees to Paris to Confirm Story of Horrible Murder: Mutilate Children: Communists Bear Brunt of Hitler's Terrorism
But Jews Do Not Escape":

> In the Hedemannstrasse in Berlin, in another Nazi barracks build-
> ing, 150 artists, arrested in Wilmensdorff [sic], Berlin's Greenwich
> Village, are lying stripped naked on the cement floor. They are
> being starved to death. They are for the most part cartoonists,
> bill poster designers, musicians and writers suspected of left-wing
> tendencies. The finding of a Socialist newspaper in a man's house
> renders him liable to arrest and death.
>
> The neighbourhood of the Moabit prison in Berlin is crowded
> night and day by people who come to seek news of arrested rela-
> tives. They can hear the cries of despair and screams of anguish of
> the prisoners as they stand in the streets. No prisoners are allowed
> to see relatives or even lawyers.
>
> Children of Communist intellectuals are kidnapped all over

Germany. Parents are not told where they are taken, but assured they will never see them again.

From a truck load of such children, who were being transferred from prison to a concentration camp, one boy of 15 jumped at the Alexander Square, although his hands were tied, right in the path of an oncoming automobile. His legs were crushed. As the ambulance arrived, he yelled out that he had been tortured. Among others, two English newspapermen heard him. The other children were pale with terror. Many were whimpering.

A child with Jewish features is not safe on the streets of Berlin. Jewish girls when recognized are taken in hand by Nazi gangs and have their breasts crushed. Jewish boys are mutilated. Refugees reaching Paris are wild-eyed and dumb with what they have witnessed. They call themselves fortunate to have had the money to escape. The poorest Jews are doomed to stay behind and bear the brunt of Nazi bestiality....

Not a single newspaper remains in Germany to protest or even to point out what is going on. The entire socialist press is proscribed. The Communists have not even their printing plants left, smashed as they are by the Nazis. Liberal newspapers are compelled to print only what the government sends out. The voice of Germany is silenced. Naziism alone talks. It talks with "long knives," gloats in its victory and promises to keep up "the present wholesome purge."

In the following days, the *Star* carried more page-one stories of atrocities, and, in an 12 April editorial, supported the reports written by its European correspondent, van Paassen. On 28 April the following headline appeared on the front page: "Swooning Men Revived for Further Torture: Salt Poured into Eyes: Twenty-Five Polish Jews 'Beaten as if We Were Carpets': Proof is Offered: Poland Protests to Germany against Nazi Outrages, But Is Ignored." The story read, in part:

Erwin Wellner, arrested in Berlin, was searched and beaten. He was taken to an apartment in Prenzlauerstrasse, where 20 people, mostly in Nazi uniform, whipped the bare soles of his feet and put salt in his eyes.

In Dresden, 15 armed uniformed men raided a synagogue and arrested 25 Polish Jews. The latter were severely beaten with rubber truncheons and rifle-butts, many suffering terrible head and body wounds.

"With several others," swears one J. Singer, "I was taken from a restaurant to a Nazi house in Schillingstrase. We were beaten with truncheons as if we were carpets. The Nazis queued up to beat us and when anyone lost consciousness he was revived and beaten again. This continued almost two hours. Then we were thrown in the street, where I collapsed. Three others with me were Horowitz, Brenner and Schomberg." Horowitz is now awaiting trial, charged with spreading atrocity stories. A Polish Jew, Ichel Weiden, was carried into a cellar by uniformed men and beaten. They pulled the hair of his beard out and shaved a swastika on his head. He was then beaten again in time to the music of a piano.

Juda Zinnet, 65, was beaten terribly in a street in Furth and went to hospital.

Rabbi Marcus Jakubereisch was beaten by uniformed men in Duisberg and later taken from a synagogue where he was preaching and paraded through the streets, wrapped in a republican flag.

...All the foregoing cases have been investigated and confirmed by Polish consular authorities.

Reports of atrocities in *Der Yiddisher Zhurnal* were not as numerous in April as they had been in February and March; Toronto Jews were preoccupied with protests against the Nazi terror and efforts to aid their German brethren. Nevertheless, the *Zhurnal* reported incidents of physical violence against Jews in Germany throughout the month. In one story the Polish-Jewish leader of the Jewish community in Gelsenkirchen reported that Nazis had surrounded a synagogue looking for weapons and had taken the Jews to prison, where they were beaten and tortured. A report from a Jewish Telegraphic Agency correspondent who had secretly gone to Berlin to observe the plight of the German Jews first-hand appeared in the *Zhurnal* on 24 April under the headline: "Jews Are Still Being Tortured and Murdered in Germany":

Not Berlin proper, not America, not even the countries that border on Germany can have an exact notion and paint for themselves a complete picture about what is truly happening in Germany. The insults, the tortures, the awful hopelessness, the absolute helplessness of the Jews in Germany today are indescribable. I personally have found the Jewish situation far worse, infinitely more horrible than I imagined, far worse than even the worst reports, and I've just arrived here. Everything that was shocking in the very first days of Hitler's *coup d'état* remains absolutely true to this very day. Jewish suffering is not only a result of the first drunken days [of victory for the Nazis]. The plain truth is that in this present sober period, as it were, the Jewish situation is worse still. Jews are continuing to disappear all the same and the whereabouts of their remains is unknown. Often they are found in the morgues. The economic terror arrives unexpectedly with complete savagery. The physical attacks have not stopped, especially outside Berlin where there is no fear of foreign observers....

CHAPTER 5 "Swastika Club Must Be Outlawed"

There is no moral justification for the existence of the Swastika Club, even were its motives of the highest order.

And this is precisely what must be taken into consideration by the mayor and the city councilors who will attend the conference bringing together [representatives of] the clubs and the representatives of the League.

—Editorial, *Der Yiddisher Zhurnal*, 9 August 1933

In spite of Chief Constable Draper's assurances that the Beaches situation was under control, tension was clearly mounting. In a 3 August story beneath the headline "Swastikas Patrol Beaches/Threat of Raid Unfulfilled," the *Mail and Empire* story began:

Several core young members of the newly-formed Swastika clubs mingled with the eastern beaches boardwalk crowd and a small detail of uniformed policemen and plainclothesmen last night following reports that certain Jewish youths were coming down to forcibly take away the members' metal Swastika badges.[1]

According to a *Globe* report, members of the Swastika Club—about one hundred in number—met on the boardwalk at the foot of Hammersmith Avenue on the afternoon of 2 August. The leaders outlined their views and told of their plans for "an orderly and strictly legal campaign to clean up the beaches."[2] Following the meeting, two club spokesmen denied any connection with or responsibility for the Tuesday night parade and anti-Jewish singing on the boardwalk. An unsigned notice received by the *Telegram* read:

We, the members of the Swastika Club do hereby declare that we are in no way connected with any political or racial organization.

The sign erected at the eastern beaches with the inscription thereon has nothing whatever to do with the Swastika Clubs.

To be verified, go to the Black and White Confectionery Store, between Leuty and Wineva, on the south side of Queen Street.[3]

According to the newspaper, inquiry at this store failed to reveal any further information on the intended activities of the club or the names of its officers. A spokesman termed untrue the report that adherents of the Swastika Club would stage a parade on Sunday along the boardwalk. "We hold no parades," he said, "but we will patrol the boardwalk in twos and threes and on seeing anything disorderly it will be reported to the nearest police constable or person in charge."[4]

The claims of club spokesmen notwithstanding, *Der Yiddisher Zhurnal*'s 3 August headline firmly maintained: "Nazi Agents Organize Swastika Clubs in Toronto." The story began by linking Swastika Club activities in Toronto with those elsewhere:

After the failure of the Nazi Movement in the United States, Nazi agents transferred their activities to Canada—and Toronto is one of the places chosen by the Hitlerite agents as a base from which to spread their activity across the continent.

This becomes clear from the secret statements and the public denials of the Swastika Club in the east end of the city over the past few days.[5]

The choice of the swastika as the club's emblem was offered as irrefutable proof of the latter's anti-Jewish bent. "The Swastika, they explained, was chosen as the sign simply because it is a 'symbol of luck,'" reported the Yiddish paper. Such an assertion lacked any credibility. "The Swastika is not a coincidence. This can be seen also from the fact that eight similar clubs have been organized in such a short time, the last at Lake Wilcox."[6] Secretiveness about the club's organization masked its real purpose, which was "to capitalize on the dissatisfaction of the Beaches residents...in order to organize a Nazi movement in Canada."[7]

In spite of the Swastika Club's plans for parades or demonstrations on the weekend, Jewish picnics and organized celebrations planned for the Civic Holiday Monday on the eastern beaches were not cancelled. The majority of organizations had no intention of abandoning their original arrangements, and S. M. Shapiro, managing editor of *Der Yiddisher Zhurnal,* reassured his readers that "We don't anticipate any trouble whatever."[8] As far as he knew, no picnics had been planned for Sunday, when an anti-Jewish demonstration was anticipated.

In a 6 August editorial, "Do Not Alter Your Plans," the *Zhurnal* said:

...Don't do it!

Do not display any weakness. We are not suggesting that Jews ought to attend their picnics in order to quarrel with someone, or to fight. Precisely the opposite. We want to emphasize that Jews must follow through on their plans in the most orderly manner... so as not to provide the enemy the opportunity to confirm their suspicions [about the Jews]. But also, Jews should not be frightened away, thus showing themselves to be afraid of them.[9]

While members of the Swastika Club were meeting on the boardwalk at the foot of Hammersmith Avenue, members of the League for the Defence of Jewish Rights were conferring at their headquarters on Beverley Street. Following the meeting a statement was issued to the press. The League downplayed the importance of the "Swastika incident," attributing it mainly to the heat wave that had gripped the city[10] and to "youngsters who were looking for a bit of excitement." After pointing to the movement's lack of sponsorship ("No one seems to have thought enough of this business to lend his name to it"), the League criticized the Balmy Beach Canoe Club for allowing "itself to become implicated in this matter by the posting of the Swastika sign on its premises." More important, however, the League's statement warned of the broader consequences for the city:

While we know that the incident was trivial, reports will go abroad that Toronto is a centre of Hitlerism.... When some unthinking individuals here in a moment of pique can suffer themselves to put up the sign, "Hail Hitler," they are doing something which will do incalculable harm to the reputation of this city. It is known that the German Government has set aside a large sum for propaganda, and if the impression is gained that the Toronto public is receptive to its ideas, we will witness the unloosing of a flood of Hitler publicity in the city and throughout this country. Toronto cannot afford to act in the spirit which is contrary to the spirit and traditions of Great Britain. Hitlerism is subversive of Canadian ideals, and our Canadian leaders should join the leaders of other enlightened countries in proclaiming Canada's adherence to the ideals which dominate life in Great Britain.[11]

Roused by the League's charges that no one connected with the Swastika Club "thought enough of this business to lend his name to it," the Swastika organization lifted the veil of secrecy that had surrounded it and appointed two members, Bert Ganter and Harold W. Mackay, as spokesmen. The newly formed committee of two immediately issued a statement disavowing any connection with Nazi or Hitlerite movements, explaining that the club's aim was to assist "the civic authorities to exclude from their local district all obnoxious and undesirable elements who tend to destroy the natural beauty and the property value of the residential districts of Toronto."[12]

Immediately following the Swastika Club statement, the *Telegram* published a rather lengthy letter from a Beaches resident indicating concern over the influx of foreigners with inadequately assimilated British ideals. The sentiments expressed in the letter show the underlying appeal of the Swastika Club for many Ward 8 residents.

> ...Since the war, there has been an influx into this country of a class of people who had no civil rights in the land from which they came; people who make no effort to absorb the British ideals and culture on which this country has builded, but would rather impose their culture, such as it is, on us. If we dare to object, immediately comes the cry of discrimination and denial of their rights. I wonder if, in the fetish we make of extending British fair play to aliens in our midst, we do not bend over backwards and thereby deny to our own Canadian people rights and privileges that are rightfully theirs....
>
> I am not a member of the Swastika Association, but I believe that it is time that some consideration be given to the rights of Canadians, to enjoy their Sundays, free from the intrusion of aliens, who make no attempt to conduct themselves in a manner befitting their surroundings to which they come....
>
> While this is not to be construed as a defence of the Swastika Society, there was a statement in your paper, attributed to Rabbi Sachs, which merits comment. In it, after stating his personal views, he remarks that "he will ask his organization, 'The League for the Defence of Jewish Rights', to look into this." This in itself, is explanatory of the attitude of his people. What other race would have the colossal impudence to deny to descendants of the founders of this country the right to an organization whose aims and principles are apparently similar to the one he calls his own.[13]

While the Swastika Club gained support in the vicinity of the Beaches, it also won qualified approval from the *Telegram*. The paper disapproved of attempts to remedy the problem by group force but unequivocally supported the Swastika Club's right to organize.

> If there is a group of Beaches residents who unite under the sign of the Swastika to preserve the character of their district, good luck to them—as long as they remain within the law. They have at least as much right to organize and demonstrate as another group of citizens to march to Queen's Park for the purpose of condemning Hitler.[14]

Though opposed to the Swastika Club—the name itself was most offensive—the leadership of the Jewish community could easily support an organization established to maintain standards of cleanliness and propriety. "If the Swastika Clubs are really sincere in the statement that their only aim is to assist civic authorities in keeping the Beaches clean, we are prepared to meet and cooperate with them," said A. B. Bennett, publicity representative of the League for the Defence of Jewish Rights.[15] But the adoption of the swastika emblem, which was seen by the Jews as an antisemitic symbol pure and simple, was unequivocally objectionable. The *Jewish Standard,* in a story headlined, "The Nazis in Our Midst," argued that it was justified in suspecting that elements in the Swastika Club were affiliated with Hitlerite groups or motivated by Nazi propaganda. The adoption of the swastika symbol was proof enough of this: "The swastika has come to be considered a symbol of oppression and terror. Jews, liberals, artists have been persecuted, tortured, murdered in the name of this hooked cross."[16]

Swastika Club adherents, of course, maintained otherwise. The swastika emblem, they said, was originally selected as a symbol of "fraternity and good luck." The Balmy Beach area, Bert Ganter argued, had once been a camping ground for the Iroquois Indians for whom the swastika was a good luck sign. "The sign," he added, "is well known in the eastend.... We picked on it solely as an emblem of good luck."[17] Ganter also pointed out that there had at one time been a girls' baseball club called Swastika in the area. A *Telegram* reporter, Fred Egan, who wrote some of the copy on the Swastika Club at the time, told us that no one seriously believed the swastika emblem had been chosen because it represented good luck to the Indian tribes of the area. Where did the idea of using the swastika come from?

Oh, that was Hitler. Hitler was just becoming.... My first recollection of that was...Hitler had come to power there or was on his way to power, I'm not sure which, and he made one speech which was carried on the radio here, and I not knowing a word of German was assigned to listen to and give my impressions of this speech. And there was this *Sieg Heil! Sieg Heil!* And I wrote the story on that which the *Tely* used on the front page. And that was about the time...people were talking about Hitler at that time. And I think there was so much in the paper then about that business...I think that the kids down there—these were not older people—I think that that's what sort of got the thing started.

Clearly, despite the Swastikas' disingenuousness, both Jews and non-Jews had come to attach a more sinister meaning to their chosen insignia. As Mr. Bennett phrased it: "The Swastika means suffering, death, and even torture to all our people. To the whole world it is an emblem of Hitlerism, anti-semitic Hitlerism." After trying and failing to arrange a meeting with Bert Ganter, he concluded:

> Either it [the Swastika Club] is a loose organization which is so disorganized that it cannot meet to decide on a policy, in which case it is not worth bothering about, or...there is something more behind it than a commendable desire to keep the beaches clean.[18]

For the *Jewish Standard,* there was indeed "something more behind it," as its editorial "A Circumstantial Chain" made clear:

> ...this [the formation of the Swastika Club] is not an isolated instance of Hitlerite activity in the Dominion of Canada. We have seen the organization of Foreign Friends of Hitler in Montreal; we have seen the organization of similar bodies in the West. We have seen a Hamburg oil freighter flying the swastika enter Toronto harbor. And now we learn on excellent authority that an intensive Nazi campaign is to be launched throughout the Dominion under the leadership of Colonel von Eisler, chief of Hitlerite publicity in this country.... We cannot ignore a chain of circumstance forged by definite events.[19]

Seeking to diffuse the controversy, the Swastikas offered to appoint four or five of their members to meet with an investigating committee.

On 4 August the *Mail and Empire* reported: "Swastikas' Group to Consult Jews."[20] Readers were informed that a committee of Swastika adherents would meet, as soon as possible, with representatives of the League for the Defence of Jewish Rights. Both organizations expressed a desire to meet face to face and discuss the developing situation. Said Rabbi Sachs: "It was quite possible when the two organizations got together they would find that they were both interested in the same thing."[21]

The proposed conference failed to materialize as planned. On 6 August, *Der Yiddisher Zhurnal* boldly proclaimed on its front page: "Leaders of Swastika Club Hide from Conference." Representatives of the Swastika Club had reneged on an agreement to meet on Friday with representatives of the League for the Defence of Jewish Rights in the mayor's office at city hall. "Instead of appearing...Bert Ganter...telephoned the Mayor saying that 'we are not yet sufficiently prepared to meet with anyone.'"[22] The story continued as follows:

> Upon the urging of the League that they should see who the "we" who are not yet prepared to meet consist of, no clear answer was given. This very answer leads us to believe, however, that Bert Ganter and Henry Mackay are not the chief leaders of the Swastika Clubs and are certainly not the organizers.
>
> It is clear that the organizers are hiding and that the rumours that the "innocent" and "law-abiding" Swastika Club is supported by paid Hitlerite agents have not been demonstrated to be false.

The same article pointed out that members of the Swastika Club had adopted the Hitler salute.

The 6 August editorial in the same paper focused on the secretive nature of the Swastika Club leadership. Entitled "The Hidden Hand," it asked:

> If the Club's purpose is so peaceful, why are they not yet prepared to meet?...
>
> That they did not appear demonstrated to the Mayor who they really are. But the Jews of Toronto must also know that the boys are creating a stir, but a secret hand is directing it.[23]

Despite hopeful rumours that the Swastika Club would disband, it was in fact intensifying its activities and reportedly attracting increasing numbers. Newspapers speculated that the membership was nearing the one thousand mark.

On 5 August the *Star* reported that the two sides were preparing themselves for trouble during the forthcoming weekend:

> Swastika emblems will be flaunted on the east-end beaches over the holiday in greater numbers than ever before, despite the fact over 3,000 Jews are scheduled to collect in various picnics at Kew Gardens.[24]

While stressing that no trouble would be sought, a "moving spirit" (to quote the *Star*) in one of the Swastika locals had informed the paper of carefully organized plans for the holiday involving "undercover men in case somebody should start trouble." Representatives of the two locals would patrol the boardwalk in designated areas. Behind them, at some distance, four men would follow each leader. All would wear swastika badges and sweatshirts with the swastika sign boldly emblazoned on the back.

On the Jewish side, according to Mr. Bennett of the League for the Defence of Jewish Rights, a group of "young boys" of the better element, students, and that sort of thing," were prepared to parade on the beaches with the intention of preventing disorder. In contrast to the "foreign" swastika, the maple leaf would be emblazoned on their sweatshirts.

Bert Ganter vehemently denied that Swastika adherents wanted trouble and reiterated that the club did not seek to foster racial antagonism. He also denied a *Star* report that he was German. "My grandfather was German," he said. "That's how I got the German name of Ganter. My father was Scotch, or a Scotch-German, but I was born in Scotland, coming here when I was about four years of age. My name is the only thing German about me."[25]

On Saturday, 5 August, the *Telegram* wrote that the weekend would see no Swastika Club parade along the boardwalk, no singing of antisemitic songs, and no demonstrations of any kind. In a story headed "Swastika Club Members Promise Quiet Week-End; No Parades at Beaches," it reported that an understanding had been reached following Mayor Stewart's personal appeal to Bert Ganter "to desist from any conduct that might cause trouble." The mayor was assured that an officer of the Swastika Club would be present on the boardwalk to prevent any demonstrations. For their part, Balmy Beach Canoe Club officials promised Stewart that persons wearing the swastika emblem would not be permitted on the premises.

Mayor Stewart warned that persons not heeding his considered advice should be prepared to accept the legal consequences of their actions and appealed for good conduct: "We have gone through a long depression, and the sun is shining on the noon of a better day. Any demonstration that might cause ill-feeling could be regrettable...."[26]

Perhaps not surprisingly, Mayor Stewart's appeals failed to prevent a near confrontation over the holiday weekend. On Sunday, 6 August, a series of clashes erupted in Kew Gardens. Under the headline "Beaches in Turmoil as Swastika Emblem Incites Near Riots," the *Star* told the story:

> Sullen clouds of tense racial feeling, brooding over the east end waterfront for days, burst during the weekend, and enveloped in a series of clashes and near riots, thousands of Torontonians who flocked to the beaches for pleasure, and for the "thrills" which they found abounded. Trouble was in the air, and it required only the appearance of the Swastika sign to make it all too actively tangible. Throughout the turmoil, the small swastika badge, emblem of the rapidly growing club bobbed and eddied as gangs of non-Gentiles, incensed by Hitlerism which they charged it symbolized, pounced on wearers. They tore sweat-shirts on which the sign was emblazoned from the backs of youths, and forced them to seek shelter in nearby houses.[27]

The visibility of the swastika emblem was cited as the cue for trouble. As the *Globe* reported: "Badges were in evidence on every hand.... In some instances, even young ladies had the emblem pinned on their bathing suits."[28]

It was immediately evident that trouble was brewing on Sunday afternoon as crowds began assembling along the beaches shortly after noon. As the *Mail and Empire* described it:

> In a tense atmosphere apparently relished to the full by thousands of citizens who flocked to the beach in an obvious search for excitement in the shape of a direct clash between the two groups, the hostile bodies of youngsters strolled up and down past, and sometimes through, each other without any pitched battle occurring.[29]

Ganter and Mackay, the two Swastika Club spokesmen, were the centre of attraction as they paraded along the walk, a husky henchman on either side. In addition to emblems on their jackets, both men wore the official badge of the club. No sooner had the pair arrived (at about 4:45 p.m.) than a Jewish man stepped out of the crowd and attempted to pull Mackay's sweatshirt over his head. Ganter and a few members of the club rushed to Mackay's aid, but were too late to prevent the assailant from tearing Mackay's swastika-stamped shirt. According to the *Telegram* account: "In a few seconds, it appeared that the storm which had been threatening all afternoon had broken loose, but prompt action by the police quelled the trouble."[30] The few other fist fights that began were also quickly squelched by the crowds.

Determined to prevent outbreaks of violence, Inspector Majury kept repeating his warning against any disturbances as he patrolled the boardwalk, insisting that the swastika emblem be removed by those wearing it. "We don't want any trouble here," he repeated. Several times he snatched badges from their owners' chests and stuffed them in his pocket. Meanwhile Ganter and Mackay were escorted, protesting all the while, to the boathouse and advised to remove their emblems. A large crowd was cheering outside. The Jewish faction, plainly delighted by the police action, called "Take them off," whenever a swastika emblem was sighted. A few minutes later another member joined the two leaders in the boathouse. With two plainclothesmen guarding the door, Inspector Majury informed Ganter and Mackay: "You can't leave here until you take those signs off. I am not going to have a riot all on account of a couple of lousy shirts. I am here for the good of the beach and I don't want any trouble."[31]

Mackay dared the Inspector to lock him up. "If I have done anything wrong, why don't you arrest me? I have been told that I have a perfect right to wear the badge and the sign on my sweatshirt."[32] The inspector refused to make any arrest, and Ganter and Mackay refused to remove their shirts. "We will stay here until morning if necessary," Ganter told Majury.

With Ganter trying to calm him, Mackay began shouting: "Where is our gang? Do you want to see the rest of my gang? Go and tell them we are here. Go and get Joe McNullty. If he says to take the signs off we will do it." (McNullty was reported to be the head of Swastika Club Local No. 6.)

"You can't stay here any longer," Inspector Majury informed them when he returned half an hour later. He pointed out that their actions might threaten the safety of women and children. The opportunity to save face and to demonstrate the law-abiding nature of the Swastika

Club was timely, and Ganter yielded. "All right, we will do it for the sake of the women and children," he said, as both he and Mackay removed their shirts and slipped quietly from the building. This marked the termination of any open hostilities for the day.

Until dark, however, the beach was a hive of activity. Scores of policemen regularly dispersed the assembling crowds. According to the *Mail and Empire,* "there were no blows struck, no harsh words heard...."[33] But this version of the story was contradicted by a number of our witnesses, who had participated in the conflict that weekend:

> So, now my brothers and a bunch of other guys, they got about two or three trucks and they loaded them up with guys, and they went out there right onto the beach. And there were slug fests there all the time.

> All of a sudden these little *shiksalach* [Gentile girls] started running around with swastikas on the front of their bathing suits and this was the big in-thing down there. And the boys went down and they put their trunks on and they wore swastikas. And if they didn't wear them on their trunks, they put them on their chests....
> We drove out there and we ran up on the beach and we tore the bathing suits off these girls.... We took bats, not real baseball bats, and paddled their rear ends for doing this and all that. They were screaming bloody murder. And we called them all Hitlerites. You know, antisemites. All this caused a furor in the paper.

Der Yiddisher Zhurnal suggested that the expectation of violence had attracted larger numbers of Jews to the Beaches than usual: "Jews who under other circumstances would have travelled elsewhere came specially yesterday, some awaiting some action and others prepared to take action lest a Jew was touched."[34]

The Jews were prepared. In addition to a "few young Jewish lads [who] appeared with Jewish stars on their lapels...a number...without an insignia paraded back and forth." Quite clearly, said the paper, an unusually large number of Jews came to see the goings-on.

The rumoured problems did not materialize, however. "They travelled there with the noble purpose of restoring order," reported *Der Yiddisher Zhurnal,* "but upon arrival did not encounter any disorder and the majority returned to the centre of town."[35]

Sensing that too many diverse parties were presenting themselves as the protectors of the Jews, thus preventing an effective, co-ordinated Jewish communal response, the 8 August edition of the *Zhurnal* editorialized on the Beaches situation under the heading "Lawlessness Must Not Prevail." It proposed that the League for the Defence of Jewish Rights should be recognized as the official representative of the community in any ongoing negotiations.

> Neither individuals nor groups must enter into negotiations with the "swastika" organizers; neither individuals nor groups must release statements to the press. For this purpose there exists an organized body in which the entire Jewish community is fully confident. Power lies only in organization and order.[36]

The *Star* reported an interesting side development of late that Sunday night. Two cars had driven to Swastika headquarters on Queen Street. Al Kaufman, who earlier in the day had headed a group of younger Jews keeping watch on Swastika actions, made his way towards the door of the store. He was officially greeted by H. W. Mackay and Bert Ganter, the acknowledged leaders of the Swastika movement. "I come as a representative of Rabbi Sachs and the uptown boys," said Kaufman in a loud voice. "I desire to know just what the Swastika Club signifies. Is its purpose to stir up racial prejudice?"[37] The Swastika spokesmen replied that the motive of the organization was solely for the betterment of conditions at the Beaches and that there was absolutely no racial animosity attached to it. Kaufman then conceded that he could sympathize with Beaches residents. "I know some of the problems you are confronted with," he declared. He continued:

> The offenders are greenhorns from Russia. They are so glad to come to a place where the sands and waters are free to all that they go wild. When they see that there are no czars they tear off most of their clothes and break the regulations which they cannot read. These are the people who must be educated.[38]

Meanwhile plans were underway for a meeting, probably under the sponsorship of the mayor, at which representatives of the League for the Defence of Jewish Rights and the Swastika Club would each state their side in the controversy. According to Ganter, he and Mackay had made several abortive attempts on Sunday afternoon to contact members of the Jewish party in order to arrange a private meeting, but police interference had prevented contact: "Each time we came together a crowd would immediately form around us and the police on seeing it broke it up before any progress was made."[39] However, the *Telegram* reported that Swastika spokesmen and Jewish youths had met in a friendly, informal fashion on Sunday and Monday and that these conferences had done a great deal to clear up the situation and straighten out several misunderstandings.

In its front-page story of 8 August, headed "Swazis Are Satisfied Objects Being Gained But Resent Police Acts," the *Telegram* reported that Ganter and Mackay, known "Swazi" spokesmen, had claimed partial attainment of the Swastika Club's aims. In an interview on Monday 7 August, Ganter told the *Telegram* that there had been great improvement in the condition of the eastern beaches district after thousands of visitors from all parts of the city had departed. Both Ganter and Mackay expressed appreciation for the co-operation of the police under Inspector Hans Majury of No. 10 station. Majury had turned back several truckloads of picnickers en route to the beaches. As always, the Swastika leaders claimed to have the wholehearted support of the vast majority of Beaches residents in their drive to keep out "undesirables."

Official announcements from Swastika headquarters on 7 August placed membership at approximately 2,500.[40] (According to the *Star*, at this time the prospective membership of the Swastika Club stood at between 3,000 and 4,000.)[41] "We have long since run out of metal badges," said Bert Ganter, though he explained that there were only thirty-one charter members. Eight of the inner group were women, he revealed. Moreover, "three prominent women of the Beach district have just formed themselves into a committee to canvass the women and young girls in an attempt to form a ladies' Swastika Club. They are doing this at their own expense."[42]

While the police successfully contained outbreaks of violence at the Beach, Swastika-related activities appeared to be spilling over into the Lake Simcoe area. On 8 August, beneath the main headline "Fear Nazi Plot Against Jews Worldwide," the *Star* announced: "German Nazi Plot Blamed for Swastikas up North." Red swastika emblems had appeared on the property of Jews at Roche's Point and other beaches. Swastikas had also been placed at the Roche's Point post office and along Balfour Beach, the site of a number of Jewish-owned cottages. The *Star* quoted a Mrs. Dunkelman—swastika emblems were found at her mother's summer cottage—who claimed that the insignia were there as part of a Nazi campaign to stir up anti-Jewish feeling:

Anti-Semitism has always been a German disease. I have no doubt that this affair is of German instigation. It was at the summer resorts that the anti-Jewish campaign in Germany first started. They hope to capitalize on Gentile feelings against the Jew, and the use of these emblems is one way to do it.[43]

However, Rabbi Sachs, in an interview in the *Star,* suggested that there was little cause for alarm. "Merely an echo of the Toronto affair," he commented. "I do not think there is any reason to be pessimistic about the matter, as I am sure some youngster or group of youngsters who heard about the trouble at the Eastern beaches thought it would be a good prank to tack up a few swastikas with the object of starting a rumpus.... I'm sure it's easy enough to get swastika emblems."

For the *Zhurnal,* the events of the busy weekend confirmed its conviction that the Swastika Club was indeed antisemitic, that its leaders were deceitful, and, most important, that the organization was a front for Nazism. Still, Jewish community leaders remained confident that British traditions would prevent the club's influence from spreading across Canada and recommended ignoring antisemitic outbursts as the wisest course of action. In a statement prepared for the *Star,* Edmund Scheuer, a prominent Jewish citizen (and former senior lay leader at Toronto's Holy Blossom Temple), endorsed this view and implored the young in the community to remain calm. A similar view was expressed in the *Star*'s editorial of 10 August. Titled "No Anti-Semite Movement Here," it read in part:

Young men who adorn themselves with an emblem or wear a shirt of a particular color and go about in numbers seeking to enforce their will upon others must know or must learn that under our system of government here there is no room for any such voluntary and self-appointed interference with the lives and doings of others....

The imitating of Hitler or of those who follow him in a country far different from ours will not amount to much.[44]

Not everyone shared this optimism. For different reasons, Mayor Stewart and the League for the Defence of Jewish Rights were not prepared to ignore the Swastika Club's presence. Unless racial differences at the eastern beaches were amicably settled, warned the mayor, drastic action would have to be considered. He asked the city solicitor for an opinion on the legality of a police ordering the removal of the swastika emblem from public display, and requested the three aldermen of Ward 8 and representatives of the Swastika Club and Jewish organizations to meet with him on the afternoon of 9 August.

The League for the Defence of Jewish Rights felt that a meeting would give them more information about Swastika Club objectives. Rabbi Sachs, the League's chairman, said: "What we desire is a meeting.... We want to find out what is behind this and we want everything stated clearly. There is going to be no back water."[45]

On 9 August *Der Yiddisher Zhurnal* reported that the long-awaited meeting was scheduled for that very day. Its first editorial expressed the view that Europe was on the brink of bloody war; its second, entitled "Swastika Club Must Be Outlawed," questioned the moral right of the Swastika Club to exist and argued that the city had no need of "these self-appointed law-enforcers."[46]

The meeting was convened in the City Council chamber and was open to the press. In attendance were aldermen Bray and Elgie, representatives of Ward 8; aldermen Phillips and Glass, Jewish members of City Council; Frank Cummins and A. J. Stringer of the Balmy Beach Canoe Club; Rabbi Sachs, A. B. Bennett, S. M. Shapiro, and M. F. Steinglass, representing the Jewish groups; T. G. Ferris, representing residents of the Beaches; and B. W. Ganter, H. W. Mackay, D. Griffin, H. J. Jordan, and two (unnamed) women, representing the Swastika Club.

The meeting lasted more than two and a half hours and produced "an exhaustive analysis of both sides of the controversy over alleged indecency, rowdyism and untidiness at the eastern beaches and adjacent streets or parks; the responsibility for such offenses, and methods pursued by the Swastikas in endeavoring to have such annoyances eliminated."[47] "Police Keep Order, Both Beach Groups Are Told by Mayor," the *Globe* announced, and reported that Mayor Stewart had appealed for the abandonment of the Swastika name and emblem and had also told both groups that the situation at the eastern beaches would be left to Chief Constable Draper's discretion. "If people conduct themselves in a manner which causes breach of the peace, they will find themselves in the courts," said Mayor Stewart.

The swastika emblem appeared as an "exhibit" only at the meeting, when one of the boys from the Beaches produced as "evidence" a large swastika button, which he then returned to his pocket.

As a pledge of their common loyalty to Canada, of their commitment to strive for co-operation among all sections of the community, and of their willingness to avoid any activity calculated to incite inter-racial animosity, the two sides sang "God Save the King" at the request of Mayor Stewart.

At the meeting the Jewish representatives voiced their appreciation of the efforts to clean up the eastern beaches park and keep it attractive, but the Swastika delegation was unwilling to alter the name or emblem of the organization unless formally requested by a resolution adopted by the entire City Council. Ganter steadfastly maintained that he had not known that the swastika emblem was offensive to Jews before the controversy erupted. When questioned by the mayor, Ganter persisted in the view that the antisemitic signs displayed about the Beaches were in no way connected with the Swastika Club. He denied that his movement was connected with offensive songs, or that it had a salute (meaning, presumably, the familiar Nazi salute), or that it was a subsidiary of any other organization. In the official greeting of the Swastikas, Ganter told the gathering, the words "ho'ya pal," and a salute with the right hand extended palm out at about a forty-five degree angle were used. When Alderman Glass interjected, "The Nazi sign," Ganter replied: "Our organization is open to all creeds and both sexes as long as they are over eighteen years of age." The aims and activities of the clubs, he claimed, were not directed against any particular group.

Presenting the Jewish view of the matter, Rabbi Sachs declared that there would be no need for additional police in the parks or on the beaches were it not for the friction caused by the formation of the Swastika Club. The resentment and ill-feeling centred, he said, on the ill-advised selection of the swastika emblem, which, though it had once been an ancient symbol of good luck, was at present universally regarded as an insignia of persecution.

> You know the power of the emblem. The Swastika emblem today is accepted throughout the civilized world as the emblem of Hitlerism. No longer does it mean "good luck." It means "bad luck." To the Jewish people the Swastika is a symbol of the wild beast crouching over 600,000 people, sucking their blood. If you are sincere and have no connection with Hitlerism, adopt the broom as your emblem should you wish to keep the beaches clean, or perhaps you might adopt the maple leaf.[48]

According to Rabbi Sachs, Swastika Club members would be stuck with the Nazi label if they persisted in using the emblem after learning what it signified to Jews and Gentiles the world over and after seeing what conflicts it had caused locally.

Only once during the meeting did the possibility of trouble arise. After Rabbi Sachs had spoken, a young man identified as "D. Griffin" shouted at the rabbi: "We are having this trouble because you have a bunch of uneducated Jews coming over from Europe." Mayor Stewart warned the young man that he would not permit a slight to be made against the Jewish people. Griffin immediately withdrew the remark.

In response to the mayor's invitation to east-end residents to air any complaints about the conduct of visitors to the Beaches, T. G. Ferris spoke on behalf of homeowners of the district. He had lived fourteen years in the Beaches, he said, and felt that the surroundings were conducive to harmony rather than strife. In his opinion, the incidents and situations resulting from the formation of the Swastika Club were "a flash in the pan" that would have remained such if the *Star* had not fanned the flames. The paper's tactics, he contended, were in the vein of yellow journalism. However, he was willing to admit that there were some difficulties:

> There is no doubt…that the conduct of some of those who have been using the eastern beaches has been most objectionable, to residents and other visitors alike. There is no denying that there have been Jews among this objectionable element, but at the same time I know that persons of native birth have been conducting themselves in a reprehensible manner.
>
> Also, we have people coming to this country from Central Europe (not Jews) who do not realize our social customs and conventions are vastly different from theirs. It is most distressing, for instance, for a man sitting on his beach-front verandah with his family to have a woman with a large family appear, sit calmly upon the edge of the boardwalk and expose her person to feed her baby.[49]

At this point Mayor Stewart assured Ferris and those in attendance that any wrongs suffered by citizens anywhere in the city could and would be righted by regulation and authorized supervision. Agreeing that dressing and undressing in open trucks should be stopped, the mayor pointed out that objectionable practices were not confined to the eastern beaches. He lived on the Island during the summer, and there too many incidents occurred that he preferred the members of his family not to see.

The future of the Swastika organization now rested in the hands of its members and sympathizers, who were to meet in the near future. As the *Telegram* reported in its front-page account of the city hall meeting, "Swastikas Plan Meeting to Decide Future Course," Bert Ganter and Alderman Elgie of Ward 8 were to convene this future meeting. Although confident that they continued to enjoy the support of the citizens of Ward 8, the Swastikas, for the time being, would neither sell swastika badges nor solicit new members.

In the Jewish press, reaction to the machinations of the Swastika organization could be understood only within the larger context of German Jewry's plight under Hitler. The *Jewish Standard's* report of the meeting, appearing alongside a story titled "A Sacred War against Hitlerism," summarized the discussion in a few paragraphs under the headline "Mayor Stewart Requests Swastika Club to Abandon Hitlerite Cross Emblem." The article reported that Mayor Stewart had issued a strong ultimatum to the Swastika Club leaders, "threatening them with court action if their demonstrations tending to provoke disturbances did not cease."[50] The weekly also drew attention to what it considered one of the meeting's noteworthy highlights:

> ...both Alderman J. J. Glass and Rabbi Sachs reported that they had seen members of the Swastika Club exchange the Nazi salute. Denying any affiliation with Nazi propaganda activities and emphatically asserting that the Swastikas were a purely local organization, Mr. Ganter explained that what the alderman and rabbi had called the Nazi salute was merely an extension of the arm in a "how are you, pal?" greeting. A ripple of laughter filled the Council chambers as he illustrated the Swastika hello with a gesture hardly distinguishable from the Hitlerite salute.[51]

For the *Zhurnal*, the meeting was worthwhile for the Jewish representatives if only because it confirmed what they had suspected all along—that discussions with the Swastika Club were a waste of time and energy. In its editorial of 10 August—"Noisy Fascism"—the *Globe* opined that most Fascist demonstrations would "turn out to be merely local effervescences, signifying little serious or sustained purpose." As for the disorders of recent weeks, these "seem to give little reason for apprehension. They would appear to represent little more than a clamor of small groups, largely made up of notoriety seekers."[52] On 11 August the *Star's* main headline informed readers: "Swastika Club Will Give Up

Emblem." Immediately below the headline, on centre page, a Hitler aide denied that the Swastika movement in Toronto was part of a worldwide campaign directed from Germany.

In response to the *Star's* query to Hitler, "Is there any foundation for the rumours current here that the anti-Jewish movement in Canada is allied with German Fascisti?" Ernst Hanfstaengl, official spokesman for Chancellor Hitler, cabled the following reply: "Absurd to say Canadian anti-Jewish outbreaks in any way connected with the Nazi movement here. The Nazi movement is purely German and is unconnected with any other country."[53]

The *Star's* 11 August headline was matched by a similar announcement on the same day in the *Telegram:* "New Body to Replace Swastika Club." Both the name and emblem of "The Swastika Clubs" were to be abandoned. In their place, a new club would be formed with the same aims and objectives. "Enlarged Club to Check Abuses Along Beaches" announced a *Star* headline: "Out of the recently organized Swastika clubs has grown a still greater organization in an attempt to put a check to undesirable conditions along the eastern beaches."[54] The decision to scotch the swastika symbol followed a conference between Mayor Stewart, B. M. Ganter, spokesman for the clubs, A. J. Stringer, representing the Balmy Beach Canoe Club, Alderman G. C. Elgie, and Police Inspector Chisholm. According to Ganter, prominent residents of the Beaches had come forward with an offer of financial and moral support in the formation of an organization to carry on the work commenced by the Swastika Club.

The purpose of the new organization was outlined as follows:

1 To assist the civic authorities to exclude from their district all obnoxious and undesirable elements that tend to destroy the natural beauty and property value of the residential districts.
2 Members to conduct themselves in a manner befitting their districts and by pointing out to the proper authorities such misconduct that may be unlawful or objectionable occurring in the district covered by their locals, and in this manner assist in keeping their districts clean, healthy and beautiful.[55]

Candidates for membership must be at least eighteen years of age, and both sexes and all creeds would be admitted. Furthermore, candidates would be required to reside in the district in which their local was formed and would pledge themselves to work for the aims of the organization. Describing how the new organization came into being, the *Telegram* wrote:

> It is understood that following the widespread publicity given the
> Swastika organization, a number of adult residents of the beach
> district have come to the assistance of the boys and are helping
> them to form a worthwhile organization. Good citizenship will
> be the watchword.[56]

As for the *Zhurnal*, the 11 August edition included an editorial warning Toronto Jewry that it was unwittingly assisting the Swastika Club in its activities against the Jews. "Don't run out for the amazing sight," it cautioned its readers, "because this is harmful for both the individual and the community."[57]

By 13 August, it appeared that the Jewish community would henceforth be spared the indignity of witnessing the swastika emblem at the Beaches. But worse was to come. On Monday 14 August, all of the Toronto dailies announced the distribution of a circular throughout the province publicizing a Swastika rally planned for Kitchener that evening. According to this circular, the two leading Swastika Club members, B. Ganter and H. W. Mackay, would participate in a mass rally of "Swastika friends." The program, signed by O. E. Becker and decorated with swastikas and the British flag, listed Mackay as the chairman; Ganter would speak on the topic "What is Canadian Fascism?" *Der Yiddisher Zhurnal's* headline of 15 August read: "Hitlerite S.S. Troops Are Established in Toronto."

O. E. Becker, forty-year-old "commander" of the Swastika Club, was also the president of the Hindenburg Club in Kitchener. As Becker explained, the Swastika Club had been formed in Kitchener "about two weeks ago—since the Toronto club was formed," and membership was growing.[58] Removing his Nazi regalia from a hanger, Becker described how the leaders would dress for the meeting—brown shirt, black tie, and red arm band with white circle and blue swastika emblem. "It is not German," Becker declared. "It is red, white and blue of Canada. Our Swastika flag will hang beside the Union Jack to-night."[59] Elaborating on his motive for forming the club, Becker said:

> I think myself that Fascism is a good thing, and that it is going
> to spread throughout the whole world.... You know what was going
> on before Hitler took power. The world was gripped by depression.... The best leaders of the world got together and tried to

solve the problem. They couldn't do it. Since Hitler took power there came another trouble. He put out the parasites who made a profit out of the Christian-born and had a good life. Since then there has been a lot of uneasiness in other parts of the world. There have been new troubles in Canada and the United States. Anyone who asks what Canada and the United States has to do with Germany has no brains. Nations must work together.[60]

According to the *Mail and Empire* report of 14 August, both Ganter and Mackay claimed to be dumbfounded when informed that their names appeared on the Kitchener program. "Why the thing's crazy, I've never heard anything about it. I've never even heard from Kitchener and anyway I can't go out of town. I have my business to attend to," said Ganter.[61] "I'll get in trouble with the police about this. I'm certainly not going to speak there. Why I don't even know what a Fascist is."

According to the *Star*, "Becker gasped when he...read extracts from the Toronto Swastika's repudiation of his program."

> I wrote to Mr. Mackay [Becker said] and asked him what was going on in the Swastika club in Toronto. He wired me to telephone him. I did and he came here last Thursday morning. He left Friday night. I talked our plans over with him and he granted me a delegation for tonight. I invited him to be chairman. He agreed.[62]

"As for the program," Becker continued, "Mr. Mackay was in the printing shop and saw it. I was busy in the afternoon and he carried them to me." For Becker there was no question about mistaken identity. His visitor carried a briefcase with Swastika material and gave his Toronto address, he said. The *Telegram*, too, printed a statement from Becker: "We [Becker and Mackay] had a long talk, and agreed on our plans for a Swastika club here. I took his word that he would be here. I trusted him to keep it. And I still believe he will be here."[63]

Becker was right. The *Mail and Empire*'s report that Mackay had repudiated the Kitchener meeting was inaccurate. On the following day, the *Star* reported that: "H. W. Mackay, one of the moving spirits in the east end Swastika Club, told the *Star* today he would go to Kitchener to take the chair at the proposed meeting of Swastika enthusiasts in that city." It quoted Mackay as follows: "I was asked if I would act as chairman, and I said I certainly would. I am not representing the Toronto Swastikas as they have no connection with the Kitchener affair officially." Of course, the connection could not be official. After all, the Toronto Swastika Club was officially no more.

Official Jewish reaction to the Kitchener Swastika Club mirrored that of some two weeks earlier when the Swastikas had appeared in Toronto. The ideal strategy was to ignore the club and remain confident that Hitlerism, being alien to the "true" spirit of Canada, would be soundly rejected. Meyer Kauffman, described in the *Star* as a prominent Jewish citizen of Kitchener, was quoted as stating: "Personally I would be inclined to ignore the whole thing.... I don't think that with British justice and fair play we have much to fear."[64] And this view was shared by Rabbi Sachs, Chairman of the League for the Defence of Jewish Rights:

> I imagine the movement will find favour with some recent German immigrants about the Kitchener district who are fired by the Hitler spirit at home, but I don't think that real Canadians there will countenance them for one moment.[65]

On 15 August the *Star* announced that "Hitlerism in Western Ontario met a speedy downfall in Kitchener last night." The *Telegram's* account, headlined "Kitchener Council Frowns on Swazis," and "Police of Kitchener End Swastika Meeting as Disorder Threatens," reported that the meeting had ended abruptly:

> Fascism in Kitchener, as personified by "Commander" O.E. Becker, of this place, and H.W. Mackey, of Toronto, died a hurried death last night amidst boos, hisses, shouts and derision and out and out antagonism. The meeting came to a close before it was scheduled to do when Chief of Police William Hodgson quietly advised both Becker and Mackay to adjourn.[66]

According to the *Star*, the hall was crowded with between three and four hundred people when the meeting was called to order. At the head of the stairs was chalked a huge sign that read: "Meeting, Swastika Friends—Gentiles Only." Swastika emblems surmounted the greeting. When the curtain was drawn for the meeting to begin, Becker and Mackay were revealed standing with right hands upraised in the Nazi salute. As a background, two Union Jacks hung beneath large pictures of the King and Queen. Between the two pictures, tacked on their frames, was a huge scarlet flag with the swastika emblem in blue on a white background.

Becker was dressed in the apparel in which he had been photographed all day—brown shirt with a swastika on the left arm and a gold "Hindenburg" metal over his heart. Mackay, reported the *Telegram,* appeared in the same "rather dirty sweatshirt emblazoned with a swastika in which he first appeared at the Eastern Beaches in Toronto."[67]

Prior to the meeting it had become known that the two former spokesmen of the Toronto Swastika Club, B. Ganter and H. W. Mackay, had come to a parting of the ways. In headline form the *Telegram* had reported: "Swastikas at Parting—Mackay Admits Interest in Anti-Jewish Body—R.C.M.P. Watch."[68] Though Ganter's name appeared on the Kitchener Swastika Club program he failed to attend. Mackay claimed that this was "for matters of his own business,"[69] and asserted that the two remained friends. In fact, the rift between them was a serious one. As the *Telegram* reported:

> Members of the Swastika Clubs have reached the parting of the ways. While Bert Ganter, one of the two spokesmen for the organization and two other original members have issued a statement reiterating that they are not connected with any anti-Jewish organization, and announcing the inaugural meeting of the Beaches Protective Association, H.W. Mackay, the other spokesman, claimed that Ganter had no right to speak for the Swastikas, and admitted that he (Mackay) was interested in a frankly anti-Jewish organization.[70]

For his part, Mackay was rather blunt about his disagreement with Ganter. "He [Ganter] let us down. He did something he had no right to do when he said we would quit wearing Swastikas."[71] He added, "Ganter is working with the police."[72]

Like the English press, *Der Yiddisher Zhurnal* provided extensive coverage of the meeting of the Kitchener Swastikas. In its very first report it linked Mackay with the new organization, which, it claimed, was patterned after the Hitler SS:

> Not only will H. W. Mackay, one of the leaders of the Toronto swastikas, chair the meeting of Nazis in Kitchener, as he announced yesterday, but he also admitted that he is affiliated with an organization that is currently being established in Toronto which has adopted the same principles as the Hitlerite SS troops in Germany.[73]

For the *Zhurnal*, however, the most important results of the Kitchener rally were its revelation of Mackay's real motives and the evidence it offered that Hitlerite agents were active in Toronto. This idea prompted the paper's 15 August editorial, entitled "Uncovered a Hitler Agent":

> When Mayor Stewart called the conference last week to which he invited the Jews and the Swastika heroes, the leaders, both Ganter and Mackay, argued that they had nothing to do with antisemitism.... It now appears that Mackay is a simple liar. Only yesterday did he change his colour and argue that Ganter had betrayed him...; that in the beginning he had really meant to organize a Fascist organization on the German model because "the Jews have made all the countries in Europe miserable and they are preparing to seize power in Canada." These are Mackay's words.
>
> So why did Mackay speak differently at the conference in City Hall last week...? What's important is that it unmasked the Hitler agent in Canada....
>
> There can now be no doubt that the Hitler agents are active in Ontario, and if they are not unmasked in time they will become a true danger for the peaceful population in Ontario and the entire country.[74]

CHAPTER 6 Kipling or Hitler?

The swastika, the official government emblem.... "Kill the Jews."
Free yourself from them once and for all! There are two kinds of
antisemitism. One, of a higher kind, limits Jewish power through
laws. The other, baser sort, kills Jews. The latter is perhaps a dread-
ful kind, but it brings the best results because it ends for a time the
Jewish question by exterminating them.
—Leaflet distributed in Berlin, quoted in *Der Yiddisher Zhurnal*,
1 August 1933

Meanwhile, back in Toronto, a meeting was finally held in the east end
in the hope of reconciling Jewish and Gentile interests. "Gentiles and
Jews Form Beach Committee: New Organization Will Take Place of
Swastika Club," read the headline in the *Globe's* second edition.

In a statement issued by Bert Ganter, Donald Griffin, and George E.
Singer, all previously affiliated with the Swastika Club in Toronto, attention was called to the meeting to be held at Kew Beach Public School
on Thursday, 17 August, at 9:00 p.m. and the objectives of the Beaches
Protective Association were outlined. The statement concluded:

> The Beaches Protective Association is an association for the car-
> rying out of its aims and objects in the Beaches district only. We
> have no connection of any type in any other city in Canada and
> we have absolutely nothing to do with Fascist, Nazi or other an-
> ti-Semitic ideas.[1]

In describing the meeting, which was attended by between three and
four hundred residents, the *Star* reported that: "Everything from what
the well-dressed bather should wear to racial prejudices, Hitlerism and
the real significance of the swastika emblem came under open discussion in Kew Beach Public School last night."[2] There was no shortage

of police at the school. Chief Inspector of Detectives George Guthrie and Inspector Nat Guthrie headed large squads of uniformed and plain clothes officers both in the school and on the grounds.

Following more than two hours of discussion, a committee representing the diverse element in the Beaches district was chosen. The committee, which was chaired by J. H. Kerr, a provincial civil servant, had nineteen members, four of whom were Jews: Mrs. Shaloff, Abe Nodelman, Miss Nodelman, and Miss Simkin. It was decided that the committee would meet the following Wednesday at 8:30 p.m. to plan for a future meeting of Beaches residents.

The 17 August meeting was chaired by Donald Griffin, and commenced with the singing of "O Canada." In his opening remarks, Griffin explained that the Beaches Protective Association had been formed for the betterment of the Beaches district. "I think you will agree," he declared, "that since the advent of the Beaches Swastika Club the conditions in the park have improved considerably."[3] Despite the different name, the new organization would absorb in its entirety the aims and objective of the Swastika Club of the Beaches. However, as the swastika emblem was considered offensive to certain persons, the new organization would also select a different emblem: a shield with a watch tower on it with the letters "BPA" across the face. About halfway through the evening, Morris Simkin, a thirteen-year resident of Kew Beach, was granted permission to speak. He drew the audience's attention to the horrors conjured up for Jews by the swastika symbol:

> "I am a Jew," he remarked quietly. "I was born that way. I had not much say in it. The Jews for the last generation and for thousands of years have gone through persecution by the Gentiles and many other people."
>
> Then he made reference to persecution in Spain and other countries years ago. "No, no," shouted the audience. "Stay in Canada."
>
> "The Swastika Club," challenged Mr. Simkin, "was formed to eliminate the Jewish people from the beach."
>
> Voice: "You're wrong."
>
> Mr. Simkin: "No. I'm not wrong. If you had been left orphans through German atrocities—the swastika is an emblem of blood. You don't realize, you don't know why the Jewish people see the red bull and are so bitter against the emblem of the swastika.
>
> "I fully agree that all of your beaches have to be clean," Mr.

Simkin went on. "Is there not any other way of accomplishing it than by wearing the swastika that is dipped in Jewish blood...?"

Mr. Ganter: "If the young people had any intention of bringing in propaganda, or inciting riot, would they be here tonight when they guaranteed safety to those present?"

"I think the proper way in the beginning," replied Mr. Simkin, "would have been to call a meeting of the Beaches residents and figure out the situation."

"Have you any reason whatsoever," Mr. Ganter proceeded, "to connect the Swastika Club with the meeting at Kitchener? You have heard the resignation of one of our more radical members [H. W. Mackay] who differs from our views."

Mr. Simkin made some response, but it was lost in a general hub-bub and din.[4]

Another speaker offered: "We as Canadians have not done our duty in teaching foreigners our Canadian laws and ideals," and went on to describe the selection of the swastika emblem as an "unfortunate mistake" due to "immature judgment."

In one of the more significant moments of the meeting, Bert Ganter read the resignation of Harold W. Mackay, who had recently presided over the Kitchener Swastikas' meeting. "I am glad that the other members understand my position and have accepted my resignation," said Mackay. "Now I can turn my energy to other affairs I have in mind." The "other affairs" were understood to be the Swastika Association of Canada, announced by J. Fair to the press the previous day.[5] The swastika would serve as the emblem this newly formed body: about the size of a nickel, it would be displayed on a badge and worn on the lapel of the coat.[6] "The new organization will be frankly anti-Jewish," declared Fair. "We are not going to parade and we are not trying to start trouble, but we see no reason why we should not wear our badges just as much as Orangemen use their regalia."[7] Formed from a nucleus of Swastika Club and Beaches Protective Association members, the association was to be national in scope. Fair claimed some fifteen hundred followers, and stressed the association's independence: "We are not going to identify ourselves with the Beaches. We hope to make this thing Dominion-wide. It will have nothing to do with the Nazis, Steel Helmets or any of the rest of them. We want to make it purely national. We are not identified with the Kitchener group."[8] Fair and ten other members of the executive planned to submit their resignations at the organizational meeting of the Beaches Protective Association, but only one such resignation—H. W. Mackay's—was actually tendered at that meeting.

The word swastika itself, according to the *Oxford English Dictionary,* comes from the Sanskrit: *"svastika* f. *svasti* well-being, fortune, luck, f. *sú* good + *asti* being (f. *as* to be)." It is defined as "(A) primitive symbol or ornament in the form of a cross with equal arms with a limb of the same length projecting at right angles from the end of each arm, all in the same direction and (usually) clockwise; also called gammadion and fylfot." According to the *Meyers Konversationslexicon,* the swastika has been found on prehistoric vessels and devices; it is also a Hindu religious symbol. For about the last five decades it has come to stand for Nazism exclusively in the public mind and to evoke images of unspeakable horror, torture, and mass death.

Although the swastika has been identified as the symbol of German National Socialism since Hitler's rise to power, its origin as an antisemitic emblem is obscure. It was probably first used within the ranks of modern antisemites by Georg Lanz von Liebenfels, a Viennese crackpot "theo-zoologist" who ran an Aryan cult group and published a magazine called *Ostara* that was devoted to expounding the features of a racially based theology. Hitler purchased back issues of *Ostara* and drank deeply from its perverted content. A group of followers of von Liebenfels was supposed to have raised the swastika flag on Christmas Day 1907 at the ruins of Castle Werfenstein, the bastion of the order.[9] After World War I, units of the Freikorps adopted it as their emblem. It was part of the paraphernalia of the Nazi party from its very beginning.

For Toronto Jewry, by mid-summer 1933, the association of the swastika with German National Socialism was unmistakable. However, the freshness of this association for the public at large, and the still lingering albeit weak images of the swastika as an emblem associated with Rudyard Kipling or a good-luck sign, enabled members of the Swastika Club to deny their antisemitism. On the one hand, it was simply not the case that the swastika symbol assumed the same meaning and significance for its Toronto supporters as it did for German National Socialists. On the other hand, the question naturally arises: having adopted the swastika as their official emblem, to what extent did the Swastika Club members, and the members of the Pit Gang who hoisted the swastika flag, identify with Hitlerian antisemitism? Were the swastika bearers seriously committed to the Nazi cause? Or was it, rather, that the emblem, while purposely selected to provoke the Jews, had little political meaning for its bearers?

Logically, we might expect to resolve the problem neatly: either the swastika bearers were identifying with Hitler, or they were not. In fact, however, the matter is not this simple. In both settings where the swastika appeared—at the Beaches and at Christie Pits—the swastika supporters publicly denied any connection with or sympathy for the Nazi cause. For the Swastika Club the emblem was claimed as a sign of good fortune with a historic connection to Indian bands in the area; for the Pit Gang it was just a joke. Yet it had to have been apparent to all that there *was* a connection between the swastika's display in Berlin and the emblem worn along the beaches and hoisted at the Pits. Though these Canadian youths were not Hitlerites—or adherents of any political ideology—nevertheless, both groups likely seized upon the swastika emblem for identical reasons: to demonstrate hostility to a "foreign" group that encroached upon, and therefore threatened, their respective territory.

Xenophobia—fear of foreigners or strangers—has played a significant role in Canada's history by influencing immigration policy, determining the relationships between the dominant British majority and the various minority groups, and shaping the way Canadians thought about themselves and their country. Fear of the foreigner was widespread among Canadians of British decent in 1933 and is one of the keys to understanding the violence that erupted in Toronto during that summer. In the Toronto of the early 1930s, any homogeneous, non-Nordic ethnic group entering the areas in question in large numbers would have met with hostility.

Although general xenophobia was more important than a specific ideology, the choice of the swastika was not accidental. The newspapers had been full of atrocity reports concerning the desperate situation facing the Jews of Germany. Many Jewish groups in Canada and in other countries were advocating a boycott of German products. Nazism and Jewry were portrayed in the press as mortal enemies. Any non-Jew would know that he would provoke a violent reaction from Jews by displaying the swastika in public.

At the same time, however, the swastika bearers in Toronto were simply not political enough to be labelled Nazis, or even German sympathizers. The swastika emblem may still have had associations with the writings of Kipling among the "British" youth of Toronto in 1933, as well as with the hysterical rantings of Adolf Hitler. Rudyard Kipling's books were decorated with swastikas; and it is highly unlikely that the young people in the Beaches district would have made a German symbol their own only fourteen years after the end of World War I—a war in which

Canada suffered many casualties. Anti-German feeling still lingered and it is improbable that these adolescents felt a deep sympathy with the new German government.

A further point to consider is the way in which the Swastika Club developed. Denying it was political in anyway, its leaders asserted that they were only interested in keeping the Beaches area neat and tidy and discouraging rowdies and other disruptive elements from entering the vicinity. All residents of the Beaches who shared these aims would be welcomed into the club, and this, the Swastika spokesmen asserted, included Jewish residents of the area. In spite of their unwillingness, at first, to adopt some symbol other than the swastika to express their purpose, the majority seemed to agree when Bert Ganter announced the decision to drop the swastika and change the club name to the Beaches Protective Association. With the exception of a handful of its organizers, the Swastika Club's public dissociation from Hitlerism was probably genuine. Excepting Mackay, an official spokesman, none of the Swastika supporters advanced an openly antisemitic view to the press. There was a sense that to do so was improper, if not shameful, in the Toronto of 1933, especially if done publicly.

This is the most charitable view that can be taken of the thinking of the youthful Swastika Club members. Similarly a charitable interpretation of the Pit Gang's use of the swastika emblem would concur with Magistrate Browne's view at the trial of the four youths: it was only an innocent joke. Judging from our respondents' impressions of the political sophistication of the Pit Gang members, it is likely that the world of politics was not part of their daily frame of reference and that the idea of a swastika flag was derived from reports of the events at the Beaches in the two weeks before the fateful ball game.

Thus, though it would have been incredible for anyone to wear a swastika in Toronto during the summer of 1933 without understanding the antisemitic statement it made; the substance of that statement was somewhat ambiguous and probably differed considerably from one person to the next. In a general way, it expressed disapproval and dislike of stereotypical Jewish character and behavioural traits and signified that the Jews were unwelcome.

As for the leaders of the Swastika Club, there is overwhelming evidence to suggest that their selection of the emblem was based upon its association with events in Germany. In the first place, the "undesirables" they wished to keep out of their neighbourhood were Jews. Moreover, the appearance of the "Hail Hitler" sign in front of the Balmy Beach Canoe Club and the singing of antisemitic doggerel by a group of "Swazis" is evidence that the swastika was more than a good-luck charm to these individuals. The public appearance of H. W. Mackay at a Nazi rally in Kitchener confirms that at least one important member of the Swastika Club was a political supporter of Hitler and his brand of antisemitism.

It is highly unlikely that the youthful adherents of the Pit Gang were worried about property values and the like. More probably they were looking for excitement and were provoked by an encroachment of other young people upon "their" turf. That these other young people were Jews made matters even worse in their eyes. In adopting the swastika they signalled to the other "gang" exactly what they thought of them. This was true both at the Beaches and at Christie Pits. In both places, the swastika was employed to deliver a clear message to "intruders" that they were not wanted on that territory.

Finally, and most importantly, the Toronto papers had firmly established the connection between the swastika and Hitlerism. The newspapers were the prime source of national and international news for most people at the time, and their repeated identification of the swastika with Hitlerian antisemitism developed and heightened public awareness of this connection.[10]

The summer of 1933 proved a dramatic turning point in Jewish-Gentile relations in Toronto. The public display of the swastika emblem and shouts of "Heil Hitler" along the city's eastern beaches and in Willowvale Park starkly revealed the contempt for Jews avowed by segments of the Gentile population and added a new dimension to the expressions of anti-Jewishness theretofore found in Toronto.

The choice of the swastika as an instrument of provocation and insult was hardly an accident. The newspapers that reported the violence, torture, discrimination, mass arrests, degradation, and murder inflicted on Jews in Germany also delivered the clear message that the wrongs perpetrated against Jews were all done under the sign of the swastika.

A front-page story (by Pierre van Paassen) in the *Star* on 27 March 1933, entitled "German Children Taught Pre-War 'Hate' Sentiment: Nazis Pump Youngsters with Extreme Nationalism of Imperial Regime: Terror Reigns," highlighted the violent associations of the swastika as follows: "Later in the day, I saw a parade of hundreds of children, between the ages of seven and sixteen, carrying the swastika and the old imperial colors, and shouting at intervals: 'The Jews must be destroyed!'" In its front-page story of 29 March 1933, entitled "Naziism Embodies Ideals

Followed by Ku Klux Klan: Extreme Nationalism, Hatred of All Aliens Common to Both Orders: Nordics Superior," the *Star* wrote: "Curiously enough, the Swastika or Hooked Cross, Hakenkreuz, the Nazi symbol, was an emblem much in evidence in the Ku Klux lodges and on the parades of the order in days gone by.... A man without a program save hatred, ignorance and vulgarity is driving a great and disillusioned people to perdition. This is a pessimistic prognosis, yet I am afraid, although I hope not, that history will bear me out in this assertion."

On 5 April 1933, again in a front-page story, the *Star* reported as follows: "'Christ himself was a Hitlerite,' the assembly was informed by the Pastor, Dr. Wieneke of Soldin, who declared, 'The Christian cross and the swastika belong together.'" In its issue of 13 April 1933, the *Star* carried three pictures of the German boycott of Jewish shops in which the swastika was clearly portrayed. The captions read:

> Campaign Against Jews Highly Organized in Berlin: These pictures from Berlin show incidents in the Nazis' antisemitic demonstrations. In (1) uniformed Black Shirts are pasting stickers on the window of a Jewish-owned shop on April 1, the date of the one-day boycott against all Jewish-owned establishments in the Reich. The large placard reads: "Germans defend yourselves. Don't buy in Jewish shops." The smaller ones say: "It is forbidden to purchase in this Jewish shop."(2) Carrying banners setting forth their principles Nazi storm troopers stand guard outside the barred doors of the Tietz store in Berlin. (3) Dr. Joseph Goebbels, chief Nazi spokesman, outlines the program calling for the boycotting of Jewish merchants to a huge gathering in front of the former imperial castle in Berlin.

And, as we have seen, the swastika was also directly associated with physical violence towards Jews.

On 17 May, Hitler delivered an important foreign-policy speech to the German parliament. The *Star* described the pageantry of the occasion as follows:

> The theatre was a vast expanse of brown-shirted figures, tense with expectancy. There was one brief salvo of applause as Hitler entered the opera house. He strode to the tribune, took his place before an immense swastika flag, and signaled for silence.
>
> The opera house, used for parliament since the Reichstag was

burned, was gaily decorated with black, white and red flags and the Nazi swastika.[11]

The swastika also figured in the tense relationship between church and state in Germany. The Nazis had been trying to bring the Protestant churches under their control since taking power. The Nazi appointee as Prussian Protestant commissioner had ordered the churches to celebrate the sabbath as a day of "thanksgiving and supplication." The *Star* wrote: "Accompanying the Nazi order are the instructions to fly not only the church emblems but also the Reich's black, white and red flags and the Nazi swastika banner."[12]

Earlier in May, the *Star* carried a report from England featuring the swastika. Hitler had sent Alfred Rosenberg, his personal foreign representative, to England and, during his trip, the Nazi emissary laid a wreath bearing a swastika emblem at the cenotaph in a ceremony honouring British war dead. This action so incensed a Captain J. E. Sears of the British Legion that he mutilated and stole the wreath.

Of the Toronto papers the *Star*, with the largest daily circulation in the city, was the most outspoken in its criticism of the new Nazi government in Germany. Though the *Evening Telegram* was the least critical of Hitler and his henchmen, it too condemned the Nazi movement as anti-democratic and deplored the treatment of the Jews in Germany. In its pages the relationship between the swastika and Hitlerism was also clearly drawn. On 27 March the *Tely* reproduced a French cartoon in which Hitler as a German Samson was portrayed as tearing down the columns of world peace; he wore a swastika on the sleeve of his left arm.[13]

In its front-page story about the boycott of Jewish stores in Germany on 1 April, the *Tely* observed the following: "On many public squares and market halls, the Nazi brass bands made the air reverberate with snappy military marches. The Nazi swastika and imperial flags were fastened to all street cars. Shops whose owners were Nazi party members flew especially large swastika banners."[14] In another front-page story two weeks later, the swastika and the Reichskanzler were identified: "From Poland to the Rhine Hitler propaganda is sweeping through the new Germany. Photographs of Adolf Hitler and Nazi emblems are displayed among Easter presents. A popular picture shows the blood-red swastika, the Nazi emblem, rising above a marsh land in the dawn of Germany's morning."

On 10 June the *Telegram* introduced the first in a series of articles about Hitler and the Nazis from its correspondent Bruce Bairnsfather. Bairnsfather had created a character called "Old Bill," who had written reports for the British papers from the trenches during the First World War. Bairnsfather now brought Old Bill out of mothballs and took him on his travels through the new Germany of Adolf Hitler to send reports back to the English public. The very first article was accompanied by a cartoon picturing a dishevelled fellow leaning over the rail of a ship (Harwich to Holland), whose head was spinning. In the speech balloon above his head were eight swastikas and a question mark. The series was introduced as follows: "'Old Bill,' noted authority on the late war, is out of retirement, called by duty and his creator, Capt. Bruce Bairnsfather. From his comfortable hostelry, 'The Ball and Chain,' Bill is going to Germany with Capt. Bairnsfather to find out what all this business of Hitler, Nazis and swastikas is about." There were five parts to this series, each preceded by a cartoon. Of the five cartoons, three featured the swastika.

In its coverage of the World Economic Conference, the *Tely* sketched a picture of the world being carried by leaders of different countries towards a building marked "World Economic Conference." The sketch was entitled "Out of the Ditch." First the procession of leaders was the British representative with a Union Jack on his hat. In second place was the Canadian figure with "Canada" written on his "Mountie" hat. The Americans were third with Uncle Sam, and the Germans fourth. The German representative was a storm trooper with a swastika armband.

Finally, on the *Telegram*'s front page of Friday, 28 July, only a few days before the emergence of the Swastika Club at Toronto's eastern beaches, there appeared a picture of a German ship anchored in Toronto harbour. To the left of the ship was a close-up of the top of the mast from which a British flag was flying above the swastika ensign. The picture bore the title: "Nazi Emblem Flies for First Time in Toronto Harbour." Only a few days later it would be flying on Toronto's eastern beaches.

Since the newspaper served as the prime source of national and international news in 1933, reports of the Nazi measures aimed at German Jewry cemented the identification of the swastika with Hitlerian anti-semitism. Coverage in the English-language press unmistakably linked the Nazi symbol with Hitler, but the *Zhurnal*'s emphasis focused less on the symbol per se. Instead, in its reports on the Nazi atrocities, it fleshed out the swastika's meaning for Jews: degradation, terror, and physical violence. By August 1933, the mere display of the swastika in Toronto was enough to put Jews on a sort of "red alert" and provoke them into taking strong collective action against those displaying it.

Although the Swastika Club existed under that name in Toronto for a relatively short time—less than two weeks—its presence attracted enormous attention and had considerable influence. Whether it was Nazi-sponsored, Nazi-inspired, or simply the work of thoughtless, prejudiced individuals is difficult to say definitively. We have seen that a few Swastika Club leaders—Mackay, for example—were very probably inspired by Hitlerism. But the split between Mackay and Ganter over whether to keep or abandon the swastika emblem indicates tension within the club. In retrospect, the leaders' reluctance to identify themselves or to meet with representatives of the League for the Defence of Jewish Rights was probably due to the squabble within the club between a minority pro-Hitler faction and a majority non-Nazi (but xenophobic and mildly antisemitic) group. Hugh Garner, in *Cabbagetown,* portrays representatives of the Swastika Club at the Beaches as asking for support from a distinctly Canadian Fascist political organization. In the book, residents of the Beaches are shown to be xenophobic and antisemitic, but not political supporters of Fascism. In an attempt to gain support for the newly formed organization, one of the characters declares:

> "We are tired of our Christian wives and girlfriends being leered at by every Abie and Izzy who ogles them on the boardwalk as they walk by. The sight of big fat Jewesses calling to Rachel and Sammy around our neighbourhood has got to stop! We don't want to persecute the Jews—"
>
> "Why not?" somebody in the audience asked, to the accompaniment of loud laughter.
>
> Leveritt smiled and went on. "All we want is that the Jews stay in their own section of town. We Christians can't go to the Islands or Sunnyside anymore on weekends because of the hordes of Jews, but we won't stand for being driven out of our own neighbourhood facilities by them too!"[15]

Whether or not Swastika Club members were really motivated or instigated by Fascist elements, they were perceived to be so. To many Jewish community leaders they represented an obvious attempt to assist Hitlerism in gaining a foothold in Canada. Moreover, the Jewish community at large, a people already battered by the prejudices of the surrounding society, generally agreed with this perception.

Mayor Stewart was therefore quite correct in believing that the presence and activities of the Swastika Club presented an unsettling situation. Noting the tensions and sporadic outbreaks of violence they had caused, he said: "It would not take a very great spark to start a conflagration in the city that you couldn't put out in a day."[16] His worst fears were to be realized on the evening of 16 August 1933.

CHAPTER 7 "Take Me Out to the Ballgame"

Every time you went to a ballgame... these guys started running around with swastikas yelling "Heil Hitler" and all this. And it got so bad that somebody came down to our area in the community, College and Spadina, and they asked the boys to organize and do something about it. So they went from College and Spadina to Dundas and Spadina and to the Jewish bookmakers, to the gambling clubs, and they rounded up everybody they knew. All of us got together, and we got a bunch of trucks. We piled into the back of these trucks and we drove en masse to Christie Pits and we piled out of the trucks and we started chasing all those characters.
—A witness

In a rather dramatic turn of events, the swastika, which had disappeared entirely from the eastern beaches district, reappeared in Willowvale Park—Christie Pits—on the evening of 14 August. During a junior softball quarter-final game, in which Harbord Playground, a predominantly Jewish team, met the team from St. Peter's church at Bathurst and Bloor, a huge swastika emblem five feet long, the *Telegram* reported, sewn in white cloth on a black sweater coat was unfurled in the final innings. According to newspaper accounts, only small sections were unfolded from time to time, "amid much wisecracking, cheering and yelling of pointed remarks."[1] When the Harbord team tied the score in the ninth inning, the two flag bearers acted. According to both the *Mail and Empire* and the *Telegram,* St. Peter's fans brought out the swastika-emblazoned flag and unfurled it to urge their team to victory. The strategy failed. To quote the *Mail and Empire:*

St. Peter's kept the lead until the ninth inning. Then the Jewish boys rallied and tied the score. The tenth inning began. The St. Peter's supporters considered desperate measures. They decided to act. In a winking they unfurled the bold Swastika emblem and flaunted it.

A Jewish boy was at bat. He looked at the large Swastika. The ball was nearly over the plate. He gripped the bat and let it fly—a hit, and victory for the Jewish team.[2]

The *Star* identified the provocateurs as members of a gang. To Jews the incident was further evidence of the growth of the Swastika Club and of general support for Nazi Germany.

Following the game, the gang held the emblem high and swarmed on to the field. According to the *Star*, they gave their "club yell" again, and gathered around the Jewish players. Spectators thought a fight would follow.[3]

Some time during the night a large swastika with the words "Hail Hitler" was painted on the Willowvale Park clubhouse. The following morning, Park Commissioner Chambers announced: "All we intend to do at the minute is obliterate the sign and turn the matter over to the police." The swastika had been painted after attendants left the grounds at ten o'clock, and the department had no information as to the vandals' identity.

The *Star*, however, was able to supply more details:

> Later, the gang met and decided to paint a sign on the roof of the clubhouse. A collection was taken up to provide paint. A member left and returned with a half pint tin. The youths waited until the attendants left the park, then two of them climbed the roof and painted the sign, amid cheers from the others on the ground.
>
> Questioned they admitted that no connection existed between the Beaches swastikas and themselves. The club had no membership cards or fees, but is merely formed by the gang which frequents the parks, they explained. "We want to get the Jews out of the park," they said.[4]

According to the newspaper, the swastika emblem had been seen during the past week on Bloor Street, and on Wednesday of the previous week a number of Jewish boys from Euclid Avenue had attacked five Willowvale lads. The Willowvale group retreated to Christie Pits for reinforcements and then returned to Euclid, whereupon the Jewish boys fled before waving clubs. The *Star* visited with a Sydney Adam of Clinton Street, father of John Adams, reported leader of the "Willowvale

Swastikas," as the paper referred to them, who termed the affair "a lot of tom-foolery."[5] Said Adams:

> I knew he was the leader of the thing because I saw him sewing the emblem on the sweater coat. It's a bunch of foolish nonsense and I have had him remove the emblem. I'm afraid he may get into trouble.[6]

On the following day, 16 August, William G. Carroll, director of the St. Peter's Athletic Association, denied that the boys of St. Peter's baseball team had had any part in the flaunting of the swastika emblem during the game:

> There were many games in Willowvale last night. Ten thousand fans watched a hardball game between Native Sons and Vermonts, and upon its conclusion several thousand of them congregated around our softball game, which had not finished. It was then that the hoodlums started their sideshow. Why should St. Peter's supporters get the blame for it any more than the supporters of the Harbord team, or, in fact, any other team in the park? It happens that on the softball team in question there were no Jewish boys, but we have a number of Jewish lads on other teams, so there is no discrimination in this respect by us.[7]

After the Monday night game, supporters of the Harbord Playground team announced that they would be back in force for the Wednesday evening game. Earlier in the day, one Harbord fan told the *Star*: "We are not going there to make trouble, but if anything happens we will be there to support our players."[8] Willowvale Swastikas, as the *Star* referred to them, aware of these plans, mustered their supporters as well. The anticipated trouble was not long in coming.

Even before the game began, one Gentile spectator was reported to have required medical attention. The "Swastika supporters" claimed that while they were cheering for the St. Peter's team, a crowd of Jewish youths arrived and ordered them to be silent. "Whatever the cause," the *Star* account read,

> it wound up in a swiftly-ending free-for-all, with an unidentified swastika supporter requiring medical attention, the result, it is claimed, of a blow from a club, while one of the Jewish leaders was thrown down the hill into a cage back of the batter's box.[9]

When the game was in only the second inning, there was another fracas—a foretaste of what was to come. The trouble began in a group seated on the rising ground above the north-west diamond on which the game was being played. Close to the more than one thousand Jewish supporters lining a section of the hill was a group consisting of some thirty "Willowvale Swastikas." "Heil Hitler," the group yelled in unison. Incensed, the Harbord supporters ran toward the group, and in the process a spectator was struck with a sawed-off piece of lead pipe. "The spectators, seeing the attack, rushed. At the same time the Jewish section flocked to the fight. Batons, lead pipes and other weapons were swinging freely."[10]

The game was stopped and many of the spectators gathered around the battling groups. The *Star* report suggested that the encounter was more than a mild skirmish:

> Blood flowed freely, faces were cut and bruised. The fight gradually worked its way up to the north hill and into the dump. Two Jewish youths took flight before half a dozen who chased them for blocks. They finally escaped through a backyard.[11]

One individual, Howard Wilson, cut and bruised about the face, his shirt ripped to threads, staggered up the hill after allegedly being attacked by Jewish rioters. Telling his story to the *Star* immediately after the fight, Wilson stated that the Jews mistook him for someone else:

> I was sitting on the hill minding my own business when suddenly four men—I afterward learned they were Jews—attacked me with a lead billy. They said they would "bash my brains out" if I didn't shut up. I said something back to them and then they piled on me. I was stunned by a heavy blow in the face. They kicked and bruised my body. Then I noticed several others were helping me.
>
> Then everything went black. The next thing I remember was being escorted up the hill by a chum of mine. Then I went to the doctor and got my cut attended to. The doctor told me to go home, but I returned to the park to get the man who struck me with the billy. If I ever get him alone I'll kill him.[12]

The next shouts of "Heil Hitler" were heard during the third inning. Despite the fact that they were vastly outnumbered, four Jewish youths drew sawed-off lead pipes and headed for the two they believed to be leading the Gentile faction. Supporters rushed to the assistance of both groups of fighters, but with some police assistance, order was restored. Matters remained relatively quiet for the duration of the game, and it was not yet dusk when the St. Peter's team ensured its 6–5 victory by catching a fly from the last Harbord batter.

Throughout the game, however, in the words of one Jewish spectator, there were a number of "pro-Hitler remarks, and anti-Jewish remarks made. There were references to Ikee and Kike to some of the ball players and there were some skirmishes in the stands." It was increasingly evident that something was about to happen. And it did. As the crowd milled about after the game, youths standing on the "camel's hump," the slope of the hill south of the baseball diamond, suddenly spread out a large white blanket bearing a startling black swastika. In the *Star's* words "a mild form of pandemonium broke loose," and in the *Telegram's*, "In a moment all was turmoil."[13] The section of the park where the emblem was displayed was only sparsely occupied, and "the sign stood out visible to the entire crowd and acted like a red flag to a bull."[14] The young Swastika enthusiasts were immediately besieged by Jewish youth intent on capturing the flag. As one witness recalled: "the Jewish ball-players grabbed their bats and dropped their mitts and charged for the hill together with a lot of spectators. There was quite a to-do, a real fist fight."

A cry of "the swastika, the swastika," that "could be heard for blocks away" swept over the crowd. Maddened Jews tearing after the Gentile flag-bearer were met by the latter's supporters, and in an instant the battle intensified. "Baseball bats, lengths of iron piping, rocks, fists and later police batons were brought into play and it seemed a miracle that more were not seriously hurt."[15] Reported the *Globe:*

> The assault upon the swastika was the signal for a general inrush of Gentile youths, who plied baseball bats and fists in a wild riot. By the time police reserves arrived the battle had gradually moved over to Bloor and Clinton Streets, where some serious casualties occurred, and where, it is alleged, bottles for the first time became legitimate weapons. From this battlefront, it is said, many injured limped away or were assisted to their various homes.[16]

And as the manager of the Harbord team recalled:

> The swastika came at the end of the ball game.... All hell broke loose. Truckloads, truckloads from Spadina Avenue came up.

Now there were some tough guys down there.... When this race riot broke out, it really broke out. All I saw was people getting hit. I herded my team together to protect the team.... I didn't want my players involved. And the bats all disappeared. We had fifteen bats and they were all gone. They were delivered to my house at three o'clock in the morning.

One witness watched the activity from his parents' cigar store on Bloor between Palmerston and Markham:

I remember I was standing outside. I started noticing dump trucks, full of guys brandishing pick axes, pipes and so on shooting along Bloor Street.... Every few minutes, another going by. Also the chicken, little chicken trucks that they used to use... also full of guys and, you know, brandishing a whatever. But anyhow, I started noticing these men shooting along Bloor going west... and, you know, I just wondered what it was about. I had no inkling. After a little while, maybe an hour or two, I saw a few guys coming back, walking along Bloor Street, who looked like they had been in a real fight, bleeding, clothes torn off. So I asked them, "What the hell's going on?" He says, "There's a big riot going on over in Christie Pits." So I ran over.... Anyhow, when I got there, hundreds of people were standing all the way around the rim.... When I walked down, I could see all this goddamn fighting going on all over the goddamn place, hundreds and hundreds of people fighting.

The crowd crossed Bloor Street and headed down Montrose Avenue, where they were joined by others armed with an array of weapons.

Thousands of people, tightly packed, now blocked the street intersection and lines of streetcars and automobiles, waiting to pass in either direction, added their horns and bells to the confusion.[17]

According to the *Mail and Empire*:

For hours after the battle for the swastika quilt crowds jammed the streets around the parks, milling and shouting and grudgingly moving along when ordered by police to clear the park environs.

Motor cars jerked along in unbroken lines on Bloor, Christie, Shaw and other streets around the park and leading to it.

Motorcycle officers drove along the streets, breaking up groups which persisted in gathering and shouting. The groups were about evenly divided between Jews and Gentiles, some of the different groups brandishing baseball bats, lengths of scantling and piping and carrying rocks. Around the park a mass of humanity wandered, swirling back to the main streets as soon as the officers had passed who had dispersed them.[18]

The combatants fought desperately for possession of the swastika banner. Caught by the Jews, the Gentile flag-bearers were beaten, and the flag was ripped into pieces. A piece of the flag was seized by an eighteen-year-old Jewish youth, Murray Kruggell, who attempted to wave it aloft in defiance of the crowd. Only the arrival of two police officers saved him from a beating. But the fate of the much-coveted white flag, according to the *Star*, was not yet settled:

Several more efforts were put forth by its champion to regain it before the augmented forces of police, realizing it was the bone of contention, forcibly seized its tattered remnants and their holders for the moment and hustled them away.[19]

Although police had been expecting trouble at the park for days, they were simply unable to contend with the outbreaks of violence and were later scathingly criticized for their lack of preparation and apparent disregard of warnings to expect violence. Although the *Telegram* reported that "an unusually large number of mounted men and constables were stationed nearby," suggesting police preparedness, the *Star* was severely critical of the police. They had been warned of the coming trouble, yet "spectators estimated the police force in the park when the ball game commenced at six."[20]

It was not until 8:45 p.m.—about an hour after the first blows were struck—said the *Star*, that the mounted police arrived. They were followed shortly thereafter by a motorcycle squadron. Using drawn batons, the officers gradually gained the upper hand, forcing the main sections of the crowd to separate into small groups. By 9:00 p.m. everything seemed to be under control and, reported the *Telegram*, "quiet gradually spread throughout the park."[21]

The peace did not last long, however. Shortly after the arrival of police reinforcements, Joe Goldstein, a centre player for the Dufferin Lacrosse Club's midget team, was chased from one side of the park to the other and knocked unconscious. Help reached him after he had collapsed. Finally, Goldstein and his rescuers (Joe Cancelli and two other boys) found sanctuary in the home of Lillian Garfield, of 47 Christie Street. When she began administering first aid to the injured youth she discovered that her patient was her fifteen-year-old brother-in-law.

Goldstein was taken to hospital with a police escort, and the rumour spread that a Jewish youth had been killed. Boys on bicycles carried the news of the Gentile-Jewish battle down to the Brunswick-College-Spadina Avenue district. The Jewish population was up in arms, and cars and trucks were quickly commandeered for an assault upon the Bloor Street sector. Reported the *Star:* "Organization only took a few moments and soon truckloads of shouting young Jews armed with anything they could lay their hands on were speeding for the centre of the disturbance."[22]

The rounding up of the Jewish youths occurred with considerable dispatch, according to witnesses:

And I remember within no time at all, almost by magic, because I don't know how the message got through so quickly, but the message got to the Spadina and College district. At that time the restaurant at the corner of Spadina and College was called the Goblin restaurant, and trucks came to the front of the restaurant and boys from the district hopped onto these trucks with sticks and... hand weapons. I don't mean firearms. Mostly sticks and maybe a few pipes, a few iron pipes.... And within what seemed to be no time at all, there were three or four of these trucks at the Pit battling with the pro-Nazi element....

When we got there it seemed to me that half of the Jews and half of the goyim of the city were there.... This is what it looked to me like. I would say that we were well armed.... There were a lot of heads broken. I could tell you that there was clashes.... A few of the guys, quite a few of that side and some of our own were taken to the hospital by ambulance. There was a tremendous confrontation, and I would definitely say that we won.... We were as proud as if we had gone to Entebbe, I mean it. I think for a week we were higher than a kite.

Der Yiddisher Zhurnal, too, mentioned the rumour in its account: "Meanwhile a rumour spread in the Jewish area that Jews were being beaten up in Willowvale Park. Cars and trucks sped there, mainly with young people."[23] Many of these vehicles were trucks used to transport chickens. One respondent who sped on his bicycle from the Pits to Spadina and College reported that College Street was cordoned off and cars and trucks were commandeered on the spot. On their way to the Pits, the boys on the trucks yelled to others on the street, "Gevalt, me shlugt yidn!" (Help! They're beating Jews.) Many dropped what they were doing, grabbed some makeshift weapon, and jumped on the trucks. Several witnesses testified that people from all segments of the community responded to the alarm. They were impressed by the fervour with which Jews in the community reacted to the call for support:

> Whoever knew about it, went up. There were rabbis with beards up there. From B'nai Brith, from everywhere.

> The great part about it is that it wasn't all tough guys that you think went to Christie Pits. There were people. Some of them couldn't even wipe their ass. They couldn't fight but they went. They got themselves a pool cue, a baseball bat or a brick, whatever. The guys who were a little more shy, and were backward and never did fight, never knew how to fight, still had that thing in them that they were Jews.

By 9:30 the battle was on again, fiercer than ever. Although police on horseback and motorcycle and on foot had formed a complete circle around the park, the trucks of reinforcements still managed to break through. "They were met by the Swastikas waving blackjacks, broom handles, stones, fists, steel and lead pipes. It took police about fifteen minutes to separate combatants," reported the *Star.* This time, instead of being confined to the park, groups fought on side streets, in lanes, and even on Bloor Street in such numbers that, in the *Telegram's* words, "traffic was completely demobilized." A second call for more police was made. In the *Mail and Empire* account:

> Arriving reinforcements for the harassed constables, however, turned the tide, which had taken an ominous appearance by

10:30. By 11 o'clock, when more trucks arrived with fresh cohorts from the College Street, Bathurst and Spadina area bringing well-armed supplies of men, police were prepared. Before a truck could come to a stop, before its occupants could alight and rush into the park area, motorcycle and mounted constables had surrounded it, ordered its driver to keep moving and compelled the truck and its crew to leave the district.[24]

At 11:10 p.m., the *Star* reported, the police sergeant in charge ordered his men back to their respective divisions. Only a handful of officers were retained at the south-east corner of the park. Just after they left, a truck carrying young Jewish men who had managed to slip through the police lines disgorged its passengers, and a further skirmish took place.

Without waiting to find out whether it was a friend or foe standing on the corner, the boys from the central part of the city, mucked in with hands, fists and feet flying.

The cries soon brought a squad of some 20 officers on the run. Hastily summoned they chased the hoodlums, who had no respect for women and children who were standing on the corner at the time of the attack.

Several times, organized gangs of Jews would attempt to get up Clinton St. to where the groups of Swastikas were gathered, but a sudden rush by police officers would send them helter-skelter, running as fast as their legs would take them.[25]

By 11:30 p.m., it appeared that the police had the situation well in hand, despite the crowds of visitors who hung around the park, particularly at the corner of Bloor and Christie streets. The crowds were kept moving by the police, who had extended their activities southward along Montrose, Grace, Clinton, Euclid, Palmerston, and other streets where outbreaks seemed imminent.

Police continued to break up gangs, scatter groups that gathered on corners, and chase men and boys away from the darkened park until past midnight. At 11:30 p.m. the crowd was still so unruly that it was even blocking the streetcars on Bloor Street. Orders were given to three motorcycle police to charge. They lined up abreast, just west of Grace Street on Bloor, and charged the mob. Their exhaust pipes spread heavy, choking fumes throughout the crowd, which broke and fled. These mo-

torcycle police were then used to clear sidewalks. "By midnight," said
the *Star*,

> there were less than 200 people within 100 yards of the park, but
> police did not relax their vigilance. Officers, plainclothesmen and
> motorcyclemen were kept patrolling the streets until well past one
> o'clock this morning watching [for] renewed activities.[26]

By 1:30 a.m. Willowvale Park and the streets in the vicinity were
practically deserted. The only disturbances were caused by small groups
of youth who shouted and yelled as they wound their way home. "When
the morning papers reached the district," wrote the *Star*, "there was a
wild rush for them and the 'newsies' did a land-office business while
the papers lasted. In many instances they sold for ten cents and more."[27]

A number of the combatants sustained injuries that required medical
attention. The newspapers published the names of the injured and the
nature of their injuries.

> John [*sic*] Goldstein, age 16, 1A Bellwoods Ave., scalp lacerations,
> treated at Toronto Western Hospital.
>
> Al Eckler, 23, 112 Brunswick Ave., head and groin injuries,
> treated at Western.
>
> Dave Fisher, 21, 46 Spadina Ave., head injuries, treated at
> Western.
>
> Joe Brown, 22, 118 Euclid Ave., head cuts and bruises, admitted
> to Western.
>
> Louis Kotick, 22, Clinton St., head and body injuries, possibly
> including fractured rib.
>
> John Matheson, 19, Christie St., head injuries.
>
> Ralph Dollery, Clinton St., head injuries.
>
> Arthur Newton, Clinton St., head injuries.
>
> Howard Wilson, Christie St., head and facial injuries.
>
> Soly Osolky, Elm St., head and arm injuries.
>
> Charlie Boustead, Sydenham St., facial and back injuries.[28]

A number of others were treated at the Toronto Western Hospital for
slighter injuries.

Only two arrests were made during the entire night of fighting. One
of the arrestees—Russell Harris, a fishing guide from Peterborough—

was dismissed when charged in police court with carrying an offensive weapon. "Leave your knife at home when you don't need it for scaling fish," Magistrate Browne advised Harris. The charge was withdrawn. The other, Jack Roxborough, was held on a charge of carrying offensive weapons with the intent to do injury to an unknown person. Roxborough was seen standing over a prostrate man with a wood and metal club raised above his head. He claimed that he had been innocently drawn into the fray, about which he said he knew nothing. As the *Star* reported: "His explanation was somewhat spoiled by his record—housebreaking." His sentence was two months or fifty dollars.

The seriousness of the riot relative to other disturbances in the city's history can be grasped by surveying the next day's headlines in the city's major newspapers and the Jewish press: "Scores Hurt as Swastika Mobs Riot at Willowvale/Mayor Promises Immediate Probe of Disturbance/ Thousands Caught Up in Park Melee/Gang Wielding Lead Pipes and Bats Sweep Streets, Bludgeoning Victims"(*Daily Mail and Empire*); "Swastika Feud Battle in Toronto Injures 5/Fists, Boots, Piping Used in Bloor Street War/'Hail Hitler!' Is Youth's Cry/City in Turmoil"(*Globe*); "Draper Admits Receiving Riot Warning/Six Hours of Rioting Follow Hitler Shout/Scores Hurt, Two Held" (*Toronto Daily Star*); "Report Gunmen Here to Slay Swazis/Communists Incited Riot, Police Authority States/Jewish Toughs Began Trouble Says Witness"(*Evening Telegram*); "Swastikas Attacks Call Forth Great Panic in the City/ Mayor Stewart Agrees to Swift Steps against Nazis/Draper Called to Report"(*Der Yiddisher Zhurnal*).

Toronto officialdom was stunned by the severity and magnitude of the night's violence. When he learned that a riot was in progress, Mayor Stewart announced to the press that:

> The repeated and systematic disturbances in which the swastika emblem figures provocatively must be investigated and dealt with firmly. The matter will engage my attention as the first item of my business day tomorrow morning. I shall call upon Chief Draper to report fully to me upon the circumstances and the police organization used to cope with the trouble and if it appears necessary to convene the police commission to deal with the situation.[29]

At the emergency meeting of the Board of Police Commissioners,

Chief Draper admitted that he had been advised earlier by the Parks Department that the baseball game would merit special police attention, but denied being warned that anything resembling a riot might occur. He also denied that there was only one policeman in the park when the trouble began or that there was any delay in sending reinforcements once the alarm was raised. "'Were...100 persons on Spadina Avenue not dispersed?' asked the Mayor. 'We could not anticipate they were going to participate in the riot,' was the answer. 'Were the lead pipes, bats and broom handles displayed in any manner to indicate the peace was about to be disturbed?' asked the Mayor. 'That matter will be investigated,' was the reply."[30]

After the police commissioners' meeting, Mayor Stewart issued a statement in which he warned all citizens that people displaying the swastika emblem would be liable to prosecution. "The responsibility is now on the citizens to conduct themselves in a lawful manner," said Stewart, claiming that his statement was supported by a majority of the police commissioners.

A representative delegation of Jews called at city hall after the emergency meeting to assure the mayor of the support of Toronto Jewry. The Jewish delegation offered a written statement signed and presented by: Samuel Factor, MP; E. Fred Singer, KC, MPP; Rabbi Samuel Sachs and A. B. Bennett, League for the Defence of Jewish Rights; H. S. Rosenberg (Chairman), Sol Kaufman, and D. B. Goodman, B'nai Brith Anti-Defamation League; H. S. Rosenberg, Zionist Organization of Ontario; R. D. Green, JP, Jewish National Association; and aldermen Nathan Phillips and John J. Glass. The statement expressed the delegation's appreciation for the city's handling of the affair and offered its full co-operation.

Mayor Stewart's statement was supported by a number of leading Jewish citizens who had appealed for restraint. The *Telegram* reported that warnings were issued from official sources, both Jewish and Gentile, that Jewish strong-arm tactics, "such as were threatened when a band of 40 muscle men from the Ward raided the Beaches when the first swastika scare was raised, and looked for trouble," would adversely affect all Jews in the city.

> Fear is expressed that a recurrence of these raids might provoke a wave of anti-Semitic feeling that could cause grave injustices to hundreds of Jewish citizens who were entirely dissociated from the recent disturbances.[31]

Gentile officialdom was anxious to secure the co-operation of Toronto's Jewish population, but without active displays of Jewish force. This was also the attitude approved by the League for the Defence of Jewish Rights. Announced Meyer F. Steinglass, managing editor of the *Jewish Standard* and a member of the League:

> It was unfortunate that the Jewish youth considered it necessary
> to take matters into their own hands, for the police, I am sure,
> would have handled the situation properly.[32]

"It may have been some young man just out for a thrill who flaunted the offensive weapon in the face of the Jewish youth," he said. But Steinglass really knew better, for he added: "But on the other hand, there may have been others behind the scene who instigated the affairs...." He nonetheless concluded that the Jewish boys who joined in the fray "shouldn't have adopted the method they did."

Jew or non-Jew, those responsible for the events at Willowvale Park should be punished in the courts, declared Rabbi Sachs, when informed of the rioting. "I have no accurate account" he said, "but from what I am informed some hotheads displayed an emblem which is hateful to our people, and some Jewish lads, equally hot-headed, tore it down."[33] He was, he said, "deeply ashamed of the conduct of the Jewish youth who seem to have let their imagination run away with their judgement."[34] Lest his assessment of the situation be considered too one-sided, Rabbi Sachs was equally critical of the Gentile youth who were involved: "I am also deeply ashamed of the Christian young people, who appeared to leave their Christianity at home or in church when they visited Willowvale Park." Said Alderman Nathan Phillips: "I counsel the people of the Jewish faith to leave the matter in the hands of the police and justice will be done.... Such disturbances have no place under British institutions."[35]

Jewish and Gentile officials' confidence in British institutions and their faith in the fair distribution of justice by the police was not, however, shared by the combatants. Once the rioting sides were separated, the Jewish boys gathered in a restaurant at Spadina and College where, according to the *Telegram,* they planned another attack on Willowvale Park for Friday evening, when the two baseball teams were to meet for the final game. Simultaneously, at the north end of the park, the Swastikas were planning their defence.

Neither group would say what it intended to do, but the *Telegram* learned that a meeting would be held on the afternoon of the seventeenth in the Spadina-College district, at which representatives of Jews, Italians, Ukrainians, and other groups would be present. One of the "spokesmen" explained:

> If any trouble starts, we'll have cars and trucks ready to get to the scene within a few minutes. Several cars drove up and down Spadina Avenue between 1 and 4 o'clock this morning, with those inside yelling "Hail Hitler!" at the top of their lungs. If they try that again to-night, we will have cars and trucks to cut them off, even if we have to force a collision. And even if they have their lead pipes with them, we'll give them something to remember us by. It would have been just too bad for these fellows early this morning if they had had trouble with their cars and had had to stop.[36]

Each of the newspapers carried eyewitness accounts of the rioting, but only the *Telegram* left the unmistakable impression that the Jews were chiefly responsible for the evening's riot. "Jewish Toughs Begin Trouble Says Witness" proclaimed a front-page headline. The eyewitness's account read, in part:

> The scene shifted to the southwestern corner of the park, where a gang of about 30 Jewish lads attacked a man aged about 50, wearing a returned soldier's button. They punched him in the mouth and he went down. A baseball bat was brought into play and the Jewish youth began to kick him at random. Several of the more sane Jewish lads pleaded with their companions "to leave him alone"....
>
> As I walked easterly from Montrose Avenue to Bathurst Street, I passed several groups of Jewish youths, boasting of how many blows they had struck. I met a Jewish friend of mine... and he told me that he regretted the trouble and hoped that the blame would not have to be shouldered by respectable law-abiding Jews. He blamed the entire trouble on the Jewish hoodlums.[37]

The *Telegram* went to even greater lengths to establish the culpability of the Jews. A front-page story headed "Communists Incited Riot Police Authority States" quoted an unnamed police authority's view that the riot was incited indirectly by young Communists acting under the thin disguise of a swastika banner. Investigations would reveal, the *Telegram* learned, that Jewish Communists affiliated with the unlawful Young Communist League "had no small part in the releasing of pent-up racial feeling that broke out into an open race riot."[38] Suggesting Jewish collusion, the *Telegram* asked:

> Who unrolled the Swastika banner that apparently kindled race hatred into open flame? Why did not the avenging Jew who manhandled those who first waved the banner, capture them and hand them over to the police in the interest of justice and peace?[39]

The *Telegram*, of course, could never prove that Jewish Communists incited the riot. Along with the *Mail and Empire*, however, it referred to the strategic role of a Jewish gang from the Spadina-College district, citing an eyewitness who claimed that "one gang of Jews, noted as one of the toughest in the city, caused most of the trouble." "There were about a hundred of them," he revealed, and "they seemed all evening to be just looking for trouble. Most of them carried wooden clubs and used them to good advantage. This group," continued the paper, "believed to have been organized in the Spadina-College district, went for the Gentiles and the Swastika banner like a swarm of maddened bees."[40]

A witness quoted in the *Mail and Empire* was convinced that most of the fighting and disorder was caused by a group of youths who had come to the game looking for trouble. Stationed behind the first-base line, they were waiting for something to happen. They were the same ones, he claimed, who had visited the east-end beaches to battle with the Swastikas after the first signs were posted around the Balmy Beach Canoe Club. This newspaper, too, labelled the gang "one of the toughest groups in the city"[41] and identified the gang as one based in the Spadina-College district.

Needless to say, the role of the swastika emblem as the single most important factor in the riot cannot be overlooked. The *Star* interviewed a young man who had sustained cuts and bruises in the riot and who admitted his attachment to the Swastika group at the Pits. "While the ball game was in progress," he said, "the Spadina Ave. crowd gathered on the west side of the park, while our gang collected on the Camel's Back, which is located in the central part of the park.... At the conclusion of the game we unfurled our emblem and that started the works. I'll admit it, if that flag had never been uncovered, everything would have been quiet." He added:

When we did uncover it, the whole mob from the other side of the park rushed at us, but even if I do say so myself, we held throughout. They were about ten to one, until our forces arrived, then it started in real earnest.[42]

In the immediate aftermath of the riot, the finger of blame was also pointed at the Toronto daily press for having spread the rumour that the Jewish boys were returning to the Pits in force to support their team at the second game in the series. An editorial in *Saturday Night* magazine accused the Toronto newspapers of encouraging inter-racial violence in the city:

We gravely question whether the inter-racial violence which has recently been noted in Toronto would have reached anything like the pitch it has if it had not been for the encouragement afforded by the flaring headlines and exaggerated descriptive reports in the daily newspapers concerning the earliest and most significant outbreak. Such publicity must have been exceedingly gratifying to the feather-brained young men who were responsible for these early outbreaks, and undoubtedly spurred them on to the further provocative measures which led to the movement getting out of their hands and into those of the regular gang leaders of the city's hoodlum element. The Toronto daily press is as a rule a most valuable force for the preservation of the rights and civil liberties of the citizens, but in this case it has hardly done itself justice.[43]

Following the riot, Jack Turner, secretary of the TASA (Toronto Amateur Softball Association), announced that no more league games would be played in Willowvale Park until the present trouble had been cleared up. If necessary games would be played indoors.

The managers of both the Harbord Playground and St. Peter's team denied all responsibility for the riot and stated that none of their players had participated in the disturbance. Interests outside of sports circles were responsible, they contended. They assured Mayor Stewart that there was nothing but friendship between the players. As the coach of the Harbord team recalled: "There was no animosity between the teams.... Most of the kids that played for St. Peter's were in the same neighbourhood."

On the following day, 18 August, the newspapers were still filled with accounts connected with the riot. Both the *Globe* and the *Mail and Em-*

pire featured the riot in their main headline, though each emphasized a different aspect: "Calm Prevails Again in Swastika War Zone" (*Globe*); "Police Stand Guard as Crowd Threatens Fresh Disorder"(*Mail and Empire*). The formation of a Beaches Protective Association to replace the defunct Swastika Club was also widely covered in all of the papers. The press made the most of the opportunity to editorialize on the riot.

Though renewed violence was expected and police patrolled the parks, especially Willowvale, there were no further swastika demonstrations. The only trouble, according to the *Globe,* was on Bloor Street, "when a motor car cruising slowly along the street loaded with a number of Jews was the target of missiles and apple cores thrown by a number of boys."[44] However, trouble had been anticipated by Gentile youths. As the *Mail and Empire* wrote: "Following Mayor Stewart's appeal for general co-operation to end rowdy conflicts in city parks... comparative peace reigned throughout the city last night despite the fact that tens of thousands of citizens packed the parks where trouble had occurred previously."[45]

The *Star* reported that more than a hundred members of the Pit Gang (described as "hoodlums") had been roaming the streets around Willowvale Park. They "struck terror into the hearts of Jewish residents in the vicinity and assaulted 22 year-old Louie Sugarman pummelling him with their fists inflicting a cut on his head with a heavy iron pipe."[46] On Harbord between Clinton and Grace streets, a couple of iron bars, sticks, and debris were heaved at a car in which two men, who were believed to be Jewish, were riding. The two Jews escaped with only slight damage to their vehicle.

The majority of people in Willowvale Park on the evening of the seventeenth were sports fans or curious onlookers, but a group of about a hundred boys and youths waited around the park clearly looking for trouble. At the Bloor Street end of the park about a thousand people watched a lacrosse game; there were another two to three thousand spread over the rest of the park. Parts of the crowd converged on hill tops at times, as though waiting for something to happen. The *Mail and Empire* reported that:

> Some of the younger boys, between the ages of ten and fourteen, were seen carrying sticks, stones and other implements. One was carrying an autoskid.
>
> A couple of them ran down hills shouting in treble voices, "Hail Hitler."[47]

Inspector Herbert Little of Ossington Avenue station, who was in charge of the operations in the park, issued instructions to arrest any person creating a disturbance. Police were stationed at Harbord Street to warn Jews that it was unsafe for them to enter the Willowvale Park area.

The weapons carried by some of the Gentile youths suggested that any Jews who showed up would have received a rough reception. For the most part, these Gentile youths were members of the Pit Gang, a group that apparently terrorized the neighbourhood. For four hours gang members hung around Willowvale Park in anticipation of another riot. They roamed the slopes of the park openly flaunting pieces of metal pipe, chain, wired broom handles, and even rockers from chairs. They shouted taunts at Jews—though none had appeared. A *Globe* reporter moving about the crowd was jostled against one of the gang, and a heavy piece of lead pipe fell from the latter's pocket onto the reporter's toe. When asked what the pipe was for, the owner replied: "I'm going to rap this across the head of the first Jew I meet."[48] Several other youngsters displayed their weapons, "and in businesslike manner demonstrated how they were going to use them."

The *Star*, too, informed its readers that youngsters, ranging in age from seven to eighteen and armed with sticks, stones, and baseball bats, were responsible for disturbances in the park. At the end of a lacrosse game they gathered on the knoll in the lower end close to Bloor Street and chanted "Heil Hitler."

> On finding no opposition in the south end of the park, the laddies still being in the fighting mood, raced up to the bank of the hill at the extreme north and again began shouting the name of Herr Hitler.[49]

The swastika sign was also in evidence in the form of brilliant yellow emblems on some of the benches around the baseball diamonds. Throughout the evening, windows of houses surrounding the park were packed with curious onlookers. Twenty uniformed officers and thirty plainclothes officers, some waiting in cars around the park, were on hand. When eleven o'clock came and no Jews had arrived, the crowd began to disperse.

CHAPTER 8 "Dismissed All Charges"

We have experienced in Toronto a night that Jews from Russia, Poland and Rumania have become so accustomed to—a night filled with the atmosphere of a pogrom.

For the first time in Toronto, a night filled with a pogrom atmosphere. For the first time—and it clearly makes one wonder if for the last time as well? Who knows? The question cannot be answered because in spite of the heroics displayed by our younger generation, just as in other countries, our fate here is not in our own hands....

—"The Night of the 16th," *Der Yiddisher Zhurnal*, 22 and 23 August 1933

Following the events at Christie Pits, each of the English dailies, as well as *Der Yiddisher Zhurnal*, outlined their respective positions on the disturbances and apportioned responsibility for the outbreak of violence. While all deeply regretted it, they were not unanimous identifying the responsible agents. At one extreme, the *Telegram*, which held the view that those who wanted to wear the swastika emblem should be free to do so, argued that the attack on the swastika wearers and Hitler devotees was unacceptable and applauded Rabbi Sachs when he condemned such behaviour as inexcusable.

The display of Swastika emblems and shouts of "Hail Hitler" are naturally resented by Jewish citizens, but that does not give any group the right to attack the Swastika bearers and Hitler devotees. They are, after all, entitled to their opinions.... Jewish citizens would be well advised not to interfere with those who persist in wearing the Swastika emblem. They are much more likely to accomplish its disappearance by ignoring its display than by attacking those who display it.[1]

The *Globe* complained that the riot was poor publicity for Toronto, and charged that those with prior information that violence was likely who neglected to inform the police must be held responsible. Far from joining in a general outcry of police negligence, the *Globe* hinted at the possible contribution of the Communists as catalysts. The editor in "Racial Fights Must Stop" explained:

> Unfortunately, Toronto, like most large cities, has elements in its population always looking for trouble, and unfortunately, also, it has an aggregation of theorists and a newspaper seemingly anxious to help them along. The Reds and their backers, with their demand for "free speech," tried to trample on constituted authority, and learned that the law had to be obeyed. The police, however, are powerless against the continued effort in the hidden background to keep things stirred up.[2]

The *Mail and Empire* also deplored the "racial war" in the city. Blame for the violence would be apportioned evenly between the two sides, but the failure of the police to heed advance warning of the disturbance was cause for dismay: "Even yet some of the [police] commissioners are disposed to forget the fact that the taxpayers of Toronto pay the costs of policing the city and that there is an ultimate responsibility to the taxpayers on the part of the police and of the Police Commission."[3]

The rioting at Willowvale Park presented the *Star* with an excellent opportunity to attack the methods of the police for dealing with large gatherings in public places. In an editorial entitled "In Two Parks," the paper noted that police behaviour towards certain groups in the city—most notably the CCF—suggested a distinct bias in the force:

> On Tuesday evening at Allan Gardens, where somebody proposed to make a speech—we do not know who, nor does it matter—there were present, before the hour at which the meeting was to take place, two policemen stationed at each gateway, four mounted policemen, eight motorcycle policemen, a dozen policemen in uniform and a number of plainclothesmen.
>
> On Wednesday evening at Willowvale Park where, according to rumors which had spread all over the northwest part of the city, serious racial trouble was likely to occur at a baseball game only three policemen were present—the same number which is there

on all occasions to keep an eye on the crowds attending amuse-
ments which occur simultaneously.

At Trinity Park where somebody wanted to make a speech
there was a strong force of police on Wednesday night—the place
was garrisoned to prevent speaking.[4]

Der Yiddisher Zhurnal, too, was severely critical of the police (the
chief of police included). As on previous occasions, the paper argued in
favour of reason and restraint:

> The events of last Wednesday evening have united all the Jews of
> Toronto. All strata are now united in the League for the Defence
> of Jewish Rights, and all Jews can be certain that the League will
> protect not only Jewish rights but also Jewish honour and the Jew-
> ish good name.
>
> At the present moment when the spilled blood upsets us and
> there is a natural thirst for revenge on both sides, reason and re-
> straint are most necessary. Toronto Jews have representatives in
> the municipal, provincial, and federal governments who are un-
> tiring in doing everything to protect the Jewish community in
> Toronto and Jews throughout the country.
>
> Let all Jews bear this well in mind.[5]

Three days later, a *Zhurnal* editorial vehemently attacked the *Telegram*'s 18 August editorial, which had suggested that Jews had started
the violence. The *Zhurnal* quoted virtually the entire *Tely* editorial—its
"glittering gem of an editorial" the *Zhurnal* dryly labelled it—and concluded: "The entire tone of the editorial is that the Jews brought on the
unrest, that it was all their fault, that if it weren't for the Jews everything
would be fine." This response, the paper noted, revealed much about the
Telegram: "When it comes to Jews everything is forgotten. The hatred
towards Jews triumphs over all. They're even prepared to '*kasher*' [to
make kosher] Hitler in order to attack Jews."[6]

Meanwhile, the *Star*'s criticism of the police continued: "Demand
Police Board Call on Chief Draper to Resign His Office" read a front-
page headline of 18 August. Captain Philpott, CCF spokesman, addressing a capacity audience of the Spadina CCF Club in the Labor Lyceum
on the evening of 17 August, had charged that "Chief Draper is a man
who is totally and utterly incapable of holding down his job."[7] During

the meeting another speaker charged "Draper and his Cossacks" with "freely using batons and nauseating gases in dispersing peaceful gatherings." This was a reference to recent police intervention at a CCF rally in Trinity Park. Captain Philpott demanded that Mayor Stewart seek an explanation for why "only six policemen were present when trouble broke out at Willowvale Park, while the rest of the force was in Trinity Park unlawfully breaking up a peaceful meeting of citizens of Toronto."[8] He added, "I am not sure that the Willowvale park outbreak was engineered by a band of irresponsible hoodlums. I sincerely believe that it is but the opening wedge to start a Fascist movement in Canada." The entire swastika situation was of paramount importance to every Canadian, whether Gentile or Jew, he stated, adding, prophetically: "I believe that the Hitler menace throughout the world is going to attain far more serious proportions than any of us at present imagine."

Mayor Stewart's warning against displays of the swastika emblem resulted in some embarrassment for a number of the city's organizations. "Must Not Flaunt Swastika Is Warning of Boy Scouts" cautioned a *Star* headline. All recipients of the Toronto Boy Scouts' "Thank You Badge" (a swastika cross surmounted by the fleur-de-lis that was given to benefactors of the scouts) were told not to flaunt "the badge in public until the current feeling against the Hitler symbol had died down."[9] The Toronto Library Board had to decide what to do about the swastika emblems decorating the thousands of Kipling volumes in their public libraries. Said the chief librarian: "Kipling placed the swastika cross on all his books. We are not going to do all our binding over just because Hitler has adopted the swastika as his emblem. Kipling had it first."[10] The swastika was also stamped on the keys to the lockers at the police motorcycle depot. And, as the *Star* reported: "A touch of irony was added to the wedding of the daughter of a prominent Toronto Hebrew family recently when she was photographed in the living room of her luxurious home, standing on a rug in which large swastika crosses were the main design."[11]

The *Star* also pointed out that the swastika was a popular shape used in designs on vases, rugs, dress goods, and wallpaper; its origins, readers were informed, could be traced to early antiquity, when it had been used in the worship of the sun gods, the Greek Apollo, and the Scandinavian Woden.

Meanwhile, the third game of the St. Peter's–Harbord Playground playoff series was postponed and rescheduled for Wednesday of the following week in an unspecified local park. "There's no particular hurry for the game," declared the group convenor of the TASA. "We have four weeks to play two series and until September to declare a city champion."[12]

On Saturday, 19 August, under the *Telegram's* headline proclaiming "Swazis Form Canadian Association," a story informed readers that three young men who were presumed to be members of the notorious Christie Street Pit Gang had been arrested the night before on charges of unlawful assembly. Both the *Globe* and the *Mail and Empire* featured the arrests in their main headlines of 19 August. "Three Held as Willowvale Park Riot Sequel/Police Question Other Members of Alleged Gang," wrote the *Globe*. "Police Arrest Three after Willowvale Park Riots/Unlawful Assembly Counts Swastika Display Sequel/22 Youths Subjected to Questioning as Officers Launch City-Wide Probe/Guards Retained at Trouble Centres," proclaimed the *Mail and Empire*:

> Three were arrested last night on charges of unlawful assembly, arising out of Wednesday night's rioting at Willowvale Park. They are:
> CHARLES BOUSTEAD, 18 years old, of Sydenham Street.
> JACK PIPPY, 17, of Crawford Street.
> EARL PERRIN, 21, of Sterling Road.
> They are all alleged to be the ones who flaunted the white quilt, on which a black swastika was emblazoned, from a knoll in the park—the act which precipitated the disturbances and fanned into flame the spark of racial feeling.[13]

(A fourth person, Jack Roxborough, age nineteen, of Ossington Avenue, had, as we have seen, been arrested on Wednesday night, 16 August, on a charge of carrying an offensive weapon and sentenced to a fine of fifty dollars or two months in jail. He was unable to pay the fine, and so went to jail.)

The four young men appeared in police court on Saturday, 19 August, and were remanded until 25 August on bail of $200 each. None of the boys had retained counsel. "For that reason, I don't want to go on," explained Crown Attorney W. O. Gibson. "Rioting is a very serious charge, and I think the boys ought to have a chance to secure counsel."[14] Magistrate Browne agreed. Pippy was released immediately on bail provided by his parents. Boustead and Perrin were unable to secure bail and were taken to the Don Jail. Perrin's sister and Boustead's mother—his father had been killed overseas—were said to be trying to secure bail.

According to police, Boustead had provided the quilt for the demonstration, the swastika had been painted in Pippy's garage, and Perrin had
carried it to the park. The three were said to have admitted carrying the
flag to the top of the knoll known as the "camel's hump," and displaying
it in full view of the crowd. About thirty members of the gang had accompanied the three to the park and had been told to arm themselves
for a fight. "These four," said a police officer, including Roxborough in
his remarks, "went over to the park with the intention of causing trouble. They were under the impression that a few Jewish boys might come
after them, and they intended to fight them. But when the Swastika was
displayed, a large number went for them and the youths with the swastika ran."[15]

Police interrogation of the Pit Gang was not the end of the investigation, according to Inspector Little of the police. Attention would now
turn to the Jewish gang and, Little warned, an arrest would be made in
every case where proof could be furnished of participation in the riot.
However, the police made no further arrests.

The police patrolled Willowvale and other parks for yet another night. Although there were no incidents, from 7:00 to 10:00 p.m. a
crowd estimated at perhaps one thousand did mill about in Willowvale
Park and along the streets for several blocks on either side.[16] Uniformed
police patrolled the vicinity, and plainclothes officers in cars passed and
repassed the park area. Nothing came of a rumour that Jews were to
organize in order to appear in the park.

The only evidence of action on the swastika front during the evening
occurred at Conboy Park. Officials there were startled to find swastika signs painted on the fence surrounding the Ossington Avenue recreation area. Eight or nine emblems were counted and the signs were
immediately painted over. Meanwhile, the final game of the St. Peter's–
Harbord Playground series, which had been scheduled for Friday, 18
August at Conboy Park, was postponed. Rounding out the activities for
the day, a rumour spread that a Jewish youth had been taken from his
veranda and fatally beaten.

In the aftermath of the riot the newspapers tried to fathom the senti-
ments on both sides. On 19 August the *Star* included a story headed,
"'Die with Boots On!' Cry of Incensed Toronto Jews." According to one
Ben Steiner, who was quoted extensively in the story, "Die with your
boots on" had become the motto of the Spadina Avenue Jews. Said
Steiner: "Rather than submit to the outrages that have been perpetrated

against our race, we would die on the streets. This is the feeling amongst the younger element of our people."

> These gangs [Steiner continued], or rather we should perhaps call them unorganized groups, are really old schoolmates, and co-workers in the various Spadina Ave. factories, who have been drawn together for mutual protection....
>   Following the row which occurred Wednesday night these groups have more or less united, so that there is one large "gang" or group of Jewish boys representing the Spadina Avenue district.
>   Boys who had not spoken to one another for years owing to old quarrels have sealed the breaches between them, and joined each other in voicing their protest against mistreatment by other racial groups.[17]

Steiner then suggested how British influences had moulded the boys' outlook:

> These boys are all British. They have been brought up in Canadian schools, and have learned something of the British bulldog idea never to give up without a fight. The teaching of passive resistance no longer carries any weight with them.
>   While we are not looking for trouble, if there is going to be more we are ready. Last night we were waiting in readiness, but refrained from going to any of the parks until scouts reported disturbances. This was done so that no incentive might be given to Swazis to start anything.[18]

The same story quoted the views on the Pit Gang of a Mr. Williams, proprietor of an ice-cream parlour at Christie and Bloor streets. "Is there such a thing as a pit gang?" he was asked. "Absolutely," he replied. "There is a gang which gather in the Pit nearly every night.... They're all good fellows, but I suppose they lost their heads on Wednesday night."[19] He felt that ultimate responsibility for the disturbances lay with the police: "But the whole trouble is in allowing this Swastika business to take root. I blame the police. I am a Christian, but I can't see why we should allow rowdies to create disturbances in our parks or on our beaches. We don't want any of these rotten Nazis in our country."[20]
    In the newspaper accounts of the riot, members of the Pit Gang were quoted as saying that they were defending *their* park, and that they

wanted the Jews out of it. If we examine the information provided by the tax assessment rolls collected in 1933 for 1934, we can arrive at a rough distribution of Jews, Catholics, and Protestants in the area of the Pits. Looking at the streets running south of Bloor across from and on either side of the park—from east to west, Euclid, Manning, Clinton, Grace, Montrose, and Crawford—we see that they were of mixed religious composition. The number of Jews was greatest in the south-east sector bounded by Bloor Street, College Street, Euclid Avenue, and Shaw Street. (See Appendix B, Table 7.) Jewish numbers diminished to the north and west of the area. North of Bloor Street there were practically no Jewish residents at all. (See Appendix B, Table 8.)

This demographic information sheds light on the remarks of the Pit Gang after the riot. The Jews were beginning to move into "their" territory; Christie Pits was the turf being contested. These territorial feelings were, of course, intensified by the xenophobia and antisemitism of the overwhelmingly British Protestant majority in the immediate vicinity of the park.

The formation of the Swastika Club in the eastern beaches was also a territorial matter, at least in part. The difference between the incidents at the beaches and the riot in Christie Pits had a lot to do with the distance separating the Jewish area from Ward 8. The beaches became hot spots only on weekends when Jewish picnickers and bathers sought relief from their toil and the summer heat. Had serious trouble broken out on the beaches, the Jewish boys would not have been able to count on reinforcements as they could after the outbreak of fighting at the Pits. Jews had not moved into the area in any numbers (there were fewer Jews in Ward 8 than in any other city ward). The situation was far more explosive at Christie Pits because Jews were beginning to move into the area in substantial numbers, and this vanguard was contiguous with the main body of Jews in Toronto, which, as we have seen, was at the time the largest non-British group by far in the city.

The demographic data suggest that Bloor Street was a kind of dividing line between nearly pure British neighbourhoods and those with a mixed ethnic composition (including a large proportion of Jewish residents) in Ward 5. When the big Jewish migration northward occurred in the 1940s and 1950s, the area between Bloor and Dupont was given a wide berth. Leapfrogging over this district, the Jews relocated north of Davenport, north of St. Clair, on either side of Oakwood Avenue, up into Cedarvale and Forest Hill (where there had been a not-insignificant contingent of Jews in the early thirties), and, somewhat later, into North York.

Jocko Thomas, the reporter who wrote copy on the riot for the *Star*, painted a picture of the anti-Catholic and antisemitic character of the neighbourhood around the Pits:

> Unless you lived in those times you wouldn't know but there was an atmosphere of hatred toward Jews. Antisemitism in an area which was largely WASPish.... A lot of Orange people lived in that area.... There used to be trouble between the Catholics and the Protestants in that area. Catholic kids going to school used to be waylaid by Protestant children coming home at lunch time and attacked. I used to see those things going on. I got my eye blackened one time by taking the part of one guy, Patty London, who was getting beaten up by some of these Orange kids, who'd come from Orange families. But there was a feeling there. The headlines were all Hitler making big speeches against the Jews, a lot of unemployment.

As late as the 1950s, Menzies, a civic candidate in Ward 5, made an issue of religion in the campaign. On the promotional blotters distributed by his workers he provided a piece of "relevant" information concerning the candidate in his area—their religious affiliation. He pointed out that his rivals were Jewish and emphasized his own United Church background. It is even more interesting that his campaign workers distributed this blotter only north of Bloor Street in Ward 5.

Although the riot was portrayed at the time and has been remembered since as an essentially Jewish-Gentile conflict, there were a significant number of Italian (and a few Ukrainian) boys who fought alongside the Jews.

Many of the people we interviewed and the Toronto newspapers at the time referred to a truckload of Italian boys who went to Christie Pits as allies of the Jews. Prominent among them were boxers and street fighters who had grown up in Jewish neighbourhoods and who belonged to the same boxing clubs and training gyms as the Jewish pugilists. One witness confirmed that:

> There were quite a few Italian boys. The Italians and Jews at that time, even now, I think they're quite harmonious, you know they get along pretty well. At least in the boxing crowd, like there were fellows who boxed, like Frankie Genovese and Steve Rocco, who's gone now. He lost a very close fight for the world's fly-weight

championship,... but Frankie Genovese is still around, he fought Sammy Luftspring.... He was always around with the Jews as was Rocco. So I knew they were there, and quite a few Italian boys.

Another witness suggested that "the Italians were pretty good friends with the Jews. Mostly they got along very well. Rocco and Genovese came down that time and fought. The Bagnatos were always very good with the Jews. They lived together. The Wasps [were] more [antisemitic] than the Italians. That's what I would think."

Confirmation that there were bonds of friendship between Jewish and Italian boys and that they fought together at Christie Pits was plentiful:

There might have been a few *shkutzim* [non-Jews] with us, help-ing us. There might have been say ten or twelve *goyishe* [non-Jew-ish] boys helping us.... Frankie Genovese, boxers, you know. Ste-vie Rocco. The Bagnatos. You know Joey Bagnato who was the welterweight champion at the time and his brothers. All of those boys, they were part and parcel of the Jewish people because we grew up together.

There was truckloads of fellows picked up which was at the Jewish centre, College and Spadina. They sent down truck loads or where the trucks come from, I couldn't tell you.... even Italian people helped us which they weren't overly—you know you couldn't count on, but they came out. They'd come out with pipes and sticks and brooms and bats, baseball bats....

We jumped in their trucks, they even sent over a truck, over to "the Ward".... In the Ward, we hung around a place, there was a guy by the name of, ah, what the heck was his name, Rotenberg. Rotenberg had a little store at the corner of Elizabeth and Ger-rard.... He had a little grocery store and that was also a hangout.... And even the Italians, I remember guys there was Charlie Difalco, there was the Romanos. They jumped on the trucks and all out to Christie Pits. And we handled that so beautifully.

One of the Jewish contingent at Christie Pits said that he was the only Jew in a truckload of Italian boys that rushed to Christie Pits:

We all, a bunch of us, I was the only Jewish boy there. They used to call me the matzo eater.... Here we had boxing clubs. Now when I went to Christie Pits I went with Italian boys... we went up with a dump truck and I had a pick axe. I went with Italian boys, I went with Steve Rocco and Frankie Genovese, and I was partners with a guy called Gene Volpi that I liked very much.... My father-in-law was Italian and we were digging the cellar, and I wasn't about to get my nose broken so I took a handle from a pick axe, I remember the kid's name that drove the truck, Andy Bartople.

An Italian witness also confirmed the Italian involvement in the riot:

Well, there was two fights then. There was that one, and there was the last one. That one, the Pit Gang as they were called, came in there one night, it was in the evening, and as usual the diamonds were dotted with playground teams, mostly Jewish boys and they went in and proceeded to beat the hell out of them. I wasn't there that night. I'd heard about it. So, about a week later, we sent the Mansfield Gang up. The Mansfield Gang was the Italian Gang. And we encircled the Pits. We'd come up in dump trucks. And we sent up about two hundred guys. We encircled the Pits. This gang always hung around.... If you're familiar with the Pits, there was the dressing-room and beyond the dressing-room there was a clump of bushes and trees. This is where they hung around. Right in that area there. Our trucks came up along Bloor Street, up Crawford, up Christie, along Barton, and they just closed in on this area. And our gang proceeded to kick the hell out of them. That was the end of it. There was never any more of that type of demonstration. 'Cause they were told that if they started any nonsense again, we'd come in again and kick the hell out of them.

In general, the relationship between the Jewish and Italian communities was very cordial and supportive. The trying conditions of immigrant life in the "Belfast of Canada" led to a sense of solidarity both within ethnic groups and between ethnic groups. One mutual-aid service was babysitting. It was not uncommon to find Italian children speaking a basic Yiddish and Jewish children being able to converse in the Italian of the street. (During the course of an interview, an Italian witness who was at the Pits supporting the Jewish side asked us a question in Yiddish.) "Italians were brought up with Jews," a witness informed us,

> and here was the system, on Saturday or a Jewish holiday when the mother would go to the synagogue, you know to a high holiday or some of them went every Saturday, leave the kids with the Italians. The Italians, we had a family that lived along the street from us, when the mother went to church, brought the kids into our house while they went to church. My mother spoke Yiddish to them. There was a kid by the name of Jimmy Garmoni, Jimmy Garmoni spoke Yiddish as well as any Jewish kid in the neighbourhood, his mother used to leave him with the Jewish mothers, and the Jewish mothers they knew no other language. They spoke Yiddish and the Italian mothers spoke Italian to the Jewish kids when they were left there, and every Jewish kid had a good smattering of the language, Italian... and sometimes you'd forget, and you'd use it, and your mother'd say to ya, "*Vos redste Talainer?*" [Why are you speaking Italian?]

The ability to speak "functional" Italian was not limited to the younger generation. A Jewish respondent who was married to an Italian woman recalls:

> Look, you go down to the Italian district in those days.... There was a dry goods store—Jaffe had a dry goods store; father, mother, all the children spoke Italian; my mother-in-law went to the store, she didn't have to speak English. Cohen's Fish Market was at the corner of Clinton and College and all the Jews were there. Later they sold it to an Italian guy, but they could all speak Italian better than.... I remember walkin' into a chicken store he gives these chickens to her, it was my wife. I was standing there and old Rubenstein was reading the Gemarah. And finally they asked for a chicken and old man Rubenstein without looking up from the Bible, said to his wife: "*Gib ir a traifa*" [Give her a non-kosher one]. And I remember my wife saying, "*Far vos gib ir mir a traifa?*" [Why are you giving me a non-kosher one?] He nearly died.

Although the Jewish and Italian populations had largely relocated farther west by the early thirties, they both first developed viable communities in the immigrant ghetto of St. John's Ward. Robert Harney describes the close relationship between Jews and Italians and how the Jews acted as "blockbusters" for the Italians in "the Ward" around the turn of the century:

St. John's Ward became the center of Toronto Italian life, a street life with a pace and purpose at variance with the dour and "indoors" north European city around it. From the outset, Italians shared the Ward with the other major group of newcomers to Toronto, the east European Jews. The relationship was not unusual. Humbert Nelli showed that even in Chicago's Little Italy, the Italians rarely exceeded 50% of the total. In New York and Chicago, Jew and Italian lived side by side. R. Glanz claims that the basis of the relationship was an essential lack of competition: Jews tending to trade and Italians to laboring and both to the garment industry. The number of street corners that passed from Jewish to Italian hands as the latter moved into the Ward suggests, however, that competition did exist, but that there was rapport at other levels. Neither group worried excessively about threats to endogamy; initially the strength of religion and family was too great on both sides. Both groups accepted high levels of street activity as the inevitable noise, "hustling," and crowding that preceded the "take-off" from greenhorn to successful immigrant. Jews in numbers had come north into the Ward before the Italians and had, in modern usage, "blockbusted" for the Italians to follow. Still a typical street of the Ward had Jewish, Italian, and older stock on it. The latter were often "mechanics" (artisans) while the Jews and Italians dominated the storefront and residential pattern. Many older Italians can recount serving as "shabbes goy," the lighters of sabbath fires and runners of errands, for the Orthodox Jews of the neighborhood. Toronto's Little Italy had along with the Italian Methodist Mission on Elm Street and eventually a parish, The Church of Our Lady of Mt. Carmel—Rumanian and Russian synagogues, some smaller congregations, several Protestant missions to the Jews, and an African Methodist Church. In that sense, St. John's Ward was not just Little Italy, it was the foreign quarter of Toronto.[21]

Growing up in the Ward during and after World War I, Jewish and Italian boys participated in local sports. Elizabeth Playground produced the famous "Lizzies," baseball and basketball teams that for years were champions or championship contenders. One Italian source told us: "Most of the Lizzie team came from down in the Ward, where the Sick Children's Hospital is now. That's where the playground was. Hester Howe School. The playground was there. Down in that area there was strictly Jewish boys and Italian boys."[22]

What drew the Italians and the Jews together in addition to the sports, the proximity of their dwellings, the lack of competition in the economic sphere, and the shared fate of immigrant life, were the discrimination, prejudice, and, on occasion, official and unofficial violence both groups suffered at the hands of the British majority. One Italian witness pointed out that Italians, too, were victims of prejudice:

> The Italians the same thing. They'd call you wop, ya. As a matter of fact we even made up a song about the Italians. If you'd like to hear it? Ya? "When I first come to this country people called me dago man, long time ago they make me feel just like an empty banan, first they called me Tony Spagoni, then they say you're full of macaroni, now its a biga shame they gimme the nickaname, why don't you tell them to stop, stop, stop. Why don't the Irish cop tell them to stop. First they called me Tony, you're full of macaroni, now they call me wop." Actually this is how it was. You lousy wop.

In describing the antisemitism at Parkdale Collegiate directed at the few Jewish children who went there, one of our Jewish respondents confirms that the Italians experienced an equal degree of abuse:

> And he had a business, it was a, it was a nice shopping area, and the Jews like I told ya, they had the ladies' store, the men's store, and this store, naturally they tried to move to that neighbourhood. So, where did their kids go to school, those kids went to school in those WASP neighbourhoods, Parkdale Collegiate was one. I remember them being asked to be transferred. If they didn't, the kids said, "We'll go all the way to Jarvis Collegiate, we'll go to Harbord, we'll go to this school, we'll go to that school, I don't want to go to Parkdale. All I keep hearing is Kike and Sheenie, Kike and Sheenie." And the Dagoes had the same thing, they had Wop and Dago, Wop and Dago, and don't let nobody tell you different, they had it as bad as we did. The WASPS only knew two words,

Goddamn Kike and Goddamn Wop, or it was either Sheenie or Dago, that's all they knew. Anything that happened, blame it on the Wops or blame it on the Hebes.

One Italian witness suggested that nationality was all but meaningless for minority youth in the immigrant districts in the thirties:

There were also Jewish people. And we all got along very, very well, and very close. As a matter of fact, we were brought up by my father and my mother I tell you the truth, a lot of us kids who were ten, eleven, or twelve years old didn't know what the hell nationality was. 'Cause it was such an ethnic group around. Ukrainian, Polish, Irish, Italians, Jewish and that there who knew one from the other? As a matter of fact I remember once that I went in and I asked my dad once, I said "Listen pop, tell me, what am I, am I Italian, Irish, Scotch, Jewish?" He says [imitating his father's accent], "Whats a difference, isa same a ting. There's no difference."

This is not to suggest that there was never any tension or physical violence between minority groups. There was a good deal of ethnic friction which manifested itself, on occasion, in violent encounters.

The fact that Italians (and a few Ukrainians) fought alongside the Jewish boys against the primarily British-Protestant youth backing Pit Gang can be attributed, in part, to the general situation of minority groups in Toronto during the early thirties. Non-British, non-Protestant youth had to take verbal and physical abuse from majority youth gangs, just as their parents faced discrimination in the labour market and the workplace from the older Anglo-Protestant population.

As suddenly as they had appeared, the press reports about confrontation and near violence between Jews and Gentiles ceased. After 19 August, there was no more large-scale violence over the matter of the swastika emblem. Over the next few days, however, the newspapers featured stories about the appearance of the swastika in and around Toronto. Fears of possible violence surfaced in Orillia, when members of the local Jewish colony received letters from a mysterious Swastika organization warning them to remain away from the Beaches.[23] On Saturday, 19 August, Jewish residents received letters, decorated with a swastika and with the word "Beware" printed on them. The message said: "You and your family warned not to appear at any of the Orillia beaches to-morrow, Aug. 20. Signed, O.S.C." The day passed without any untoward incident, and no displays of the antisemitic emblems were found in the town's parks. In Orangeville, on 17 August, two Jewish chicken pedlars hurriedly left town after discovering a swastika marked on their parked truck.[24] And in Toronto on Sunday, 27 August, elderly Jews who warned some boys against carving swastika emblems in a cemetery fence were threatened by several men. But no threat or acts of organized violence transpired between members of the Pit Gang and the Jewish gang.

The English-language press published editorials on the riot only on 18 August. *Der Yiddisher Zhurnal*, however, continued its warnings about the activities of the Swastika Club. It judged the threats received in the mail by Orillia Jews as qualitatively different from earlier threats, and on 22 August published an editorial headed, "It Is No Longer a Local Matter." It asked: "But what will the federal authorities answer now that the Hitlerites have organized themselves to use the mail services of the country for propaganda and 'blackmail'? Will they also refrain from acting by arguing that this, too, is a local matter?"[25] The paper also concluded that a threatening letter sent to Alderman Nathan Phillips required decisive action.

In a lengthy article, "The Night of the 16th," the writer, L. Eminadab (pseudonym of S. M. Shapiro, editor of the *Zhurnal*), assessed the position of Jews in Canada, evaluated the actions of the Jewish youth who had participated in the riot, and judged the role of the League for the Defence of Jewish Rights in its handling of the entire swastika affair. While the current trouble had erupted suddenly, claimed the author, it was entirely consistent with the precarious position of Jews in Canadian society.

> This night will occupy an important place in the history of Jews in Canada. It is the first time since Jews have lived in this country that they have been beaten for the simple reason that they were Jews.
>
> Which means: can the history that we have experienced in different countries and in different times also occur here and at the present time?...
>
> Did we have any justification for so believing? A certain British justice, Anglo-Saxon gentility, old humanitarian tradition, and Jewish quietness planted in us such a sense of temerity that

were someone to have appeared two months ago and predicted that Gentile youths would present themselves with iron clubs and beat up every Jew that they met we would have been the first to brand this individual a lunatic.

And not only did we believe in their honesty, but we more fully believed in our innocence. After all, we did not overstep our boundaries. We are so quiet that we are hardly noticeable in everyday life.[26]

The writer remained impressed by the response of Mayor Stewart and the majority of the non-Jewish population. He had praise for the League for the Defence of Jewish Rights, particularly the contribution of Rabbi Sachs. He also congratulated the Jewish youth whose behaviour had been so severely criticized by certain sectors of the Jewish population. More important, however, he exhorted these youth to recognize the reality of Jewish life, even in Canada: "Meanwhile... we must thoroughly teach them a few uncomfortable truths with which our Jewish fate is closely bound."[27]

Finally, the author speculated about the outlook for the future:

There exist two opinions. There are those who contend that the entire swastika movement is but a game for local immature Gentile youths. They engage in a different game each season. Last year they played "yo-yo" and this year they are playing with swastikas. And if they are left alone, they will have their fill and be bored with swastikas after a few weeks, just as was the case with yo-yos and miniature golf.

But there is a different opinion, that the swastika movement is to be taken very seriously and that it is supported by Germany and that now it will only begin to spread out.

In any case, the League for the Defence of Jewish Rights will have to continue to be vigilant. It must not alter its methods. If the situation deteriorates, it will have to extend its activity.

We have already indicated that the police alone are not capable of eliminating Hitlerism.

We will have to mobilize and, aside from the use of police, adopt other social means as well. Thanks to the tactical methods of our leaders, there exists an opportunity to found, along the lines of France, a purely Christian society to battle antisemitism along French lines....[28]

The question remains of why displays of the swastika sparked instant violence at the Pits and not at the Beaches. Demography and the lack of a strong police presence at the Pits would appear to account for much of the difference between the two situations. Had Chief Draper and his lieutenants responded to Jack Turner's request for police reinforcements before the game began, it is unlikely that a riot of such proportions would have resulted. In part, too, the very distance of Kew Beach from the Jewish areas militated against a large-scale outbreak of hostilities. The Jewish boys who went to the Beaches to challenge the Swastika Club were far from home and had little chance of getting reinforcements in case of trouble. Christie Pits, on the other hand, was very close to the edge of the Jewish ghetto. The neighbourhood around the park north of Bloor was mostly inhabited by lower-middle and working-class people of British extraction and of the Protestant faith. Many of them had been severely affected by the Depression, and a large percentage, especially among the young, had been unemployed for some time. At the same time, the Jews were migrating northward and had reached Bloor and Christie streets; thus, the actions of the Pit Gang can be understood as a defensive response to a perceived threat to their territory by upwardly mobile "foreigners."

It is not surprising that the riot erupted on the occasion of a baseball game between a local team (St. Peter's) and a visiting team (Harbord Playground). Many of our witnesses emphasized how important local sports, particularly baseball, were to the youth of Toronto during the Depression years. S. Armstrong, head of the playgrounds for the City of Toronto, encouraged sports and athletics in part as a way of keeping the boys out of trouble during this all-too-troubled period.

For many young people, of course, ethnic rivalries compounded territorial rivalries that surfaced on playing fields. There were no Jewish players on the St. Peter's team. The majority of players on the Harbord team, however, were Jewish. A number of them also played for the Lizzies (Elizabeth Playground coached by the legendary Bob Abate). Both the Lizzies and Harbord Playground were generally thought of as "Jewish" teams, and the press often identified them as such. After the riot, the press attempted to stress the mixed composition of these and other teams. Under the headline "Jews, Gentiles Play Together," the *Star* reported:

> Amateur sport puts up no racial barriers if the personnel of many of Toronto's most successful baseball and basketball teams

with Jews, Gentiles, Italians and other central Europeans playing together is any criterion. Irish boys in minority groups play on predominantly Jewish teams. Jews, singly and in groups, team with Gentiles, and throughout all there is no friction of a racial character, according to sporting authorities, closely in touch with the teams....

Most striking examples of this interracial team work is [sic] seen in the Lizzie's basketball team, 1932 champions, the University of Toronto basketball team, Big Five champions last year, and Greenwood Park Senior League, all of which have several races represented in their lineups.[29]

The area surrounding Willowvale Park was the claimed territory of the Pit Gang, a group of adolescent working-class Protestants. The Pit Gang was known for actively seeking excitement, which the Jew's increasing presence in the area readily provided. A walk near that park required one to be on alert for the sudden appearance of members of the Pit Gang. As one witness recalled: "When you walked by the Pits in the evening in that particular summer, you always walked with your fists clenched. You were ready." Another remembered experiencing problems with the Pit Gang as far back as 1931. He claimed he would never forget the gang's yell or cheer before an attack: "There was almost a call, the call was 'Niccy Oyup'.... When you heard 'Niccy Oyup' you dropped whatever you were doing and you ran for your life because somewhere over the hill they were coming around the bend. This gang of guys was coming.... 'Niccy Oyup' and that was it."

Not surprisingly, gang members preferred to start trouble when they outnumbered their opposition:

The only time they would attack us is when there was one or two of us and there was ten or twelve of them. But any time...it was near an even amount, they wouldn't go near you. They were scared shitless. They were real troublemakers. The very strange thing about it...was that if it was one on one they would never seem to challenge anybody, but if there was four on one, they'd almost always beat you up.

None of the witnesses, Jewish or Gentile, ascribed motivations of political antisemitism to this group:

But whether this gang was consciously antisemitic, I don't think they had enough brains for it.... I doubt very much if anybody in that group really had a handle on antisemitism as we know it today. I doubt it. That there was resentment, ya. But I think it was based on local sports pride.

They were mostly kids... who weren't particularly political animals. They just used Nazism to vent their hatred for the Jews and to bully. They figured they outnumbered the Jewish boys in the crowd and this was a good occasion to beat some people up and to have a little fun and excitement and not get hurt in return. But they were sorely mistaken.

The Pit Gang was willing if not eager to provoke agitation, and if the swastika served that purpose, they would not hesitate to use it:

Jews were outsiders. They were good bait and that was it.... The atmosphere of the city at this particular time was one in which the Pit Gang would be encouraged to, in my opinion, be antisemitic. It was just young drop-outs with nothing better to do. And if you tell me there was a swastika, that was enough to lead them that way. I don't think that the gang had enough brains.

Though gang members, too, disclaimed any serious political motive or affiliation, the Jewish community felt at the time that use of the swastika tied the Pit Gang to the Beaches Swastika Club. While the gang members maintained their sole motivation was "to get the Jews out of the park," there is fragmentary evidence to suggest that some outsiders were involved. For example, one of the injured Gentile boys arrested for supplying the quilt lived on Sydenham Street, near Queen and Parliament, a good deal closer to Cherry Beach than to Christie Pits. Charles Boustead may have been the link between the Pit Gang and the Beaches Swastika Club. We will probably never know for sure, but it is interesting that he was identified by the press as a member of the Pit Gang, even though he lived miles away from it.

The Pit Gang may simply have learned of the Swastika Club's actions at the Beaches through the reports and discussions in the press and through rumours. Or possibly a few of the Beaches Swastikas came to the Willowvale Park area and, with or without the knowledge of the Pit

Gang, acted as provocateurs. *Evening Telegram* reporter Fred Egan believed that members of the Beaches Swastika Club helped instigate the trouble at the Pits:

> I remember being down there and talking to some of these people and some of them were saying we've got to keep the Jews [out].... There's too many Jews coming down here. And that was newsworthy and that feeling did exist over there. So I went back and talked to the city editor and I wrote my story on that.... Now I had the impression that that's where the whole thing [the riot] started. I'm pretty sure of that.... You see, there was.... I don't know what happened after that down at Balmy Beach.... I think on a weekend, there were some Jewish people who'd come down, or people who took objection to these other people. And there was a confrontation of sorts. But it wasn't, as I recall it, there wasn't any real fighting or real rioting at that time. It was just a question of these people from the other end of the city to go back where they came from. My recollection is that as an aftermath of this thing a gang of people went up to Christie Pits and put out this swastika there because they seemed to think that these other people had come down and that they must go back and confront them.

Star reporter Jocko Thomas, who claimed considerable familiarity with the members of the Pit Gang, was also quite convinced that outside influences were at work, and he thought the German Bund was responsible for both the Swastika Club and the Christie Pits riot:

> They blamed the Pit Gang for the thing [the riot] but there was a lot of other people that were around there the first night... that I never saw there before. And I suspected that they were from the German Bund.... But there was somebody in the park that night during the first game; there were strange people. And they had caused some trouble, yelling "Heil Hitler".... A lot of the Christie Pits Gang were in on it, you know. They were down there that night. And some of the guys were just looking for a fight. Been drinking rubbing alcohol, you know, things like that.... But the ball game didn't have anything to do with it, it was just first that the trouble had been started because of these guys standing on the hill yelling "Heil Hitler".... There were strange faces in the park.

And so everybody thought they were the Bund. I think they're the same ones that went down to the Beach and started trouble down there.

It is, however, highly unlikely that the German Bund was behind the Christie Pits riot. The Bund was not officially formed until January 1934,[30] and it was always careful not to get involved in activities that would alienate the majority of the German-Canadian population and bring the full weight of the authorities down on it (as happened to the German-American Bund). Moreover, the Nazi government was still in the process of consolidating its power in Germany and agitprop of this nature in foreign countries was only in the planning stages. More likely provocateurs, a number of the witnesses suggested, were the actively antisemitic members of the Kew Beach Swastika Club. Certainly the "Heil Hitler" epithets shouted on the evening of the first game and re-peated at the conclusion of the second game were not the usual fare for the lads who made up the Pit Gang. One would have expected them to use home-grown slurs like "dirty Jew," "Sheenie," and "Kike." The words "Hail Hitler" and the swastika painted on the clubhouse roof on Mon-day night echoed the sign that had appeared in front of the Balmy Beach Canoe Club two weeks before. The writing of the German word "Heil" as the English word "Hail" makes it unlikely that any native German speakers (such as the Bund) were directly involved in the incident. The white swastika on the sweater coat also follows the Beaches Swastika Club pattern of using the emblem on shirts, sweaters, and jackets.

It is highly probable that the members of the Pit Gang were aware of the Hitler phenomenon, which had recently received such massive news coverage. They would almost certainly have known about the goings-on at the Beaches, and they would have seen in the swastika emblem an easy way of provoking a reaction from the Jewish boys. What we may never know is the precise nature and extent of the relationship between the Pit Gang's challenge and the activities of the Beaches Swastika Club or any other antisemitic group.

Charles Boustead, Jack Pippy, Earl Perrin, and Jack Roxborough—the young men charged with unlawful assembly after the riot—all pleaded not guilty. For reasons unknown, the Crown immediately withdrew the charge against Jack Pippy, who was discharged. Pippy explained that he was at Willowvale Park "because I heard a bunch of Jewish boys were going to beat up the Gentile boys." He admitted helping to prepare the swastika quilt, but claimed not to know who had brought it to the park. "We took it as a joke," he said.

"And I think the whole charge is a joke," interrupted Magistrate Browne. "Dismissed all charges."[31]

The final game of the St. Peter's-Harbord Playground series was played at Conboy Park the following week. St. Peter's won the game by a score of 5–4 and went on to the semi-finals, where they lost to the Millionaires.

CHAPTER 9 Protest

Members of the Jewish community in Toronto are following the example of their fellows elsewhere in calling a meeting to denounce the injustice to which their people in Germany are exposed. Notwithstanding the sympathy which the purpose of the meeting will evoke, it must be regarded as a mistake that the gathering should be called for Sunday, and an impertinence that criticism should be directed against the Mayor for adhering to his rule to refuse to attend political gatherings on this day or to delegate anyone to act for him on such occasions.
—*Evening Telegram*, 1 April 1933

When we look back upon the riot at Christie Pits, we view the event through the prism of the Holocaust. The violence is inconceivable apart from the context of Hitler's assumption of power at the time. This is perhaps the most important reason for the telling and retelling of the story of Christie Pits, especially within the Jewish community, across three generations. Many Jewish veterans of the riot believed that unlike the millions who were fed into the killing machine set up by the German state, the Jews of Toronto fought back, and they did so at the very beginning of the long road that led to the Holocaust. Of course, this is a post-Holocaust judgement of a prior event. The boys who fought in Christie Pits at the appearance of the swastika could not possibly have known what was to happen at Auschwitz, Treblinka, Chelmno, Belzec, Sobibor, Majdanek, and other places of unspeakable horror.

And yet the question of resistance at that time is perhaps one of the most important issues to be raised in connection with the riot. By viewing the riot at Christie Pits in the context of the general resistance to National Socialism's triumph in Germany, we see that it was truly part of a larger response to this catastrophic event. Whereas "cooler heads" in the community advocated peaceful means of protest—diplomacy, rallies, boycotts—the Jewish street gangs opted for a violent response to the display of the swastika. Here too, there had been several precedents in the months following Hitler's rise to power.

On 24 April the *Star* reported an outbreak of violence near the German embassy in London, England:

> Despite elaborate police precautions, violence broke out to-day in the vicinity of the German embassy following renewed agitation for an anti-German boycott in protest against alleged mistreatment of Jews.
> William Dunlee, a 32-year-old seaman, was charged with throwing a bottle through a window of the embassy. Police declared the bottle contained this message:
> "Hitler you butcher, you have gone too far."
> A heavy cordon of police guarded the building throughout the night, following a tip received by Scotland Yard officials that a demonstration on behalf of Jews or a raid was planned.

On 8 May the *Star* reported on a street fight that had taken place in London's Piccadilly Circus between black-shirted Fascists and Jews and Communists. "The fight broke out," wrote the *Star*, "when the anti-Fascists attacked a dozen of the Fascists, half of them girls, while they were distributing their newspaper. Both sides were swiftly reinforced."[1]

The *Tely* noted that when chief Nazi ideologist Alfred Rosenberg visited London on 11 May to act as Hitler's proxy in laying a wreath on the cenotaph, someone ripped the swastika from the wreath; later a Captain Sears stole it in protest.[2] In a *Star* article of 19 May, M. H. Halton described a street brawl involving Fascists and Jews in London in terms unsympathetic to the latter:

> You cross from Piccadilly to Coventry St., and see a band of smartly-dressed Fascists in black shirts and gray flannel trousers parading up and down and offering for sale copies of Sir Oswald Mosley's Fascist paper, *The Blackshirt*. They are bold men, for they have been attacked before by Jews, and Coventry St. and Leicester Square is always full of Jews.
> The theatres disgorge their late showing crowds, and sure enough, a mob of 40 or 50 Jews, men and women, gather round the half dozen Fascists and start jeering at them, cursing them,

insulting them. The Fascists ignore them at first, but after a while there are a hundred of them, and the Black Shirts lose their heads, answering insult with insult. A red-haired Jew throws an empty cigarette package at a Fascist, accompanying it with a particularly nasty insult—and gets what you must admit was coming to him, a sock in the jaw. The Fascists are mobbed. Women fling themselves at them and scratch and bite. The bobbies rush up. Two Fascists are arrested, eight Jews. A smartly-dressed woman shakes her fist at the Jews and cries: "You cowards! The only time you dare to fight is when you're a hundred to one!"

"Not at all!" rebukes one of the arrested Fascists. "The odds were equal—one Fascist to a hundred Jews!"

The young German diplomat turns to us triumphantly. "You see!" he exclaims. "Can you blame us for being anti-Semitic. These Jews, once they feel themselves secure, will do anything!"[3]

Both the *Tely* and the *Star* covered a riot that broke out in Brooklyn at the North German Lloyd Line pier on 25 May as a crowd waited for Hans Weidemann, Hitler's envoy to the World Fair Exposition in Chicago. About one thousand people became enraged when they learned that Weidemann had been transferred from the ocean liner *Columbus* to a tugboat and brought to land surreptitiously. Both papers described the scene as follows:

Displaying banners condemning "the Nazi murder and terror regime", the crowd turned on the 50 uniformed police and 30 plain-clothesmen, throwing brick and bottles at them.

Police engaged in hand-to-hand combat with the rioters, and after a struggle arrested thirteen men and women, the latter wearing red hats. The prisoners were locked up in a garage near the pier, and rioting broke out afresh. Additional police arrived on foot, on horseback and in automobiles. Order was restored only after police drew their guns and levelled them at the crowd.

During the melee more than a score were injured, including four policemen....[4]

The Hitler issue was the focus of smaller violent encounters too: "Hitler Causes Toronto Fight," the *Telegram* headlined a story about a workplace fight that led to a court case:

"Take a smaller brush," said Foreman Wilinski to Sam Green, a Hebrew, in the plant where they worked.

"What for?" asked Sam.

"Give him a broom," interjected Frank Lentgeb, an Austrian and fellow worker.

Then the fight started! Words were passed about Hitler and Germany between Sam and Lentgeb. The latter charged Sam with assaulting him, and proved that he had been kicked in the abdomen.

Sam declared that he was hit first and that Lentgeb had said he'd "do what they do in Germany." He said: "I only put my foot up and he ran into it." "He has no right to kick a man like that," said Magistrate Tinker, ending the Nazi argument with a fine of $5 or ten days.[5]

A Pierre van Paassen front-page story on 30 May about the rise of Fascism in France told of violent encounters between Fascists and anti-Fascists under the headline "Riots, Fights Follow Wake of Fascist Rise in France."

These and similar stories helped set the stage for the Christie Pits riot. And when the papers reported the trouble during the first game of the quarter-final series, on the Monday evening, they served as the primary transmitters of the rumour that the Jewish boys would be back, in strength, on the Wednesday evening. In short, the newspaper reports made a violent encounter between the opposing sides practically inevitable.

To the Toronto police, however, the violence in Christie Pits on 16 August was only one in a series of violent encounters in Toronto parks. Although other parks were better known for being perennial sites of violence, a tradition—an expectation—of violence was associated with many Toronto parks. The fighting youth did not have to break a taboo; they were following a long-established pattern. Nevertheless, the specific content of the provocation and response on that August evening has to be given greater emphasis.

Young Jewish (and some Italian) boxers and street toughs formed the nucleus of the "Jewish" fighting contingent at the Pits. The stories of atrocities and degradation coming out of Germany must have had a particularly frustrating impact on this group of youngsters, who were used to fighting back when Jewish honour and persons were attacked. Here we have a particularly poignant example of fighting back where the real fight cannot be joined. Their frustration had probably been heightened by recent news stories about the fate of Jewish boxers in Hitler's Reich. On 25 April the *Star* and *Tely* carried the same report on the expulsion of Jews from every aspect of the fight game in Germany:

> A new climax in the complete ostracism of Jewish athletes from organized German sports life has been reached by the Verband Deutscher Faustkaempfer (Union of German Professional Boxers).
>
> The organization issued 10 regulations designed to eliminate Jews from the fistic industry, thereby joining the movement that resulted in the dropping of Daniel Prenn from the Davis Cup team, forced the resignation of Theodor Lewald, chairman of the German Athletic Federation, and to a lesser degree has resulted in a ban on all foreign competitors. Lewald is part Jewish but the family has been Christian for more than 100 years.
>
> With full sympathy of the Nazi press, which commented that the boxers did all the work anyway while managers, trainers and doctors or lawyers "got all the gravy," the master minds of the boxers union issued the following decrees:
>
> "All Jews, including those baptized, are ruled off the lists of members; all honorary members of Jewish blood are asked to hand in their cards; every German boxer is ordered to tear up any contract with a Jewish manager; Jews are barred from the club rooms; Jewish capital is barred from participation in the financing of boxing shows; union members are forbidden to engage Jewish doctors, dentists or lawyers; foreigners are hereby suspended until further notice; all club officials, not in harmony with the New Germany, should resign; all members out of harmony with the new movement should also quit; men in the confidence of the government are to sit in at all meetings."[6]

The frustration on the part of the Jewish community in general and the Jewish pugilists in particular was played upon by clever fight promoters in North America who used the German-Jewish animosity as a drawing card to boxing matches. The motivation of some promoters was revealed in a *Telegram* article by Henry McLemore. Under the headline "Harry Ebbets Jewish Boy till Saturday, at Least," McLemore exposed one fight promoter's gimmick as follows:

A character opened the door and started putting the old blast on Johnston for using two German fighters on Friday's card right when the papers are loaded with anti-Hitler stuff.

"What are you talking about," Johnston roared back. "I've got two Germans on the card and they're both fighting Jewish boys. What could be lovelier? The Jewish customers will come to see the Germans killed and the German customers will come to see the Jewish boys knocked bow-legged. In the semi-final I got Hans Birkie and Al Lasky, and in the wind-up I got Adolph Heuser fighting Harry Ebbets."

"Do you mean to tell me," shouted the character at the door, "that Harry Ebbets is a Jewish boy?"

"He certainly is," answered Johnston. "He certainly is—until Saturday morning, anyway."[7]

The most celebrated of these German-Jewish boxing contests was held in Yankee Stadium on 8 June 1933 between Max Baer, the Jewish hero, and Max Schmeling, the German champion. Baer beat Schmeling with a TKO in the tenth round. Newspapers carried a picture of a victorious Baer with a Star of David emblazoned defiantly on his trunks standing beside a dazed Schmeling. Baer's father, however, while descended from Jews of Alsace-Lorraine, was not a practising Jew, and his mother was of Irish-Scots descent. It appears that the Baer-Schmeling fight was contrived to match a "Jewish" with a "German" champion.[8] But in spite of the "hype," Baer's victory was significant to North American Jewry. In his column in the *Zhurnal,* M. Vogel noted:

> In fact Schmeling caught the blows, but Maxie aimed them at the Nazis: an uppercut for Hitler, a left-hook for Goering, a body slam for Goebbels, and enough whacks for a Rosenberg-Wiedemann-Bismarck.[9]

The riot at Christie Pits was merely one of the violent incidents that occurred as a protest against Nazi oppression of Jews in Germany in the months following Hitler's accession to power. But how did these violent responses relate to the reactions of the Jewish and non-Jewish communities in general to Nazi barbarism? Did the Jewish community in Canada utilize other forms of protest against the actual and potential threat of Nazism during the first half of 1933? It is clear that the gory details of Nazi persecutions of Jews were extensively reported in the Canadian papers. It is also clear that protests against Hitler's anti-Jewish actions and policies were not confined to the Jewish community. The first initiatives, however, were taken by Jewish organizations.

Jewish communities worldwide were not slow in responding to the calamity that had befallen their German brethren. According to a report in the *Zhurnal,* the Yiddish daily *Haiynt* (Today) in Warsaw, Poland, called on 12 March for a general boycott of German goods—even if such a boycott should prove damaging to Jewish businesses. The Warsaw paper also wondered why the American Jewish community had not yet followed its English counterpart in protesting against antisemitic activities in Germany. But the call to protest was heard also in America. *Der Yiddisher Zhurnal* reported, on 13 March, that a meeting of Jewish authors had been held in New York to protest Hitler's persecution of Jews and to call for massive protests by American Jewry.[10] With the threat of protest, the Nazis began to make conciliatory statements, which for a day or two were accepted as genuine by the *Zhurnal.* But by 15 March, an editorial in the Yiddish paper was calling for the Jews in Toronto to join the worldwide protest, and on the following day the *Zhurnal* was able to report that the community had created a committee to organize a protest meeting against the persecution of German Jews.

On the following Monday, 20 March, the *Zhurnal* reported that 2 April had been selected as a "Day of Protest" in Ontario against Nazi persecutions. A protest meeting had been called in Massey Hall, and similar meetings were scheduled to take place in Jewish communities across the province. The question of whether to organize a boycott of German goods had yet to be resolved.

Jewish communities around the world had begun to organize protest demonstrations and boycotts. The *Zhurnal* reported on a protest demonstration before the German consulate in Philadelphia and another against the raising of the swastika over the German consulate in Tel Aviv. On the same day, 20 March, the *Star* reported that American Jews had decided to hold mass protest demonstrations against the atrocities perpetrated upon German Jewry by the Hitler regime:

> A call went out to-day for the Jews of the United States to set aside a day—tentatively fixed for next Monday—for a united protest against the treatment of Jews in Germany by the Nazis. The New York mass protest will be held in Madison Square Garden.
>
> A resolution calling for the protest was passed last night at a meeting sponsored by the American Jewish Congress, after Dr.

Stephen S. Wise, noted rabbi, demanded that Jews speak out against what he assailed as "the damnable outrages of Hitlerism."

Turmoil and hisses greeted an objection by Former Justice Poskauer of the appellate division, that the mass meeting might only inflame the Hitlerites and make the plight of the German Jews graver.

"If this thing can happen in Germany to-day," Rabbi Wise said, "it may happen next year in some other place. The time to challenge this thing that comes out of the depths of hell is now, while it is happening."

In the same story, the *Star* reported that representatives of all Jewish organizations in London, Ontario, had met the previous day to protest against the Nazi outrages and plan a course of action.

Two days later, in another front-page story, the *Star* reported on the growing momentum of the official and unofficial protest movement in the United States as follows:

Nationally prominent Christians, including former Governor Alfred E. Smith, Newton D. Baker, former secretary of war in Woodrow Wilson's cabinet, and John W. Davis, 1924 Democratic presidential nominee, joined the Jewry of America to-day in condemning the persecution of Jews by the German government....

Simultaneously the state department at Washington called on the American ambassador and consular officials in Germany to send a complete report of alleged German excesses against Jews. This action was taken after Rabbi Stephen S. Wise had called upon the House foreign relations committee and the state department to act to protect Jews in Germany, or to protest against their mistreatment.

A monster mass meeting is scheduled for next Monday evening at Madison Square Garden at which Jewish, Catholic and Protestant leaders will unite in condemning the persecution of Jewry in Germany.

On the same day, the paper reported that a meeting of the Hebrew Liberal League at the Eppes Essen meeting hall had passed a unanimous resolution to protest the antisemitic campaign in Germany and to support the mass meeting to be held in Massey Hall.

The Canadian government agreed to investigate the situation of the

Jews in Germany, according to *Der Yiddisher Zhurnal*, at the behest of the three Jewish MPs, Sam Factor, A. A. Heaps and S. V. Jacobs. The Yiddish paper reported that Premier Bennett had telegraphed to the Canadian foreign minister in London to provide him with a report on the situation of Jews in Germany and that the German ambassador to the United States had assured Washington that Hitler would create order in the country. In Toronto the second meeting to plan for the mass protest took place in the Zion Institute. Legionnaires and veterans met as well to consider how they could most effectively join the protest movement. In its editorial "The Righteous Action of America and Canada," the *Zhurnal* referred to inquiries made by both governments and the reminder given to Hitler that what was going on in Germany was being seen by the whole world. The British government was taken to task for not taking any action.

On the same day, the *Star* reported on a protest march in New York City organized by Jewish war veterans and on the protests planned across the country: "With U.S. and Zionist flags whipping in the raw March breeze, 10,000 Jewish war veterans and numerous assemblages of women marchers began to-day a parade of protest against the Nazi oppression of their co-religionists in Germany." The *Star* report went on to say that protest was "sweeping across the nation with the speed of a prairie fire." The American Federation of Labor, the various councils of churches, state governors, senators, and bishops were all adding their voices to the chorus against Nazi oppression and were calling for a trade boycott against Germany. At the same time,

> State department officials at Washington were surprised at the action of President von Hindenburg in signing a decree cancelling all charges against Nazis and Nationalists who prior to Tuesday had engaged in anti-Semitic disturbances.
>
> It was recalled the German foreign office gave officials of the U.S. Embassy assurance that those arrested in connection with recent attacks on U.S. citizens of Jewish faith would be punished. The state department was awaiting word from the embassy as to whether the amnesty also applied to those implicated in the attacks on U.S. citizens.

The *Star* also reported that the unofficial boycott against German goods had already begun in Toronto. Lighthouse Knitting Mills in the city announced that it had refused to buy German-made goods because of the maltreatment of Jews in that country.

The *Telegram* reported on the following day, 24 March, in a page-one story, that Britain had already undertaken to investigate "outrages against Jews" in Germany. In relating the story, the paper described the growing protest against Nazi terror:

> Protest meetings of Jews throughout the world in the next few days will have a profound effect on the economic future of Germany, dispatches from the various world capitals to London revealed today. Anti-Jewish demonstrations in Germany are resulting in widespread direct economic reprisals, it was indicated.
>
> A spontaneous boycott has begun in England, where Jewish master bakers passed a resolution boycotting German flour. Jewish silk manufacturers in London have written German firms cancelling their contracts, and dealers in razor blades have similarly decided not to trade with German houses.
>
> A new society has been founded in London by Louis Golding, author, to combat anti-Semitism. To-day's issue of the *Jewish Chronicle* contains an editorial urging a total boycott of German goods.
>
> Similar activities are reported from Continental Europe and the western hemisphere. Meetings are being held in both North and South America....
>
> Answering Chancellor Hitler's complaint that a campaign of slander is being waged against him in foreign countries, *News-Chronicle* declared editorially:
>
> "The only real cure of the campaign is the removal of the suspicions on which it rests, suspicions fostered by attacks on Jews, suppressing of a free press and the air of indiscriminate menace marking almost all the utterances of the Hitler Government."

In a continuation of this story the *Tely* looked at how the German government was responding to the protests and boycotts: as well as lodging diplomatic protests, Hitler's "supporters set about to disprove reports of Jewish persecution."

The *Telegram,* however, indicated that it was not in sympathy with the attempt by the protest movement to put pressure on governments to intervene on behalf of German Jews. A *Tely* editorial of 24 March took the view that the Jews of Germany had only one source from which they could seek justice and protection— the Nazi government:

Sympathy is naturally evoked by the unfortunate position of the Jews in Germany. In spite of denial from Berlin, it is apparent that anti-Semitic excesses are one phase of the disorders which have come with the Nazi accession to power....

But however great the sympathy of the outside world with the unfortunate victims of disorders in Germany, the remedy for these conditions will have to be found in Germany and not through the intervention of other nations. The administration of justice and the protection of its citizens is the domestic concern of every nation, and interference from without would be naturally resented. German citizens, whether Jew or Gentile, can only look to the rulers of Germany for succor.

In news from Toronto, the *Zhurnal* informed its readers on 24 March that the conference to organize the mass protest meeting had decided to go ahead with the boycott of German goods. Furthermore, Toronto rabbis had declared the coming Monday a general day of fasting, to reflect on and protest the maltreatment of German Jews.

On 24 March the *Star* carried a front-page story about the planning meeting for the Toronto Jewish community's united protest against the treatment of German Jews. Representatives of more than one hundred Jewish organizations met at the Zionist Institute in a highly charged atmosphere to voice their opposition to the "medieval and brutish persecution" of German Jews and to plan for the boycott.

The assembly passed a three-part resolution stating: (1) that Hitlerism was the enemy, not the German people; (2) that both Jews and Gentiles should be called upon to boycott German goods; and (3) that the boycott should be proclaimed by rabbis from their pulpits throughout the city. The tension in the meeting was such that maintaining order proved a challenge for Chairman J. Grainer:

> "Our women and children are being butchered in Germany," he cried. "You are saying the same things over and over again. I know you all want to talk. I know you all want to give vent to your feelings. But this is no time for talk. We must act."

The flood of impassioned oratory continued unabated, until as midnight approached, the meeting was whipped into unison with but a single dissenting voice....

The *Tely* went on to note on 25 March that the boycott of German goods by British Jews had been extended to include German films and restaurants.

On 27 March the *Star* described the progress of the protest in New York:

> Sponsors of the meeting were assured that the Garden would be packed to its capacity of 20,000, and estimated that more than 1,000,000 persons would participate in protest meetings in 300 cities and towns in the U.S. Speakers at Madison Square Garden meeting: Rabbi Stephen S. Wise, honorary president of the American Jewish Congress, will preside. The speakers include Governor Herbert H. Lehman, former Governor Alfred E. Smith, Senator Robert F. Wagner, Bishop William T. Manning, Bishop John J. Dunn, representing Cardinal Hayes; Bishop Francis J. McConnell, Charles H. Tuttle, Mayor John P. O'Brien, and William Green, president of the American Federation of Labor. The speeches will be carried to all parts of the United States and to thirteen foreign countries. A force of 700 police has been assigned to preserve order.

A full report of the protest meeting held in Madison Square Garden the previous evening was also provided by the *Zhurnal*. It called attention to the fact that twenty-two thousand people inside and an additional sixty thousand people outside had heard impassioned speeches by prominent political and religious leaders—speeches that sent a clear message to the German government. However, the *Zhurnal* also noted that the Nazis were retaliating by threatening the Jewish population with increased persecution and using the demonstrations as an excuse for further violence against the Jews within Germany's borders.

In a front-page story on the following day, the *Tely* confirmed that the Nazi party had called for a boycott of Jews and Jewish goods and services in Germany. The Ontario Protest Committee was quick to react to the announcement:

> Never in the history of any civilized country has a government become the open instigator of organized attacks upon Jews, as the Hitler power in Germany has done.... He admits that the reign of terror will now be carried out, because of the false reports. It was a case of out of the frying pan into the fire for the Jews there. If

nothing was reported he would have no cause to stop his shock troops carrying out their horrors, while now he will proceed with his revenge tactics.[11]

Der Yiddisher Zhurnal, referring to the announcement of a German boycott of Jewish businesses, responded: "Only a lunatic of the worst sort could have devised a plan to answer the outrage of the civilized world at the Jewish '*tsores*' [troubles] in Germany with an antisemitic campaign organized by the government."

The *Star* and the *Zhurnal* announced that protest meetings would be held across Ontario on the coming Sunday, 2 April. Among the cities and towns hosting protest demonstrations were: St. Catharines, Welland, Hamilton, Brantford, London, Kitchener, Windsor, Galt, Peterborough, Toronto, Belleville, and Kirkland Lake. Both papers reported that a boycott of German goods and movies had been proclaimed in Palestine. The Yiddish paper also noted that Brazilian Jews had joined the protest movement and that the Polish stock exchange had closed in protest against the anti-Jewish actions in Germany.

In its revealing 29 March editorial "Why Do They Keep Silent?" the *Zhurnal* attacked the four Toronto English-language dailies for not using their editorial voices to protest the treatment of Jews in Germany. On the following day, the paper announced that Premier Henry of Ontario would support the protest meeting on 2 April. The Ontario Masonic lodges were also joining the protest.

On 29 March a front-page story in the *Telegram* informed readers that many Nazis had already jumped the gun on the boycott of Jewish establishments set for Saturday, 1 April. All over Germany, storm troopers were setting up barriers around Jewish businesses, handing out leaflets to passers-by warning them not to buy from Jews, smearing windows of Jewish stores with stars of David and words like "Jude" (Jew) and "Juda Verrecke" (Judah perish) in yellow paint. The paper also reported incidents of vandalism directed against Jewish shops. In Göttingen, practically every Jewish shop had its windows smashed in what can only be described as a dress rehearsal for the *Kristallnacht* five and a half years later. The Nazi paper *Der Angriff* wrote that the cause of the boycott was the "criminal" propaganda of world Jewry: "'The stories of atrocity,' the *Angriff* said, 'are calculated to slander the German people in the eyes of the world. The German forbearance is now ended. In the course of a national revolution, the German people have treated the Jews with exemplary consideration. Its thanks have been to see a world Jewry organized for criminal propaganda.'"[12]

On 30 March the *Star* reported that German Jews had made an appeal directly to von Hindenburg to intercede and have the boycott called off. The same report was carried by the Yiddish paper the following day. The *Star* reported further that more than 1.5 million Nazis had been mobilized throughout Germany to carry out the boycott plans.

The *Star* reported in the same issue that the Nazis had announced that photographs would be taken of all patrons of Jewish shops as long as the boycott was in effect. For the Nazis, the boycott was the beginning of a war on Jewry throughout the world. According to the *Star*: "Chancellor Hitler's old battle cry that 'Jews and the stock exchanges started the world war' was revived in to-day's proclamation issued by the central boycott committee."

Meanwhile, Ontario's Jewish communities were preparing protest demonstrations of their own. Horrified at the impending boycott of Jews in Germany, they concentrated on making their own protest a success. According to the *Zhurnal* of 31 March, leaders of all segments of the population had been involved in the protest plans. Rabbis would be exhorting their congregants to attend meetings. French Jews had organized protests and a boycott of German goods, it noted, and protests had also taken place in Morocco and Salonika.

On Saturday, 1 April, the day of the German boycott of Jewish establishments, the *Star* reported that Jewish banks had stayed open and Jewish newspapers had continued to operate, but that most other Jewish businesses had been affected by the massive Nazi effort. The rationale for the action was proclaimed once again in a statement by the Federation of Nazi Women: "Jews want to continue the fight until the destruction of the German people is complete. We will continue it until Jewry has been destroyed. The Jew must forever be eliminated from our people and our state. German women, you are fighting a holy war."

The *Tely*'s front-page reporting of the boycott cast the Nazis clearly in the role of villains. *Der Yiddisher Zhurnal*, which didn't publish on Saturdays, carried news of the boycott on the front page of its Sunday edition. No better appeal could have been made to the Jewish citizens of Ontario to attend the protest meetings scheduled for Sunday evening than the reports of the boycott in Germany. Although Goebbels had announced that the boycott would last only one day, its impact upon the Jewish communities in Canada was powerful. In a story entitled "All of Western Canada Will Protest Today," the *Zhurnal* quoted a statement made by Alderman M. A. Gray of Winnipeg to the effect that "all cities and towns in Western Canada have now reported that they have organized protest meetings for the coming Sunday, the same day that the big protest meeting occurs in Winnipeg, and, as I understand, the same day as in your city." The meeting in Hamilton was to be held in the Grand Opera building on James Street, and to be broadcast over two local radio stations. The meeting in St. Catharines, at the Capital Theatre, would include participants from Welland and Niagara Falls. Peterborough, Oshawa, Belleville, Ottawa, Windsor, Kirkland Lake, Brantford, Galt, Timmins, Kingston, and Cornwall were among the other cities and towns that also held meetings. In Kitchener, members of the German community supported the protest.

A *Zhurnal* editorial issued a last appeal to the Jews of Toronto to attend the meeting at Massey Hall:

> Only the sick among us, only the weak and the small children, should stay at home. Every Jew, man and woman, young and old, who can stand on his feet, must be on the street, must come to Massey Hall, must be at the protest site, must see to it that every voice be mixed together with the voices of all Jews over the world in a powerful call:
>
> Stop the blood-letting of our defenceless brothers, sisters, and little children in Germany!

The *Evening Telegram* did not support the anti-Nazi protest in Massey Hall, maintaining instead that it was an affront to the Christian community since it was called on a Sunday. The *Tely* considered this a "mistake." Worse, it was "an impertinence that criticism should be directed against the Mayor for adhering to his rule to refuse to attend political gatherings on this day or to delegate anyone to act for him on such occasions. If the gathering is regarded by the Jewish community as a religious one, the appropriate day for it would be Saturday. This is a day to the use of which for this purpose Christian members of the community could take no exception."

On Monday, 3 April, *Der Yiddisher Zhurnal*, the *Star*, and the *Telegram* reported on the protest meeting of 2 April. Headlines in the Yiddish paper read: "Ontario's 3 1/2 Million Citizens Protest against Nazis, Says Henry. German Industrialists and Hindenburg Force Hitler to Give Up Boycott—Massey Hall Overfilled—Thousands Turn Back Due to Lack of Seats—Meetings in Bay St. and University Ave. Shuls [synagogues]—Captain Philpott Speaks Sharply about Hitlerism—Sam Factor, Controller Simpson, S. M. Shapiro and Others Call to General Struggle against Hitlerism." The *Star* summed up the sentiment expressed at the Massey Hall meeting: "Adolf Hitler and his followers 'may wade ankle-deep through Jewish blood and tears,' but eventually they will pay for it, every drop, and the Jew will be present at the funeral of Hitlerism...." The *Evening Telegram* described the proceedings largely by quoting from the officials who spoke at the meeting.

A. M. Holzman, writing in the *Zhurnal on* 3 April on "The Biggest Jewish Protest in New York," answered the charge that the protest movement by Jews in other countries would bring misfortune to the Jews of Germany. His words were prophetic:

> And if the Hitler regime continues with its plans to exterminate the Jews of Germany, as they announced earlier, even before Hitler was raised to the office of Chancellor, it won't be the fault of the American Jewish Congress which "made matters worse." It will only happen on account of the anti-Semites present in the Hitler regime who are unshakeably agreed on turning the entire German government into a dark murder-machine against helpless Jews whom they aim to exterminate entirely.

On 3 April the *Telegram* reported that many Christian churches in Toronto had responded positively to the Jewish request for support of the protest meetings. According to the *Tely,* "many Christian ministers commended the Toronto protest meeting to their congregations, and prayers for the Jews of Germany were said in the course of several services." Among those in sympathy with the protest were: Rev. E. Crossley Hunter of Carlton United Church, Rev. O. E. Leichlitter of College Street Baptist Church, and Rector J. E. Ward of the Church of the Epiphany.

On the same day, the *Star* carried a denial from Meyer F. Steinglass, editor of the *Jewish Standard* and spokesman for the Ontario Protest Committee, of reports that Jews were retaliating against Germans living in Toronto for the atrocities committed against Jews in Germany. "On the contrary," said Steinglass, "Joseph Lewis, president of Dominion Printing, had given an unemployed German youth the money to buy tools to enable him to accept a job."[13]

On 4 April *Der Yiddisher Zhurnal* reported on an anti-Hitler protest by forty thousand people in London, England, on a large protest meeting in Belleville, Ontario (attended by people from Napanee, Kingston, Picton, and Trenton), and on a protest statement (too little, too late, said the paper) sent by Moscow to Germany. In his column of that day, M. Vogel appealed to the Jews of Toronto to refrain from venting their anger on German workers in Canada; to do so would make them no better than Hitler. On 5 April the *Zhurnal* carried news of protest demonstrations in Greece, France, India, and Poland, and reported that the German government had accused the American embassy in Berlin of being "a factory of atrocity lies against Nazis."

On 6 April the *Star* and the *Telegram* described a Montreal protest meeting in the Mount Royal Arena, attended by ten thousand Jews and Gentiles. Speakers included Senator Raoul Dandurand, Bishop J. C. Far- thing of Montreal, and the Hon. Mr. Mercier who spoke on behalf of the premier of Quebec, the Hon. L. A. Taschereau. A message sent by Sir Robert Borden was read at the gathering:

> German citizens of the Jewish race have given to that country and the world an imperishable service.... Recent reports from Germa- ny have stirred the people of all civilized countries with deep emo- tion, but the events that have been recorded cannot be regarded as the expression of the normal sentiment of the real nature of the great German nation, but rather the temporary effervescence of unfortunate passion that will soon pass away.[14]

While the English-language papers were debating the truth of the atrocity reports and the nature of the Hitler regime, *Der Yiddisher Zhur- nal* was reporting on the growth of the protest movement, searching desperately for some silver lining in the dark clouds hanging over Ger- man Jewry. On 10 April it covered the meeting between the Pope and a German delegation that included von Papen and Hermann Goering, and suggested in a headline that the Pope would "prevail upon the Hit- ler government to end persecutions." In the same issue, it noted a state- ment by Goebbels that the Jewish question would remain unresolved if the Jews were allowed to leave Germany in peace. It also reported that French political leaders Herriot and Blum had attended a protest meet- ing in France, that a Zionist youth group in Toronto, Poalei Zion, had called upon other student and young-worker organizations to join in a mass protest meeting on 13 April, and that police in London, England, had removed signs calling for a boycott of German goods.

On 14 April the *Zhurnal* reported a debate in the British House of Commons about a possible revision of the Treaty of Versailles to give Germany equal rights with other nations. Sentiment was against Ger- many. Many MPs argued that it would be impossible to make new arrangements favourable to Germany when it was a crime to be a Jew in that country. An anti-Fascist demonstration in the Royal Albert Hall by ten thousand London workers was also covered. On 16 April the *Zhurnal* reported Germany's displeasure at the debate in the British House of Commons and noted that the Toronto protest committee had been transformed into a committee to raise money for the Jewish refugees fleeing the "German hell."

The *Star* carried a counter-protest story of sorts in its edition of 21 April. At a meeting of Les Jeune-Canada, speakers denounced the participation of high-profile Quebec political leaders in a mass protest against German atrocities a few weeks earlier:

> Protest against appearance of prominent French Canadians at a recent Jewish mass meeting was voiced by five speakers last night at a meeting sponsored by Les Jeune-Canada, an organization aiming at revivals of nationalist sentiment in Quebec....
>
> Gilbert Dansereau, at last night's meeting, charged Jewry with attempting to create "a special minority enjoying the rights of French and English."

For the rest of April, *Der Yiddisher Zhurnal* carried stories about the growth of the protest movement, about German denials of atrocities, and about the fate of the refugees. On 20 April the Yiddish paper called attention to the pro-Nazi sympathies of the *London Daily Express,* and reported on a resolution passed by Italian Jews against Nazi persecutions, a boycott against Jews called by Croat nationalists, and Spain's efforts to attract German-Jewish refugees. On 21 April the *Zhurnal* carried stories about a publication by British Jews that offered proof of anti-Jewish persecution in Germany, about the growth of a fund to help German Jews settle in Israel, and about a trade boycott in Montreal against German goods. On 28 April there was a report of protest demonstrations in Australia, in which thirty thousand dollars had been raised at a mass gathering to help German Jews. Government ministers, party leaders, and church officials had taken part.

As with the atrocity reports, the number of articles in the English-language papers about protests, denials, and boycotts diminished between May and August 1933. *Der Yiddisher Zhurnal* carried news of protests almost daily to its readership, but such items were more sporadic in the *Star* and *Telegram.* The big stories in May included: a parade of some 200,000 to 250,000 marchers in New York City on 10 May protesting book-burnings directed against Jewish, leftist, liberal, and pacifist writers in Germany; a declaration of an economic boycott against Germany by the major Jewish organizations in New York, New Jersey, and Connecticut on 15 May; Hitler's assertion, reported in the *Zhurnal* on 22 May, that no non-Communist Jews were persecuted and that he would pay passage plus 20,000 Reichsmarks for each Jew, if the Americans allowed the German Jews to immigrate *en masse;* the walkout of German delegates at the PEN meeting during an attack on Hitlerite terrorism by Sholem Asch (reported in the *Zhurnal* on 28 May); and the apparently successful attempt of the League of Nations to force Germany to grant Jews equal civil and political rights in Upper Silesia (reported on 30 May in the *Zhurnal).*

In June most of the protest news centred on the boycott of German goods. On 2 June the Toronto League for the Defence of Jewish Rights met to plan a national conference of representatives of all major Jewish communities in Canada, to be held on 10 and 11 June. The meeting took place and laid the foundation for the new Canadian Jewish Congress. However, an alliance of delegates from Montreal and Western Canada thwarted the Toronto community's attempt to have a national boycott declared against German goods. In a bitter complaint in the *Zhurnal* of 19 June, K. Revitsh suggested that:

> Montreal and Western Canada came to the conference with the decision made to vote against the boycott, and they carried out their intentions.
>
> The conference dealt with the question, and their votes prevailed in favour of a struggle of words against Hitler, not a concrete, not a fighting struggle.
>
> Why? Because the clever Jews from Western Canada are afraid lest a Jew in Western Canada lose a few German customers, and the clever Jews in Montreal have figured out that a boycott would pour oil on the fire of Quebec antisemitism....

In July, the most important protest for the Jews of Toronto was on the eleventh (one day before the Orange Parade), when some 12,000 persons marched from Wellington Park, up Spadina Avenue, along Dundas Street, and up University Avenue to Queen's Park to protest Hitler's anti-labour and anti-Jewish persecutions. Organized by a coalition of some fifty-six Jewish organizations, including the unions in the needle trades, the protest was joined by leftist groups and parties throughout the city.

The parade was an important one and was held with the permission of the city authorities—the first time such permission had been granted in twelve years. The *Evening Telegram* was outraged that Communist and other radical groups had added their banners to the demonstration and that the cenotaph—a memorial to Canada's fallen soldiers—had been "desecrated" by those radical banners and signs. Under the headline "Reds Butt in as City Jews Hit Nazi Acts," the *Tely* wrote:

> Taking advantage of the official permission granted Jewish organizations to hold the procession, Toronto's Communistic organizations were out in full force and for once were left undisturbed by the few police who were on hand. Banners crying such things as "Long Live the Soviet Republic" and "March to Victory with Stalin" were openly carried, and one group even gathered on the front steps of the Parliament Buildings and wildly sang the "Internationale."
>
> Those who participated in or witnessed the unveiling of the 48th Highlanders cenotaph at the north end of the park, would, however, to say the least, have been horrified to have witnessed the arrival of the parade in the park. Straight to the cenotaph at the north end of the park they marched. The steps were soon filled, and round the cenotaph marched the paraders in thousands. Against and on its ledge were rested some of the printed cards on poles, such as "We demand compulsory insurance." Directly to the south of it was held the Young Communist banner....
>
> While the parade was ostensibly one to protest against Hitlerism, it would have been hard for anyone witnessing it to understand what it was all about.

An editorial on 13 July returned to the theme, concluding that "it is necessary that they [the 'foreign' protester] should learn that the peace and liberty which they are assured in Canada is conditional upon their conforming with the traditions of Canada."

The League for the Defence of Jewish Rights did not support the march. In fact, after the parade had been joined by the radical organizations, Rabbi Samuel Sachs condemned the introduction of banners and slogans that brought a different message to the demonstration than the one "intended by the well-meaning workers who planned it."[15] Rabbi

Sachs's condemnation of the march brought a sharp reply from Maurice Spector, one of the organizers:

> We are well aware that soft and apologetic Jews, monied Jews and those anxious to make an exclusive club will find such a demonstration as ours naturally distasteful. These people are merely agitated over the anti-Semitic feature of Hitlerism. Mussolini and apparently Pilsudski have become acceptable to them. The Jewish workers, however, protest not only against the pogroms but against the whole system of tyrannical and labor-hating Fascism of which German anti-Semitism is but a single link....

The protest march was the subject of two *Tely* editorials, the "cenotaph" piece, and one pointing out that the presence of Communists in the parade had harmed the Jewish cause. To emphasize its point the *Tely* cited as the "natural reaction of many Canadians" an anti-Jewish letter it had received after the march. The letter said in part:

> An article in today's *Telegram* describing the Jewish anti-Hitler parade would give one the impression that there were no Reds in the Jewish population of Toronto. A check-up as to the birthplace of thousands of these Jews would reveal the fact that a great percentage of them are of Russian birth and in sympathy with anything Russian.
>
> The parade on Tuesday did, as your article stated, give the Reds a chance to display their Soviet tendencies but they were Jewish Reds. There may have been a few of Stalin's followers in the procession, but they were welcomed by their Russian Jewish anti-Hitlerites.
>
> Too much leeway has been given to the Jews in this country, and if we don't wake up soon things will be in the same condition that they were in Germany. Perhaps the Jews will do the fighting for us in the next war and the unemployed Canadians and war veterans will have a chance to get in a few days work before they get back.

On 21 July, the three papers reported that an international conference of Jewish organizations had called for a worldwide boycott of German goods. A report to the conference suggested that export of German goods had dropped by 30 per cent to some countries. The president for the international committee, Samuel Untermeyer, attacked Rabbi Stephen Wise for his opposition to the boycott and appealed to the League of Nations to come to the assistance of the German Jews.

CHAPTER 10 "...Lies, Lies, Lies"

Everyone who knows Germany, the German character and culture of the German people, must feel at once that the news spread at present about the putting out of eyes, the mutilation of corpses, the searing of parts of the body, etc., must be just as mendacious as the war-time tales of horror about the mutilation of Belgian children, the crucified Canadian and the factories in which corpses were to be turned into soap.

—Letter from a former crown prince of Germany to a friend, *Toronto Daily Star*, 28 March 1933

The reasons why Jewish youth responded violently to the swastika provocation in Toronto during the summer of 1933 should now be apparent. It is less clear, however, what led the "British lads" at the Beaches and in Christie Pits to adopt the swastika as an emblem. The evidence suggests that the swastika was not used as a political symbol. With the exception of Mackay and a few of his supporters, members of the Swastika Club and the Pit Gang were not interested in National Socialism as a political ideology or program. To be sure, they didn't like Jews; but they also didn't like Italians or Catholics. In fact, they didn't care much for anyone who wasn't like them. They did share a stereotype of the Jew that probably derived in large part from traditional Christian images of Jews; but it was not this home-grown, xenophobic antisemitism that provoked the riot at Christie Pits. It was the swastika flag and the "Heil Hitler" shouts.

In spite of the massive evidence of Nazi barbarism towards Jews in Germany, there was a significant movement to deny atrocity reports, minimize them, or explain them away. This effort was led by the Nazi government in Berlin, but there were a significant number of journalists and editors who were prepared, wittingly or unwittingly, to assist Berlin in its attempts to deny or downplay stories about persecution of the Jews. Thus, the meaning of the swastika was ambiguous for many. Did it or did it not stand for "excessive" antisemitism? Did the atrocity reports reflect merely ephemeral conditions in post-Weimar Germany or something more fundamental? Were some of Hitler's more enthusiastic followers merely over-reacting in the flush of victory? Were Jews not over sensitive; were they not simply crying wolf again?

In order to understand how the meaning of the swastika was contested in Toronto following Hitler's coming to power, we must turn to the pages of the Toronto newspapers.

In the *Telegram's* weekly op-ed-page column reviewing world events, entitled "Keeping Pace with Time," an 11 March article portrayed Hitler as an effective, dedicated leader, not nearly so terrible as his own propaganda had led the world to believe:

> ...Hitler is sitting pretty. Last Sunday he rolled up the largest majority ever recorded for any man in that country; and so now he can sit back and say that the people have spoken.... He did say that he would gain power only by legitimate means, and this, we must admit, he has done. There are very few but will sympathize with him in his desire to keep the germ of Communism from growing to full bloom.
>
> But now he is the boss, and the hardest work of all is to begin. Hitler wants, and rightly too, to build the Fatherland once again to higher levels, physically and mentally, back to its old position of world power. Now that he is ready to begin there is no doubt but that the Reich will place the Cabinet in practically a dictatorial position, and then adjourn to leave the fiery little boss to get things underway. It is not believable that 17,000,000 voters put Hitler into power for him to experiment. They must be convinced that he is going to speedily and safely lead his country to peace and prosperity. Much of the little man's noisy talk seems to have been just that, and no more. He is quieting down now and beginning to get to business.

It was precisely this image that Hitler wanted to present to the rest of the world. Already, on 3 February, a headline in *Der Yiddisher Zhurnal* proclaimed: "Hitler's Government Wants to Calm Jews outside Germany: New Cabinet Seeks to Secure Peace for All Citizens, States Government Press Department."

This was to become a standard Nazi trick to ward off hostile criticism from foreign countries and groups. Whenever Nazi barbarism reached new heights and the world started to react, Hitler and his henchmen would adopt any one of a number of strategies. H. R. Knickerbocker, Berlin correspondent for the New York *Evening Post,* described the Nazi tactics as follows: "First, they never happened; second, they will be investigated; third, they will never happen again."[1]

Reports of atrocities, expulsions, exclusions, and indignities committed by the Nazis against the Jews of Germany were met with horror, shock, and outrage by some and disbelief, or only qualified acceptance, by others. There were those in the Canadian population at large who greeted the reports carried by papers like the *Toronto Daily Star* with indifference or skepticism. The *Evening Telegram* consistently urged that the reports be verified by "objective sources," and very often ran stories in which pro-Nazi elements were given prominent space to deny the atrocity reports in the *Telegram* and other papers. The unwillingness to take the part of the aggrieved party and the attempt to present the "quarrel" between the Germans and the Jews as having two legitimate sides allowed a significant number of Torontonians to turn their backs on Jewish appeals for assistance.

It is also likely that the *Tely's* skepticism with regard to the reports coming out of Germany played some sort of role in the adoption of the swastika emblem by the youth of the eastern beaches and the young hoodlums at Christie Pits. The *Evening Telegram* cast a web of doubt over the Nazi revolution, covered the reported atrocities and indignities with an aura of uncertainty, and implicitly suggested that any "improprieties" were, first, the work of over-zealous supporters of Hitler flushed with victory, secondly, blown out of proportion by sensationalist reporters and newspapers, and thirdly, soon to be stopped by Hitler and the party brass, who were to reassert their control over their followers. These were precisely the official explanations given by the Nazi press bureau itself.

The message conveyed by the *Telegram* may have been interpreted by certain groups of youth with an ingrained hostility to Jews and other "strangers" as a sort of permission to adopt the swastika as an emblem. This is not to suggest that the *Tely's* editorial policy was the chief ingredient in the decision to embrace the hooked cross. In public, the spokesmen of the Swastika Club never tired of denying any link between themselves and the Hitlerites. Whether or not the connection between the Swastika Club and the Nazis was clear in the minds of the club members (and there is every reason to think that it was), club spokesmen realized that it would have been politically unwise and perhaps even shameful to make such a connection public. However, the fact that these young people could "play" with the swastika at all was probably the result, at least in part, of the kind of atmosphere created by the *Telegram*.[2]

The Jewish press was not fooled by protestations from the Nazi side. On 6 February, for example, in an editorial entitled "Hitler's Promise to the Jews," *Der Yiddisher Zhurnal* quoted liberally from Hitler's statements and warned that "this alone is sufficient reason for Jews the world over to be more than concerned for the fate of the German Jews. If the government press bureau finds it necessary at this time to calm Jews, it's a sign that a danger is hovering over the Jews."

The same edition of the paper carried two stories about apologetic statements made by Goering to Jews in an attempt to calm them. One story described a promise, made by the Prussian Minister of the Interior, of full protection for Jews who were loyal to Germany and the German government. But pressure began to mount in the following days on the heels of further atrocity reports and inquiries from both the American and British governments. On 10 March the *Zhurnal* headlines of a page-one story read: "Attacks on Jews and Arrests Continue in Germany, in Spite of Government's Reassurances: Goering Assures That Loyal Jews Will Not Be Touched—Prussian Police Promise American Consul to Find a Way to Stop Attacks." Again the Yiddish paper was not fooled: "In spite of the fact that the Nazis, in their official statements, deny all responsibility for the organized attacks on Jews, the fact undoubtedly remains that they perfected the machine for this purpose."

On 10 March the *Star* carried an interview with Dr. Walter Kotschnig, Secretary of the International Students Service. Kotschnig was in Toronto to address the Canadian Club on "the significance of Hitler." Although he didn't minimize the potential for violence, he did attempt to blame the victims, in this case the Jews, for Hitler's accession to power:

> "You ask me about the Jews in Germany. There will certainly be bloodshed. But if this report is true, that an influential Jew was indirectly responsible for the Hitler government, it makes it evident what is portending. It has been suggested that Von Schroeder, fearing that Hitler would get supreme control of Germany, with his violent anti-Semitic tendencies, arranged this meeting in order that the other two leaders, Von Papen and Hindenburg, would share the power. They are not nearly so anti-Semitic as is Hitler."

Whatever becomes of the small Jew in Germany, Dr. Kotschnig thought the wealthy Jew, banker and financier, would remain unmolested....

Jews, who knew from bitter experience that wealth was no protection against antisemitism, took no comfort from this, but began to unite behind the protest movement.

On 24 March *Der Yiddisher Zhurnal* clearly illustrated the devious tactics of the Nazis, who were simultaneously denying that violence had been practised against the Jews, promising an end to it, and threatening yet further violence! The Yiddish paper reported that the Nazi government had threatened foreign journalists and newspapers with reprisals for spreading "atrocity propaganda." At the same time it hinted that private debts owed by Germans to Americans would not be paid if there were to be a boycott of German goods. An unnamed representative of the German government referred to the atrocity stories carried by the foreign press as "propaganda tales which call to mind the propaganda [about supposed German atrocities] at the time of the war...."

In response to building pressure from outside, Hitler stepped in to calm the troubled waters. Under a front-page heading of 25 March—"We Don't Blame Hitler, He Can't Prevent Attacks Jewish Veterans Declare—Only Eastern Refugees in Official Disgrace—Plan Demonstrations in Many Nations"—the *Evening Telegram* brought the reassurance that the worst was now over. In a move to limit the damage, Hitler shifted the blame to post-war eastern Jewish refugees, promising that the issue would soon be resolved.

Hitler's reassurances were echoed by Goering, who was pressed into action to pull the wool over the eyes of foreign correspondents. The *Telegram* carried his message to a Toronto audience:

> Persecution of any man simply because he is a Jew will not be tolerated, said Captain Hermann Goering, minister without portfolio, in an impassioned address to-day to foreign correspondents.
>
> He also expressed the opinion that Jews and socialists abroad were rendering their German friends poor service by making unfavorable reports on German conditions or by holding protest mass meetings.
>
> "Every German," he said, "smiles when he learns that on next Monday prayer meetings will be held in America."

Backing up Hitler and Goering in a co-ordinated effort were a variety of German sources who tried to blame the violence on "disreputable" Jews—that is, Communists or eastern refugees.

In another front-page article on the same day, wired specially to the *Telegram*, the point was more forcefully made that German-Jewish organizations considered atrocity reports to be propaganda created by foreign newspapers. The centrepiece of the story was a statement by the Central Union of German Citizens of the Jewish Faith, the most important Jewish voice in the country, to the effect that:

> All such reports are free inventions. The Central Federation states emphatically that German Jewry cannot be held responsible for the inexcusable distortions which deserve the severest condemnation.

Both the *Toronto Daily Star* and the *Evening Telegram* were astute enough to suggest in their 27 March editions that statements from Jewish groups in Germany denying the alleged atrocities were made under pressure from the Hitler regime. The *Tely* printed a comment from Rabbi Samuel Sachs:

> We must not allow these obviously spurious statements of the situation in Germany to mislead us into relinquishing our protests.... The widespread feeling of horror at the attacks upon the Jews has so keenly affected Germany's economic relations with other countries that only such a statement coming from the Jews themselves could have stemmed the tide of resentment.

On the same day the *Star* carried a page-one story under the heading: "Claims Jews Abused High Posts They Held to Undermine Germany: Must Be Ousted 'Until House Cleansed' Says Dr. Hanfstaengl: Hitler Perturbed: Hundreds of Thousands Expected at U.S. Protest Meetings To-night." The story reported that the Nazi government would take action if the protest demonstrations, especially the one scheduled for Madison Square Garden that same evening, were not called off.

> The government... is prepared to countenance retaliation in exact ratio to the extent foreign governments countenance the atrocity propaganda. Retaliation will take the form of a boycott, a sharp reduction of the number of Jewish students permitted at German

universities and curtailment of the licenses granted to practising Jewish physicians and lawyers to the proportion of the Jews to the German population which is less than one percent.

The *Star* also reported that Hitler had summoned Goebbels to his mountain retreat in Berchtesgaden to draw up plans to curb "untrue stories of Jewish massacres emanating from obscure sources." In front-page stories on the same day, *Der Yiddisher Zhurnal* concerned itself with the Nazi response to planned protest demonstrations and with the denials of atrocity reports from a variety of German sources.

On 28 March, as part of its front-page story on the Jewish situation in Germany, the *Star* printed a letter by the former crown prince of Germany to a friend, George Sylvester Viereck, in which he denied the truth of the atrocity reports. But the paper also printed two separate confirmations of the atrocity stories. The first was a letter from a man living in Hamburg who had been sent a clipping of a *Star* report on the Nazi violence. He was able to confirm the terror. The second was a letter sent to Sam Bornstein of 76 St. Patrick Street in Toronto by Jews in Elberfeld. Written in Yiddish, it reported that a friend of his had been shot to death and went on to say:

We are in a terrible condition.... We are not sure of our lives and any moment we may get killed. We are afraid to go on the streets—every day they shoot a few Jews.... They have closed all the big Jewish department stores, and stand on guard in front with carbines, hollering to the people not to buy from the Jews. The Jewish butcher here had all his windows smashed in, and armed guards set in front of the store.... You can imagine the condition we are in—we can never go out—we've no money—there never was a time like this before. The worst thing is that we have nowhere to go. Every country is closed to us. We've nowhere to run to.... All we want is to get away with our lives. We're willing to leave everything, if only we can get away safe. We know you people in Canada can't help us, and it's no pleasure having to write you like this, but we must tell someone.... We're at a loss. Any hour or minute, no one knows what may happen. You should be glad you are not here now. Maybe times are not so good, but at least you're sure of your lives. Won't you send us some of the Toronto papers, so that we can see what the world thinks about it all, and see if we have any hope?

On the following day, the *Star* took an editorial stand on the boycott and the denials by the German government of the atrocity stories:

> The Nazis are calling for a boycott of Jews to begin on April first, which is not an "April fool" joke, but criminal folly.
>
> One charge made by Hitlerites against German Jews is that they libel the fatherland. But nothing has brought so much discredit to Germany since the war as the conduct of Hitler's followers.

On the eve of the boycott, the *Evening Telegram* carried an interview with a member of the German Nazi party living in Toronto. Gerhard Kantorowicz, who had lived in Canada since 1930, had joined the NS-DAP in 1927. He informed the Toronto papers that the reports of persecutions in Germany were simply untrue.[3] On the same day the *Star* carried a more detailed report of Kantorowicz's denial and of his accusation that Jewish firms were firing their German employees in Toronto. The headline ran: "Toronto Jew Firms Dismiss 75 Germans, Says Nazi No. 57312: Declares Propaganda Abroad Only Make Matters Worse for German Jews: Staunch Fascist." And the report read:

> What firms in Toronto have reacted to the stories of Jewish persecution in Germany by dismissing their German employees, the young Nazi refused to say. Neither would he reveal names.
>
> "I can only say that if it keeps up a cable will be sent to Hitler from Toronto.... "
>
> Like his leader, Kantorowicz claims the stories of the persecution of the Jews by the Nazis are exaggerated. "They sound like stories you used to hear about the atrocities in Belgium, and like the ones we used to hear about your soldiers during the war," says Kantorowicz, who is 28.
>
> "You know the whole trouble is the Jews began to howl just as soon as they saw Hitler becoming strong. Those Jews who since the war have bought their way into positions knew they were doomed. Hitler would clean them out, they knew quite well, and so they are trying to gain sympathy."[4]

The German government used the atrocity reports, according to the *Star*, as an excuse to ban scores of foreign newspapers in Germany on grounds that they had spread atrocity "lies." Meanwhile, Jewish refugees were pouring across the German borders into Denmark and Czecho-slovakia.

On the day of the boycott, the *Evening Telegram* took up the issue of the persecution of Jews in Germany in its weekly op-ed-page column "Keeping Pace with Time." The uncertainty expressed in the column was typical for the *Tely*, which tended to leave room for doubt when it came to the atrocity stories emanating from Germany: "Who is wrong and who is right?" the *Tely* asked, and, after setting out the case for both sides, concluded:

> On the other hand the Jews claim that he [Hitler] is mercilessly persecuting them, just because he hates them; and that his follow-ers expect him to permit them to do as they like with the Jews. They claim that he is rabidly anti-Semitic, always has been and always will be.
>
> So you see, both sides have common sense and logic in their argument. Germany to-day is undergoing terrific changes, and it will be hard for a few days yet really to get a straight slant on the panorama. That Hitler is working hard to bring back the Germa-ny of old is quite apparent; but for him to fear the Jews seems a bit ridiculous when we remember that the total Hebrew population of Germany is only about 600,000—just a little over one per cent of the total population.

In his column in the *Zhurnal* of 2 April, entitled "The Blood Cry," M. Vogel examined the Nazi claim that only criminal Jews were singled out for attack:

> And not a single Jew was brought to justice before a court—not even before a Nazi court—for swindle, and laws were passed, even before we began our "Katzenjammer," to throw Jews out of pub-lic office, not to give employment to Jewish labourers, not to buy from Jews. Jews were shot and tortured alive and in not a single case was effort given to dream up even a false accusation that the expelled Jew, the tortured Jew, the murdered Jew, was a swindler, a traitor, or a criminal.

The *Evening Telegram* at the same time published a front-page report to counter Pierre van Paassen's reports of atrocities in the rival *Star*. The refutation was based on information supplied by E. K. Simpson, a former German newspaperman.

> "Racial hatred is promoted rather than dissipated by publication of the van Paassen articles," Mr. Simpson maintained, and he added his opinion that "no responsible paper ought to print such sensational reports"....
>
> [Simpson] suggests that, in his recent articles from Germany, van Paassen has distorted and exaggerated the facts either to make his "copy" more acceptable to his newspaper or as deliberate anti-Hitler propaganda.

This "denial" report in the *Telegram* was matched by a "protest" report in the *Star* on the same day. The *Star's* story concerned a protest meeting in France at which refugees from Germany told their harrowing story:

> Thousands wept as one of the German speakers gave a sober account of what he had witnessed in a Nazi prison. The speaker's name is an honored one in international scientific circles. He is a personal friend of Ramsay MacDonald and Sidney Webb. The account of the atrocities this man gave can not here be repeated. All I can say is that the deeds of Naziism described by him are so bestially depraved that their like is not known in the annals of the darkest middle ages. They make one's hair stand on end—yes, and cause one to clench one's fists in impotent rage against these violators of decency and humanity. What is happening in Germany establishes once and for all the truth of the thesis of liberalism, but recently restated by Mr. Mackenzie King, to wit: Suppressive measures, instead of crushing popular movements of discontent, serve to furnish them with a more bitter, a more determined resolution to resist. Hitlerism is turning hundreds of thousands of people in the Reich into unconscious Bolsheviks. It is destroying its own ends, or it blazes the way inevitably for a day of reckoning.

On 6 April both the *Evening Telegram* and the *Star* carried a story in which Hitler suggested that the treatment of the Jews by his regime was no different from the treatment of Orientals by the American government: "Chancellor Adolf Hitler," wrote the *Tely*, "pointed to the United States Exclusion Act against the yellow race as a precedent in explaining today his purpose in removing Jewish intellectuals from medical, legal, artistic and scientific positions in Germany." Another *Tely* "denial" story in the same edition, from the paper's London correspondent, W. T. Cranfield, accused German Jews of grabbing all the best positions in the turmoil following Germany's defeat in the Great War and thus bringing upon themselves the attacks of the German government and the hatred of the German people.

Der Yiddisher Zhurnal on the following day attacked the Cranfield story as a whitewash of the Nazis that displayed their prejudices. Was Cranfield an agent of Hitler or simply an antisemite, the editorial asked.

Not at all abashed, on 8 April the *Telegram* carried two more "denial" articles. The first was an interview with Dr. Otto Hahn, director of the Kaiser Wilhelm Institute of Chemistry, Berlin-Dahlem, who was in Toronto to address the Royal Canadian Institute. Dr. Hahn

> ...arrived at the Union Station this morning to find confronting him a poster of a Toronto newspaper screaming in blue letters:
> "Nazi Fiends Scourge Jews—First Hand Accounts of German Atrocities."
> Dr. Hahn looked at it and somewhat sarcastically remarked, "Is it nice?"
> He denounced it as downright exaggeration. It reminded him, he said, of some papers in the United States which spread across their front pages lurid description of violence and torture of the massacre of prominent Jews.
> "And the next day," he said, "in the back pages, inconspicuously small, was a little interview with the same massacred gentleman."

The second item was the weekly op-ed-page column, "Keeping Pace with Time":

> The Jews say that they are being persecuted, and this past week we have tried all over the lot to get the low down on the whole thing, with the result that we have come to the conclusion the picture is not anything like as bad as certain parts of the press are trying to make it....

Towards the end of the article the columnist dropped the non-committal "on the one hand...on the other hand" approach (which was in any event but a thin veil over his pro-Hitler stance) and came out against the latest move by Hitler:

> However, the latest Hitler move is of much more import. He intends to do away, so we hear, with the Old Testament. He claims it has nothing to do with living to-day and that it is merely the history of a number of quarrels that don't help the world at all today. Here's the one spot in the picture that doesn't sit so well with us. Hitler, or no living man, in our belief, has any right to interfere with any other man's religion. It makes no difference to us what a man's belief may be, he is entitled to it....
>
> So there you have the picture at the moment in Germany. The entire country is rent and if we are not mistaken, trouble lies just around the corner and it won't take as long to find as the much mooted prosperity. Germany is going through a chemicalization period that is most unpleasant to behold, particularly when we can't see the outcome ahead.

The *Telegram* might be still casting doubt on the atrocity reports, but the *Star* was by now the Toronto crusader for German Jewry. In a Pierre van Paassen column on the editorial page on 6 April, German antisemitism was put into historical perspective, along with Hitler's place in that tradition:

> To-day Hitler has taken up the sordid task of Jew-baiter. Again the Jew is the scapegoat. Again he is doomed to assume the role of the sacrificial victim, the *salutaris hostia*, whose death and suffering is to bring salvation to the German nation. This time it is Hitler's Germany which has chosen the Jew as a vicarious atonement, that old device, by which man avoids the ultimate facing of reality, by which he seeks to escape guilt and the duty of accepting the consequences.... Always a son of man must be nailed upon the cross, to carry the sins of his brethren. This time, as it was a thousand times before, that man is the People of Israel....

In an editorial on 7 April, entitled "Certain Evils Coming to a Head in Germany," the *Star* contended:

> These shocking stories of cruelty to Liberals and Communists

and, most grievous of all, to the great people to which Christian nations owe the most precious elements of their civilization, have called to memory war stories we were gladly forgetting. Those war stories of German cruelty were doubtless exaggerated. That might easily happen in the heated atmosphere of war. But these stories have the same characteristics and there has been no war to provoke them.... It is impossible, therefore, to believe that these "atrocity stories" were inventions of Jews. They are not only convincing but they almost compel one to believe that there was some measure of truth in the atrocity stories reported of the Germans in Belgium and France.

On 10 April the *Star* carried a front-page report of fresh evidence of Nazi persecution provided by Jewish refugees arriving in London. Under the heading: "Jews Flee to London Still Bearing Scars of Nazi Atrocities," the *Star* gave details of what it described as "one of the worst anti-Semitic persecutions in history." It also took note of a threat made by one of the German newspapers against Germany's Jews concerning bloody reprisals if an attempt should be made on the life of Adolf Hitler.

In the same edition of the *Star*, Pierre van Paassen answered his detractors at the *Telegram*. He began with an outline of how well-meaning liberals, democrats, clergymen, and intellectuals had, since the end of the Great War, worked hard to bring about a reconciliation with Germany and to dispel anti-German prejudice. But Hitler's accession to power had destroyed the results of their labours:

To-day that sympathy has been wiped out. In a few weeks' time, the atmosphere of goodwill, which it took years of patient and persistent effort to build up, was dispelled by the actions of Hitlerism.... The men and women in Germany who responded to the approach of good will and friendship, exactly they and no others are being crushed under the barbaric dictatorship of the Nazis. Junkers, militarist sabre-rattlers, feudalistic landlords, the whole clan which represents brute nationalism and insolent militarism once more have the great German people under their heel and in their power....

They expel foreigners by the thousands. Hundreds of Serbs, Bulgars, Russians and Poles have been beaten up in the last few weeks, according to the special correspondent of the *Manchester Guardian*. Hitler writes openly that the French are an inferior

race, half-Jew and half negro. The moment they came to power they began, as they had promised for years, to persecute the
Jews....

Newspapers which tell their readers what has occurred lately
in the Reich are banned. Correspondents who brought the deeds
of Nazi storm-troopers to the attention of the world are discredit-
ed. They are denounced as cheap and vulgar liars in the pay of the
Jewish world syndicate. The terror is denied.... Their stupid belief
in our gullibility is so grotesque that it is almost pathetic.

Van Paassen also considered the attacks levelled at him personally,
and in his defence cited a testimonial given him by none other than the
German ambassador in Washington.

The controversy over van Paassen's reports continued, however. On
the following day the *Star* printed a statement from Ludwig Kempff,
German Consul-General in Montreal, denying the atrocity allegations
in van Paassen's reports. The *Star* cabled the text of the statement to
van Paassen, who wrote a reply defending his reporting of the situation in Germany and suggesting that Kempff was acting under strict
orders from Berlin: "This was as plain a case of intimidation as can be
imagined."

The *Star* backed van Paassen in its edition of 12 April, but the *Telegram* published an editorial on the same day, entitled "Report of Atrocities Appear Largely Exaggerated." In a thinly veiled reference to van
Paassen, the editor asserted that:

Tales of anti-Semitic atrocities in Germany are met with official
German denials. Accounts of barbarous practices have been related by peripatetic correspondents somewhere outside Germany
and have been contradicted by those who speak for the German
government.

If this were the only evidence available, it might be difficult for
the outside world to reach any satisfying conclusion....

But communication with Germany has not been cut off. And
unless Germans generally are linked in a conspiracy to suppress
the facts it is difficult to believe that a pogrom is in progress. Letters from German individuals indicate that the country is tran-
quil....

To this internal evidence must be added the reports of the

Associated Press specifically denying some of the worst atrocities which have been reported. Non-German travellers who have recently arrived in Toronto from Germany also report that they have seen nothing to lead them to believe the atrocity reports which have been circulated.

That members of the Hebrew race have been made the victims of oppression in Germany under the Nazi regime, and that there has been a considerable exodus as a result, need not be doubted. But it appears that too much reliance has been placed in reports of the extent to which the anti-Semitic movement has gone.

In order to introduce some measure of "objectivity" into the situation, George Hambleton, European staff correspondent of the Canadian Press, was instructed to go to Berlin on 5 April and provide as accurate a report as possible to Canadian readers. The *Star* carried the report, which he filed from London on 12 April.

According to Hambleton:

The conflict with Jewry has brought wild propaganda from both sides. One hears strange stories of alleged ill-treatment of Jews in the "brown houses," the quarters of Hitler's brown shirt army. Polish authorities in Berlin claim to have 81 authenticated cases of physical violence against Polish Jews.

But the actual facts are difficult to obtain. Special courts are busy meting out terms of imprisonment on those caught spreading reports of German frightfulness. One photographic agency which widely supplies news pictures to the foreign press had an operator present during a recent Nazi raid. The police afterward visited the dark-room as the operator developed his plate. Any negatives which showed evidence of violence were confiscated. Only harmless ones were allowed out.

Hambleton went on to consider the tough lot of the Jews who had been barred from practising their professions in medicine, law, and the arts and sciences.

Unconvinced by the reports, on 15 April the *Telegram* carried as front-page news the denials of a Mr. Mittelstedt, a German businessman who had recently left Germany.

198 THE RIOT AT CHRISTIE PITS

"Utter lies" and "gross exaggerations" are terms applied by Hermann Mittelstedt, German businessman, to some of the press reports emanating from Germany regarding the German-Jew situation. Mr. Mittelstedt, who left Germany within the past three weeks, told the *Telegram* that much of the "propaganda" was "unbelievably ridiculous."

He declared that there were no such things as "atrocities," that the press was "not muzzled," and that there was no such thing as press censorship. Since he left Elberfeld, centre of the German textile trade, letters from his wife had confirmed his belief that all was quiet near his home.

The vigorous blue-eyed German representative of a big textile firm was indignant that Canadians should for a moment believe that the "German people could be guilty of the cruel acts attributed to them" by certain sections of the press.

UNCONNECTED WITH RACE

"We were told they killed a Jew in Elberfeld," said the *Telegram*.

"Ridiculous! A Jew was killed," he explained with his quick English, "but he was a Communist, and was killed in a fight between Nationalists, Socialists and Communists."

He added that the incident had nothing to do with the victim's race.

Mittelstedt happened to have in his possession a letter written by Walter Peltzer, "of the great Peltzer organization," which Mittelstedt believed represented the true sentiments of the Germans in the textile trade. According to this letter:

No personal actions against Germans of Jewish confession have taken place, nor have any assaults endangered the life of a German Jew. Our Government guarantees the personal security of each citizen living in our country, no matter whether he is a Jew or not....

Peace is needed throughout the world! Instead of fighting with each other, let us co-operate.

We believe that this is the only way of overcoming the world's crisis.

Please assist us in our efforts to re-establish the truth in our mutual interest and to the benefit of the whole world.

In the same edition of the *Telegram,* the "Keeping Pace with Time" columnist was once again concerned with the question of anti-Jewish persecution in Germany. Once again the writer refused to take a definite stand but, as in the past, continued to present German rationalizations for atrocity propaganda:

NOT REAL JEWS

But on we go down to Berlin, Germany, to gather in the noise that is escaping from there—and how it is bubbling out. Stories are reaching our ears of highways being crowded with Jewish refugees, forced from their homes and deprived of everything they hold dear. But, at the same time, comes the voice of Hitler assuring us that the Jews who are being persecuted are Communists, and not in any way to be considered real German Jews. These people, so he says, are Jews from other parts of Europe, who came into Germany during the Great War and who are profiteers and a lot of other unpleasant things.

WORTH SOME THOUGHT

Some of the ex-leaders in German politics were Jews who haven't a very good name in Germany. They have been known for a long time as a hard lot, and so we are a bit slow to swallow all the dope being pumped out in the name of "humanity" about the Jewish persecutions.... We must remember that Germany has just come through a revolution; the whole country has been in an upheaval, and it would seem to us that, while there have doubtless been many unpleasant things happening in that country, it hasn't by any manner of means gone berserk altogether.

As if in response to such denials, Pierre van Paassen, in a front-page story in the *Star,* reported on the organized campaign launched by Hitler to stem the mounting tide of protest in foreign countries against the Nazi persecution of Jews. He concluded:

It should not be forgotten that the entire opposition press in Germany is muzzled or utterly silenced. It should not be overlooked that those in prison can not tell of the sufferings and indignities they undergo at the hands of Hitler's brown-shirted henchmen. Neither should it be forgotten that the thousands of refugees abroad are still too horror-struck to speak freely and prefer to keep silent in order to save left-behind relatives from reprisals by the Nazis.

The full extent of the terror is not yet known, although the mass of evidence is constantly growing. There remain many in this world determined to bring the full light of day on this episode of contemporary history which throws back the cause of civilization for a hundred years. Humanity is no stronger than its weakest link. Germany is that link to-day. Some day or other we are all bound to feel the repercussions of that defeat of the forces of democracy in the Reich.

On Hitler's birthday, 20 April, the *Telegram* carried yet another denial story on its front page. A Toronto businessman, A. C. Burke of Inglewood Drive, had just returned from a business trip to Germany and claimed to have seen nothing that would corroborate the atrocity stories carried by some newspapers. According to Burke:

Undoubtedly there is a strong feeling of antagonism toward the Jews.... They are said to dominate the medical and legal professions, besides many business enterprises to an extent that amounts to a virtual monopoly. Rightly or wrongly, too, they are blamed for much of the Communistic agitation, and, having bet on the wrong horse in the German political readjustments, are not particularly popular with the dominant party. In Berlin, and other great cities, I went out of my way to find evidence of this harsh feeling having manifested itself in violence, and found none.

Although Burke claimed to have been an impartial observer, he went on in the article to say that he had been

...a week-end guest of Count Bernstorff whose castle is in the centre of a vast estate about thirty miles from Hamburg....

According to Bernstorff, the Nazi movement was forced upon the German people as a defensive measure. So audacious had the Red element become that even in the comparatively secluded section of the country where the Count's estate is located, sniping had resulted in three fatalities among the more conservative people deemed objectionable by the Communists. After that, Bernstorff organized the men of his neighborhood, and drilled them—and, while neither fatalities nor even serious injuries resulted for the Reds, they were "cleaned up," particularly in one village.

In the same edition, Burke's "observations" were buttressed by a letter, dated 2 April, from a University of Toronto graduate who was studying in Germany. The letter read, in part:

> I suppose you have read about the agitation, especially in America and England, caused by "atrocities" against Jews in Germany. Unlike most of my Canadian and English friends in Goettingen, I am siding with the Nazis in the affair. The National-Socialist program is, of course, anti-Jewish—that is inevitable. But there were certainly no atrocities nor any active anti-Semitism until the foreign Jews began to make such a fuss and concoct such lies....
>
> Altogether the lot of the Jew in Germany is not enviable just now, but I still persist in thinking that it is the result of misguided activities of their fellow Jews in America and England. Incidentally, Einstein is making a terrible fool of himself....

On 24 April the *Star* once again came to the defence of Pierre van Paassen. Prominently displayed on the front page the newspaper ran a picture of his face beside Hitler's in order to show the physical resemblance between the two men. Among the accusations levelled at van Paassen was the charge that he was a Jew. The heading above the picture read: "PIERRE VAN PAASSEN IS NOT A JEW."

On 29 April the *Star* published a front-page article in which van Paassen challenged the German authorities to throw open the country to a free commission of inquiry into the atrocity stories. A letter sent by van Paassen to the ex-German crown prince—who through a spokesman named Viereck[5] had denied the allegations of government terror—received no reply. Van Paassen concluded: "But Herr Hitler and Herr Goebbels do not want investigators. They want men who will deny the atrocities and the terror."

In the same edition, also on the front page, the *Star* carried an article by M. H. Halton,[6] another correspondent who had been writing of the terror hanging over German Jews. Halton's willingness to blame the German Jews for their misfortunes under the Nazi regime strikes a discordant note, however. "Jews Are Not Blameless for Scourge, Says Rabbi: Gross Sections Fattened in Germany While Others Suffered...," the headline ran.

> Down in a London slum last night I stood talking to an old Jewish rabbi. In the same room were a score of men, women and children, Jews, who have fled from the curse which is scourging their race in Germany.
>
> "Young man" said the rabbi, "I thank you for the zeal you are showing for the welfare of my people in Germany. But I would not have you think that we are entirely blameless."
>
> He was silent for a moment, and I turned in surprise to hear what he had to say. He took me aside.
>
> "I would not have you forget," he said, "that there are two sides to modern Jewry. On the one hand you have, in the ghetto, the fine noble flame of Jewish genius and Jewish idealism—the white, mighty flame which 2,000 years of persecution has [sic] been unable to extinguish.
>
> "But on the other hand—and I say it with the deepest regret and sorrow and shame—you have the side against which our teachers and prophets have been thundering since the dawn of history—since the days of the golden calf. I say it plainly, that there are rich gross sections of our people, especially in Germany, who have fattened themselves while others have suffered."

In its weekly column "Keeping Pace with Time," the *Telegram* once again drew the link between Communism and the Jews that was the habitual defence against criticism of the Nazi persecutions. As well, a *Telegram* editorial in the 29 April issue repeated the Nazi line that the violence that was occurring in the wake of the Nazi revolution was no worse—and in fact was less serious—than the violence that was part of the fabric of American society. Using a false analogy the editors wrote:

> Americans who were sitting in judgment on Germany might ponder an item sent out by the Associated Press from a small town in Iowa where a crowd of more than one hundred farmers dragged a judge off the bench, beat him, carried him blind-folded in a truck to a crossroads, put a rope around his neck, choked him until he was only partly conscious, smeared grease on his face and left him in this pitiable state after removing his trousers. This outburst of

mob law was occasioned by the judge in the discharge of his duties granting foreclosures on farms....

Pierre van Paassen, meanwhile, received confirmation of his atrocity reports in the accounts of Dr. Georg Bernardt, former editor-in-chief of the pre-Nazi, liberal Berlin newspaper *Vossische Zeitung*. Bernhardt, who had escaped to Sweden, continued to report from there on the situation in Germany:

> Dr. Bernardt "fully and unhesitatingly" confirms the reports published by the *Toronto Star* and other foreign liberal papers on the Hitlerite wave of terror, naming many instances of gruesome atrocities which came to his personal attention....
>
> Another matter to which Dr. Bernardt draws attention is that the thousands of letters written by individual German citizens, many of them Jews, to foreign friends, acquaintances, business relations and public bodies, newspapers included, abroad, were ordered by the Nazi authorities under threat of reprisals....
>
> Certain startling examples are given of letters written by people who, on reaching safety abroad, at a later date, promptly informed their correspondents that they had written the commendations of the Nazi regime under pressure, either moral or physical.

On 13 May the *Toronto Daily Star* was banned from Germany "for [publishing] articles by a Dutch Jew." The *Star* carried the news on the same day in a front-page story in which it included a short biography of the journalist who had so offended the Germans. Van Paassen, the *Star* reported, was not a Jew. Born in Holland of Dutch parents, he had come to Toronto as a young child. He was a member of the Church of the Ascension in Toronto.

> "There is not one drop of Jewish blood in Pierre," declared Adriaan van Paassen, father of Pierre van Paassen, when interviewed by the *Star* at his home, 9 Temple Ave. "He is Dutch of the Dutch on both sides and we can trace our ancestry back hundreds of years."

Two days later, the *Star* commented on the ban:

> The Hitler government of Germany has banned the *Toronto Daily Star*, the *Manchester Guardian*, the *New Statesman* and the *Week-*

End Review. These publications will not be allowed to enter Germany.

In being thus excluded, the *Star* finds itself in good company.

The *Star's* and the *Tely's* reporting of atrocities—and the controversy about it in both papers—died down for the rest of May and June. *Der Yiddisher Zhurnal* had never had any doubt about the extent of the persecutions and commented on the denials primarily in order to express its outrage either at the tricks used by the Nazis to dupe the public or at the gullibility of those who bought the Nazi line.

By 11 July, the *Telegram* was reporting that Hitler had declared the Nazi revolution over. The stressful events of the past months would now give way to a period of peace and order. Once again, Hitler had attributed the terror to revolutionary exuberance.

This "explanation" was echoed by Friedrick Krogmann, president of Hamburg, in a 21 July interview with M. H. Halton of the *Star.*

> "In a revolution you must expect a terror. But I tell you, 99 percent of all the stories you have heard about atrocities in Germany are lies, lies, lies!"...
>
> "Herr Krogmann, how did it happen that so many lies were circulated throughout the world?" I asked.
>
> "Jewish propaganda," he said.
>
> "Were all the terror reports that appeared in the *Times* and the *Manchester Guardian*, the *Toronto Star* and other papers—were they all lies?"
>
> "Jewish propaganda," he said.
>
> "What!" I protested, "in the *Times*?" "Certainly," he said, "Jewish or Socialist propaganda. The *Times* may be conservative enough, but its correspondents—that is a different matter."
>
> "Herr Krogmann," I continued, "I saw Jews who had been tortured. Was that propaganda on their part?" "In a revolution," he repeated, "you must expect a terror. Ninety-nine per cent of the stories are propaganda."

Finally, despite its tendency to play down the atrocity reports, on 29 July the *Evening Telegram* published a convincing article by Henry J. Haskell that clearly established the fact of anti-Jewish terror in Germany. Haskell began by describing a book that was on sale in Berlin in German, English, and French. The book was entitled *Atrocity Propaganda Is Based on Lies, Say the Jews of Germany Themselves,* and contained statements from high-ranking Nazis denying the atrocity stories, including a denial from Hitler himself:

> "All these accounts," says the Hitler statement, "are vile lies. During the course of the present revolution, which was the most orderly and peaceful revolution in the world's history, unavoidable friction occurred between small groups of political enemies. There has been, however, no singling out of Jews and non-Jews for individual treatment."
>
> Then follow communiqués from various Jewish organizations to the general effect that "the tales of atrocities committed against our race are based on lies." The Board and Rabbinical Committee of the Jewish Community, Berlin, goes so far as to admit that "Germany's Jewish families have been plunged into uncertainty and sorrow. But we have full confidence in the president and government of the Reich that measures leading to economic ruin of the German Jews will be avoided."

Haskell then contrasted these denials with his own information, which included reports of beatings and torture. None of the beatings and tortures were conducted in public, however, and censorship prevented them from being reported in the press. It is conceivable he argues, that "multitudes of Germans do not know that they took place." Nevertheless, in his view, "there is not the slightest question of the facts, and in many instances the brutalities were unprintable." Seeing through the denials, he accurately portrayed one common defensive tactic of the Nazi regime:

> The official defence in a word is this: "We have been conducting a revolution. It has been comparatively gentle. Only a few people have been killed. (There is no way of knowing how many Jews and Communists died from their beatings.) If we had slaughtered our opponents wholesale so the streets of Berlin had run with blood, outsiders would have said, 'What can you expect in a revolution?' But because a few Jews were beaten, the world has resounded with protests."

Debate on "the Jewish question" could also be seen in the letters to the editors of the *Star* and *Telegram*. Although stimulated by the reports and denials of anti-Jewish persecution in Germany, these letters often expressed views about the Jewish minority in Canada. Though these comments are not necessarily representative of sentiment in Toronto as a whole, they nevertheless provide clues to opinions about Jews and the nature of antisemitism at the time.

Readers' letters published in the *Star* and the *Telegram* generally reflected the differing views of the two papers. The letters in the *Star* tended to be pro-Jewish, anti-Hitler, and liberal in character. The letters printed by the *Telegram* were, for the most part, highly skeptical of atrocity reports, soft on Hitlerism, and anti-Jewish.

On 25 March the *Telegram* printed a letter from a student who identified the radical leftist youth at the university as Jews:

> A glance at the names of these youthful orators and strife fomenters is revealing. They all suggest a central European origin. These boys are possibly all the sons of Polish, German, or Russian folk of Jewish faith, emigrants who have fled the endless suppression and possibly persecutions of centuries in Europe where they found opportunities of bettering their lot always denied. They came to this new British land where equality of opportunity was not denied them, where they have escaped mindless poverty, and where their children find high schools and universities with open doors and no bounds set to their advancement.
>
> These are their sons who are showing their ingratitude and lack of appreciation of all that this land offers them by deriding the things Canadians hold dear, scorning the very institutions that gave them this freedom and great life chances, fomenting hatred. In short, working to set up the bitter things their fathers and mothers fled from.[7]

In a letter of 22 April, again in the *Telegram*, a reader equates Communists and Jews, and argues that Hitler is justified in his firm actions against the Communists:

> Comparing the German Jews with the Russian Jews: In 1913, perhaps the most terrible massacre in the history of the world took place in Russia. Most of the leaders of that disgraceful carnage are said to have been Jews, acting on the teachings of Karl Marx, who

was also a Jew, and most of the leaders in Soviet Russia since that time have also been Jewish....

But now when the Communistic Jews in Germany have failed to secure the upper hand after having given no end of trouble to the German people, they issued misleading reports about injustices they claim to have suffered in Germany....

According to authentic reports from Germany, there has been little or no injustice there. The Government is simply trying to keep the Reds in their place, the same as our Governments have had to do.... Jewish Communists in Germany have been sending out false reports in the hope of gaining world sympathy.

The Reds are out to destroy all responsible government and all religions, and home life, and nearly everything that is pure and good. They are not entitled to our sympathy.[8]

On 4 May the *Star* published a letter that took issue with M. Halton's story blaming the Jews for their own misfortunes. The reader denied that Jews were the corrupters of morality in Germany:

Jews have served their respective countries faithfully. In Great Britain Disraeli founded the empire with Rothschild's millions, and all those lords of Jewish extraction who have distinguished themselves in their service for the country. Could you imagine their kind to be running nudist parties, brothels, obscene nightclubs, etc.? Do you think Rathenaus, Einsteins, Teuchenbroenger, Nordaus, etc., to be the demoralizing element the Hitler side alleges the Jews to be in Germany? Mr. Halton does not believe it, of course; no one does.

The Jews are supposed to be in control of the press, theatre, cinema, etc., and through this medium polluted German morals. Do you think Mr. Reinhardt's production of *The Miracle* would have such an effect, or Emil Ludwig's biographies, or Mendelssohn's music or Bruno Walter's interpretations of music, and countless journalists and scientists who have caused the whole world to respect Germany? It is Hugenberg, Hitler's ally, who controls the press, the theatre, cinema and radio in Germany, and no one accuses him. The Germans lost the war and blamed the Jews! Stinnes, a German Gentile, ruined Germany through the inflation and wiped out the German middle class and now the Tietz and Wertheim, etc., etc., department stores are blamed for it....

You may ask why Jewish professionals are so successful in Germany. The answer is simple. The Jewish student has to work hard to get by. What the Gentile student gets served predigested the Jewish student has to chew himself, with the result that in practice the Jewish lawyer or doctor is better equipped.

The German student wastes his energies on *Mensuren* (duels) and *Kneipen* (beer-drinking orgies), staged by his Corp, *Burschenschaft*, etc., to which Jews are not admitted. Instead the Jewish student indulges in his studies, cultivation of art and literature, and finishes on top.

I have had the experience, I have passed examinations at a university where in physics, for instance, our professor's first question was "What is your religion?" and out of 28 Jewish candidates that year only six of us passed. However, we are Jews born to suffer—and to forgive.[9]

A letter from L. J. Solway to the editor of the *Star* about the attack launched upon Jewish medical practitioners by the Nazis quoted from a letter written some fifty years earlier by Sir William Osler—a letter occasioned by an outbreak of antisemitism in Berlin during the 1880s:

The modem "hep, hep, hep" shrieked in Berlin for some years past has by no means died out, and to judge from the tone of several of the papers devoted to the Jewish question they are not wanting some who would gladly revert to the plan adopted on the Nile some thousands of years ago for solving the Malthusian problem of Semitic increase....

Should another Moses arise and preach Semitic exodus from Germany, and should he prevail, they would leave the land impoverished far more than was ancient Egypt by the loss of the "jewels of gold and jewels of silver" of which the people were "spoiled." To say nothing of the material wealth—enough to buy Palestine over and over again from the Turk—there is not a profession which would not suffer the serious loss of many of its most brilliant ornaments and none more so than in our own.

Two days later, on 12 May, the *Star* included among its letters to the editor a note from a German-Canadian denying the atrocity stories. He had sent clippings from the *Star* to his mother and brothers in Germany and he wished to report their reactions:

I now receive an answer which might interest you. These stories of maltreatment and terrorism they say are untrue and made in the foreign press to hurt Germany. It is true that there have been acts of personal revenge.

In the summer resorts of the Rhine valley (where I come from) the foreigners are welcomed with the same hospitality as ever.

On 22 May the *Star* published a letter from a G. Brooks who had sent along an item printed on 14 April in the *Nasz Przeglad,* a Polish periodical published in Warsaw. The Polish article ridiculed the Nazi attack on Jewish doctors, arguing that if consistency were to be followed, many modern medical discoveries could not be used by the Nazis.

The National Socialists in Germany have announced a boycott of everything that is Jewish. In every sphere of life they search for traces of Jewish influence. In order to facilitate their work at least in the sphere of medicine we would suggest the following:

A Nazist suffering from syphilis must not cure himself with salvaran... because this medicine is an invention of Dr. Ehrlich, a Jew. It should also be forbidden to make blood tests by the method of Wasserman for the purpose of ascertaining if a patient is suffering from syphilis, because Wasserman was a Jew.

No heart disease should be treated with digitalis. It is admitted that this is a wonderful treatment against heart diseases and that medicine would be helpless without it, but we must not use it as a Jew, Ludwig Traube, discovered it.

Against toothache a Nazist must not use cocaine, because it comes from a Jew, Solomon Stricker.

When there is suspicion of typhoid fever, better make no blood test for ascertaining the diagnosis as this is also a Jewish invention. People often get headaches, and then generally use pyramidon or antipyrin. This must be stopped. Better let the head ache stay then use medicine discovered by a Jew, Filege.

In cases of severe convulsions in children and adults it is strictly forbidden to use a treatment discovered by a Jew, Oscar Libreich.

In an anti-Jewish letter to the *Telegram,* published on 25 May, W. W. Byers argued that the Jews were playing for sympathy, but that most Canadians would support Hitler if they knew the truth:

I hope all the criticisms directed at Hitler are his curtailment of Jewish activity in Germany are not general among Canadians. The Jews in this country, especially in this city, are endeavoring to gain the sympathy of the citizens in their cause of so-called justice....

Hitler would no doubt be welcomed to Toronto by most Canadian citizens if it were known to them that certain Canadian firms were employing cheap Jewish labor in place of their former employees who are now walking the streets.

On 21 June, Grant Balfour had a letter published in the *Star* in which he asks why no statesman in present-day Great Britain had the courage to denounce the "Nazi cruelties" as Gladstone had denounced atrocities committed by the Turks in Bulgaria.

The 11 July anti-Hitler march to Queen's Park drew considerable ire from readers of the *Telegram*—a predictable response considering that newspaper's coverage of the event. On 14 July two anonymous letters expressed outrage at the "desecration" of the cenotaph by the printed signs and placards carried by the marchers. Letter one read:

Persecuted people and malcontents from all over the world have found sanctuary in Canada under the British flag. They have been made welcome and have prospered. We are not asking for any expression of gratitude. You can't expect much but a grunt from a pig, but we will not see our war memorials desecrated or tamely submit to public demonstrations of rank treason.

...If the Jews of Germany encouraged disloyal parades of the kind witnessed here on Tuesday, is it any wonder that Hitler planted his iron heel on their necks?

Letter two demanded to be shown

...any other civilized "white man's" country where foreigners would be allowed to debase a monument erected to commemo-rate the passing of those who gave their lives for their country. It is simply "abominable" that the foreigners who have found sanc-tuary in this city or other place in this fair land should be allowed to besmirch a monument erected to our faithful dead with their rotten Communistic performances.

Because a state of affairs in Germany, brought about by the Jews themselves, is disastrous to the said Jews, then those in To-ronto who wish to show their disrespect in all matters pertaining, and I suppose we have to sit by, be "doormats" and let them go to it. Why should these foreigners be allowed to stir up trouble in this country and make ill-feelings towards us in Germany while our statesmen are at the present time trying to bring about peace in the world?

After two such letters on 17 and 18 July, the *Telegram* finally printed one short letter from "a Canadian Jew," in which the antisemitism of other letters is roundly criticized. This letter points out that many Jews died in defence of Britain in the Great War, asks whether the antisemitic letter writers are of German descent, and then addresses the charge of Communism:

We have "Reds" amongst the Jews just as every nation has them and we despise them, as you do yours. In closing may I ask the writer if he made a personal check-up of the Jews or was he merely guessing, and to remind him that amongst the nine Communists in Kingston only one is a Jew, so why pick on us?

On the same day, the *Star* published a letter from M. Tate of Markham Street criticizing an anti-Jewish editorial in the *Telegram* on 13 July. The editorial had quoted from a letter that claimed the Jews were encouraging antisemitism by their behaviour. Tate selected several points for specific refutation:

The letter reads "a check-up of the birthplace of thousands of Jews would reveal that most are of Russian descent and in sympathy with anything Russian." It would be interesting to learn whether the writer made the mentioned check-up. Apparently not as he would have discovered that there are a great number of English, Polish and German Jews in Canada. And of the horrible "Roosian" Jews, he would have found that many had, through their own toil and courage, built up large businesses which now employ and furnish a livelihood to vast numbers of Gentiles.

Our anti-semitic friend states further: "Too much leeway has been given the Jews of this country and if we don't wake up things will be like they were in Germany. Perhaps the Jews will do the fighting in the next war, etc., ad nauseam."

Just what is meant by "too much leeway" is hard to understand when it is realized that Jews have the same citizenship rights as any other racial group in this country. Jews have earned this right through giving the British Empire unwavering support and loyalty for generations. Britain's greatest era of prosperity occurred under the leadership of Disraeli—a Jew. Yes, and even in the late war in which our anti-semitic correspondent insinuates there were no Jewish soldiers, the leader of the Australian and New Zealand forces was a Jew—General Monash.

It is about time that anti-Jewish writers and newspapers cease using every little pretext as a basis for an attack upon the Jewish citizens of this country. The inclusion of the few pro-Communist placards in the anti-Hitler parade is no reason for the *Telegram* blowing a few editorial fuses. It would be just as ridiculous for Jews to consider all Gentiles Communists simply because Tim Buck is a Christian.

Both the *Star* and the *Telegram* provided their readers with reports of the atrocities German Jews faced at the hands of the Nazis. As we have seen, however, the two newspapers diverged widely in the degree of credibility lent to these reports. Regardless of how the newspapers covered and analyzed the Nazi rise to power and the deteriorating situation for German Jewry that resulted, they did provide their readership with a frame of reference within which to understand these occurrences. In short, each newspaper aimed to convey a particular message about the reported events. It is not far-fetched to suggest that the message offered by the *Telegram* helped to sustain unfavourable stereotypes of Jews and provided both organizers and supporters of the Swastika Club a measure of legitimacy—both in their adopting of the swastika as their symbol and in their purported desire to rid the area of obnoxious elements.

Conclusion

The swastika battles in Toronto during August 1933 were among most violent expressions of ethnic animosity in the city's history. Situated within a more or less homogeneous "British" city, the Jews were the most visible minority group in town and such were the target of xenophobic and antisemitic attacks, verbal and physical. Toronto at the time was little more than a loose federation of wards and neighbourhoods, and the concept of territory was clearly demarcated in the different cognitive maps of the city held by various ethnic and religious groups. The concept of territory has also to be seen within the context of the Orange Order's influence throughout the mid-thirties on the political, social, and religious life of the city. The widespread identification between Jews and Communism increased both the xenophobic and the antisemitic response to the Jewish minority. The police under the leadership of Chief Constable Draper were employed to disrupt and demoralize the labour movement and leftist political parties; they also exhibited an anti-Jewish bias. The Italian and Ukrainian allies of the Jewish fighters at the Pits were motivated by ties of friendship with fellow immigrant youth and by animosity towards the majority British youth by whom they too were victimized. Christie Pits can thus be seen as an attempt—and a rather successful one—to settle an old score.

All of the above, however, must be set against the background of the rise of Hitlerism in Germany. The appearance of the swastika and the club formed around it on the eastern beaches, and the defiant display of a swastika flag before Jewish youth at the end of the softball game, were the catalysts of violence. In the minds of Jewish youth, the swastika tied the city's "everyday" antisemitism to the anti-Jewish excesses of the Hitler regime. As *Der Yiddisher Zhurnal* commented, when reporting the knockout handed Max Schmeling by the "Jewish" hero, Max Baer, Baer hit Schmeling, but he was aiming at Hitler. So too the Jewish boys fighting the Pit Gang were also expressing their hostility towards the German brownshirts.

This book has been about a rather unpleasant chapter in the history of Toronto and Canada as a whole. It brings out the character of the society that turned its back on the Jews of Europe and did all it could to keep them from reaching a haven on its ample shores. And yet the book is a tribute to the city today, for Toronto has become a human success story measured against other cities the world over. Although a product of human artifice and thus fraught with problems, Toronto has taken great strides towards making the scores of different ethnic groups who constitute the multicultural mosaic of the city feel safe, secure, welcome, and at home.

The tremendous change in attitude from the pre- to the post-war period is exemplified in the significantly different response of the people of Toronto to a later "Nazi" disturbance. On Sunday 30 May 1965, a riot broke out at Allan Gardens after a self-styled Nazi führer, William John Beattie, declared that he would be there with his supporters to hold a public talk. Several thousand angry members of Toronto's Jewish community, the majority of them survivors of the Holocaust, went to the park to prevent him from speaking. Rumours which spread through the park concerning the arrival of "Nazis" led to attacks upon at least three innocent bystanders, as well as upon Beattie and one of his associates, by the angry crowd.

But no two riots could be as dissimilar as those at Allan Gardens and Christie Pits. At Allan Gardens, the police turned out in force and acted quickly and efficiently to minimize the violence. Beattie and his few followers encountered practically unanimous hostility from all sectors of the population. The *Toronto Star* expressed the view of one of the residents of Rhodes Avenue, the east-end street where Beattie and his Nazis set up their headquarters a month before the riot: "'When I saw that young kid say "Heil Hitler" I could have knocked his block off,' said the grandmother whose three sons served with the Canadian armed forces in World War II and whose relatives were bombed in the London blitz."[1] The police had to guard Nazi "headquarters" around the clock to protect it from the wrath of the Gentile neighbours. The swastika had lost its ambivalence for Toronto's "British" citizenry. In fact, Beattie had no chance to show the swastika. He was attacked the moment he left his vehicle. Alderman David Rotenberg said he saw a swastika on the ground and that it was turned over to the police. But it had played no role in generating the violence.

The riot at Christie Pits saw two substantial, antagonistic groups representing different constituencies in the city ranged against one another.

The Allan Gardens riot pitted thousands of Holocaust survivors and their supporters against less than a handful of misfits and ghosts of the past.

Perhaps the great reconciliation that has occurred can be expressed symbolically in the following story. We contacted a senior citizen living in the Beaches who, we were told, had information concerning the Swastika Club. He declined to meet with us or to provide us with any information. When we pressed him to give us the names of any individuals who might still be in the city who might have been part of or associated with the Swastika Club, he curtly informed us that they were all in Europe. We were puzzled by this until he explained that they were buried there. "Which is more than I can say for some on the other side," he added. The malicious intent of his comment aside, it was a useful reminder of an ironic dimension we had overlooked. Long-time residents of the area around Christie Pits informed us that many members of the Pit Gang never returned from the war in Europe. So, too, some of the Jewish lads who had fought at the Pits fell in Canadian uniform on the European battlefields a decade later. Some of the Jews and Gentiles at odds on the beaches and at the Pits fought side by side for Canada against the army of the swastika. And some of them found eternal peace beside one another.

The story of Christie Pits has been told and retold as part of the mythology of the city. This book will preserve details that might otherwise fade from human memory.[2]

Postscript

On the morning of 17 August 2008, a plaque was unveiled at Christie Pits by the City of Toronto to commemorate the 75th anniversary of the worst race riot in Toronto's history. The story of the riot and the build-up to it has been told in the pages of this book, reissued as an essential work in Canadian Jewish history. This new postscript considers the significance of the riot from the perspective of our current time, for much has changed since the book's first publication in 1987. Marcus Gee, in the new Foreword, rightly points out that, over the last fifty years, multicultural Toronto has become a place of relative harmony and peace between ethnic and racial communities. A riot of the sort experienced at Christie Pits in 1933 is unthinkable in today's city.

And yet there are new manifestations of antisemitism at home and abroad. One of the hottest debates within and without the Jewish communities of the Diaspora concerns the relationship between antisemitism and anti-Zionism. This debate is especially acute on our university campuses where the Israeli-Palestinian question has become the focus of student attention in much the same way, although not quite to the same degree, that the war in Vietnam did for the student generation of the 1960s. And not a few Jewish students participated in events organized by Jewish and non-Jewish organizations which have been critical of Israeli governmental policy. Ranging from what some call the moderate opposition of groups such as J-Street, the New Israel Fund, and some local Hillel chapters to the more radical opposition by groups such as BDS and Justice for Palestine, tensions on and off campus have been increasing over the last decade. Pro-Israel speakers have been attacked and police have had to be called. In Canada, Toronto's York University has become an iconic representative of this conflict and Jewish students wearing *kipot* or displaying the Magen David have reported being verbally assaulted and pushed around. American campuses have experienced similar incidents. Ironically, the same sorts of tensions have arisen on Israeli campuses where left-wing Jewish students have been active in criticizing government policy, which both exemplifies the active character of Israeli democracy and is emblematic of its political tensions. But what is most telling and disconcerting about all of this is that there are opposing assessments of the significance of anti-Zionist and anti-Jewish manifestations by Jews themselves. We have spoken with colleagues on the left and right; the former arguing that the extent of anti-Israel/anti-Jewish manifestations on the campuses is greatly exaggerated and the latter arguing that it is a clear and present danger and a growing threat to the Jewish community as a whole.

Why is all of this relevant to a reconsideration of the riot at Christie Pits? Because the riot was a response to antisemitic provocation, to a culture of antisemitic prejudice, to exclusionary practices and discrimination, and to the calculated display of the swastika in the city at a time when the chronicling of Nazism in Germany was daily fare in the local press. Today it is not the blatant antisemitism of the Nazis and the polite "gentleman's agreement" WASP exclusionism that Jews face, but an antisemitism that is couched in terms of anti-Zionism. Yes, it is possible to be a critic of the policy of the government of Israel without being antisemitic, as indeed is true of at least the majority of Israel's opposition parties. And this is not to say that some, especially younger, Jews in Toronto, elsewhere in Canada, and throughout the Diaspora more generally are not concerned about certain trends in Israeli society. Many are troubled by the predominance of Orthodox Judaism with regard to issues of conversion, marriage, divorce, as well as its hostility toward intermarriage; large numbers of non-orthodox and certainly religiously unaffiliated Jews find it an affront that their offspring would not be considered Jewish by the dominant religious authority in Israel. There are those concerned about what they see as anti-democratic trends in Israel. There is much less unity within the Jewish community in Toronto and in Canada more generally today than there was in the thirties—or even in the eighties when the book first appeared.

The Riot at Christie Pits was first published in 1987 and there were many people living in Toronto who remembered the riot and its impact on the city. It was considered a badge of pride that young Jews had stood up to the provocations of the Swastika Club at the Beaches and the Pit Gang in Willowvale Park (the official name of Christie Pits at the time). But the pride in the violent altercation was also felt in relation to the general culture of antisemitism at the time, reflected in City Hall, in the Orange dominance in the hiring of city workers, police and fire fighters, in the smug prejudice of the WASP elite with their exclusionary clubs, the polite antisemitism of some of the press, the *numerus clausus* at the universities, restrictions in housing, and so on. After World War II, the situation for the Jews improved. The Legion Hall replaced the Orange Lodge as the preferred gathering place for our vets. The coalition of organized labour, the Canadian Jewish Congress, and the liberal churches supported legislation in the late forties and early fifties that ended legal discrimination in employment, housing, recreation, and higher education. The pace of change accelerated with the entrance of the Canadian Civil Liberties Association into the fray, with the moral authority of the Catholic Church through Vatican II, through the voice of Martin Luther King Jr. and the actions of thousands of civil rights volunteers. And it was Martin Luther King Jr. who suggested that anti-Zionism was equivalent to antisemitism.

Judea Pearl, however, father of the brutally murdered journalist Daniel Pearl, drew a clear distinction between the two: "Anti-Zionism rejects the very notion that Jews are a nation—a collective bonded by a common history—and, accordingly, denies Jews the right to self-determination in their historical birthplace. It seeks the dismantling of the Jewish nation-state: Israel. Anti-Zionism earns its discriminatory character by denying the Jewish people what it grants to other historically bonded collectives (e.g. French, Spanish, Palestinians), namely, the right to nationhood, self-determination and legitimate coexistence with other indigenous claimants. Antisemitism rejects Jews as equal members of the human race; anti-Zionism rejects Israel as an equal member in the family of nations."[1] And in the mind of most Jews, the collective memory of the Christie Pits riot is seen through the linkage of the older form of Jew-hatred and contemporary anti-Zionism.

And another consideration: the riot at Christie Pits took place during the depths of the Great Depression, while the book was first published during a period of relative economic stability and prosperity. We tend to assume that conditions that obtain during our own times are "natural" and we fail to understand the context of historical developments. It may seem idle to speculate whether there would have been a riot with nearly full employment in 1933. We are of the opinion that prejudice, discrimination, racial and ethnic hatred, and violence, although not created by economic hardship and dislocation, are significant contributing factors to the violence of its expression. Would Hitler have come to power in Germany with nearly full employment in the Weimar Republic? Would FDR or Mackenzie King? One may repeat the phrase "It's the economy, stupid," the unofficial slogan of Bill Clinton's successful 1992 presidential bid—surely an oversimplification of the complexities of political life—but there is no doubt that a population that experiences sharp economic dislocation and hardship is open to demagoguery and racial and ethnic hostility and incitement.

Finally, world politics and economics have changed drastically since the release of the first edition of the book. The relatively sudden rise of anti-globalist, nationalist forces manifested in the Brexit election, the elections of antisemitic governments in Hungary and Poland, the election of Donald Trump in the United States, and the entry into the Reichstag of the extreme right-wing *Alternative for Germany* have caused a shiver to run through the Jewish world. But perhaps, most symbolically, the gathering of the alt-right and white supremacist groups in Charlottesville, Virginia in the summer of 2017, the flaunting of the swastika amidst the violence of the occasion, and Donald Trump's insistence that both sides ought to be equally condemned for that violence, will cause readers of this account of the riot at Christie Pits to read it with greater present concern and alarm. Reports of increased antisemitic activity—the smearing of swastikas, the prevalence of slurs and epithets on social media, videos of a neo-Nazi assembly with members giving the Hitler salute and yelling "Hail Trump!" have been widely circulated in the mass media. Debates carried on in the mainstream Jewish media (*Tablet, Moment,* the *Forward,* etc.) as to the meaning of a Trump presidency and the nature of the threat from the antisemitic right are currently raging and have caused a level of alarm and consternation within the Jewish communities of North America not seen since World War II. Comparisons with Germany in the late 1920s are legion while others caution against overreaction and recommend a wait-and-see attitude. But whatever the reality of the threats may be, readers of this book will be absorbing its content with a different mindset than readers of the first edition thirty years ago. Although today's reader is significantly less at ease and less assured than was the reader in 1987, we take some comfort in the successes of Toronto as outlined in the book and emphasized by Marcus Gee in the new Foreword, even as we express our concern about new dangers and threats to the Jewish community and indeed to the free world.

1

2

1   The Nazi campaign against the Jews was front-page news in the Toronto papers in the spring of 1933. (*Toronto Daily Star*, 13 April 1933)

2   Pierre van Paassen, a foreign correspondent for the *Star*, blew the whistle on atrocities committed against Jews by Nazis in the wake of Hitler's accession to power. Here the *Star* responds to Nazi claims that van Paassen was of Jewish descent. (*Toronto Daily Star*, 24 April 1933)

1

2

1 Jewish picnickers at Toronto's eastern beaches aroused the ire of residents. They
   complained of a "foreign invasion" and of the "immodest" behaviour of the
   visitors. (Photo courtesy the *Globe and Mail* Photo Archives, 30691)
2 One of the many signs that sprang up across Ontario in the 1930s. (Photo
   courtesy the Toronto Jewish Congress Archives)

Early in August members of the Swastika Club organized parades on the board-walk at the eastern beaches. Club members, many sporting swastika emblems on their shirts, taunted Jewish visitors to the area. (*Above: Daily Mail and Empire*, 7 August 1933; *below: Toronto Daily Star*, 8 August 1933)

1

2

1   The activities of the Swastika Club provoked an angry response from Toronto's Jewish community, who called for an immediate disbanding of the group. (*Evening Telegram*, 1 August 1933)

2   Following a baseball game at Christie Pits on 14 August, a swastika symbol and the words "Hail Hitler" appeared, painted on the clubhouse roof. (*Toronto Daily Star*, 15 August 1933)

Pictured are members of the Harbord Playground Juvenile team of 1931. Players whose names are marked with an asterisk went onto play for the Harbord Playground Junior team in 1933, and were present on the night of the riot at Christie Pits: *(left to right, seated)*: Bill Simon*, Phil Zarnett, Meyer Reitapple, Sam "Chief" Brooks*, Irv Letofsky (Lasky)*, Coach Mike Sansone, Lou Rubin*, Mickey Bockner*; *(left to right, standing)*: Syd Paul, Coach Ben Goldofsky, Joe Bluestein, Manager Bob Mackie*, Ben Lockwood.* Seated in front is the team mascot. (Photo courtesy City of Toronto Archives, DPW 52-1492)

1 Mayor William J. Stewart became a hero to many in the Jewish community by banning the public display of the swastika in the aftermath of the riot. (Photo courtesy City of Toronto Archives, 9.2.4.G#45)

2 The Chief of Police, Chief Constable Brigadier-General Dennis C. Draper. Calls for his resignation were heard from some quarters over his handling of the riot. (Photo courtesy the Metropolitan Toronto Police.)

This page and the following three pages contain a representative selection of newspaper headlines covering the events of August 1933.

… THE TORONTO DAILY STAR … THE WEATHER

41ST YEAR — JULY CIRCULATION, 200,027 — TORONTO, THURSDAY, AUGUST 17, 1933—40 PAGES

DRAPER ADMITS RECEIVING RIOT WARNING

SIX HOURS OF RIOTING FOLLOWS HITLER SHOUT
SCORES HURT, TWO HELD

Jewish-Gentile Ball Game Is Marked By Disorder As Swastika Flag Raised

LEAD PIPE WAS USED

Six Constables Only on Hand Though Impending Clash Was Forecast

HOME AND SPORT EDITION

DID NOT BELIEVE IT WAS SERIOUS HE TELLS BOARD

Parks Board Advised Him as They Opposed B Mested Attention

MAYORS REQUEST

COL. HARRY M'GEE TO BE HONORED AT HUGE RALLY

Rounding Out 50 Years of Continuous Service With T. Eaton Co.

EXPECT OVER 12,000

PREMIER R. B. BENNETT EXPECTS 15 P.C. CUT IN OUTPUT OF WHEAT

DUKE FALLS OFF MERRY-GO-ROUND

MANY ARE INJURED IN PARK RIOTING

HALIFAX SOLDIER PREFERS INDIA TO NATIVE CANADA

INSTRUMENTS STOLEN
RECORD HOP DELAYED

113,226 — The Mail and Empire. — THE WEATHER — Partly Cloudy and Warm at First, Thunderstorms Before Night.

VOL. LXII. — TORONTO, THURSDAY, AUGUST 17, 1933—EIGHTEEN PAGES. — NO. 19,187.

SCORES HURT AS SWASTIKA MOBS RIOT AT WILLOWVALE
MAYOR PROMISES IMMEDIATE PROBE OF DISTURBANCES

HYDRO EXPLORES NEW POWER SITE

Government Authorizes Survey of Albany River Project.

WILLING TO DEVELOP

Mines Seek Energy at Low Cost, Officials Claim.

Carriages, Bicycles And Roller Skating Return to Hollywood

MAKES TOUR OF U.S.

NIRA MAY BENEFIT CANADIAN PLANTS

MacNicol Reports Plan to Use Factories Here for Exports

Thousands Caught Up in Park Melee
Gangs Wielding Lead Pipes and Bats
Sweep Streets, Bludgeoning Victims

Mayor's Statement

Five Taken to Hospital, Others Nurse Gashes, Bystanders Beaten as Hoodlums Swarm Area—Police With Drawn Batons Split Crowds, Block Trucks Bearing Mob Reinforcements—Guarded Autos Remove Wounded From Field.

POLICE ROUT MOB IN TRINITY PARK

Exhaust From Officers' Motorcycles Used on Crowd of 5,000.

MOUNTED MEN WORK

Speech Attacking Capitalistic System Abruptly Terminated.

70 ARE DROWNED IN JAMAICA FLOOD

Kingston and Suburbs Swept by Worst Storms in Eighty Years.

DAMAGE IS SERIOUS

Teams Blame Outside Groups For Swastika Riot in Park
Offer Aid in Keeping Peace

The Mail and Empire.

VOL. LXII.   TORONTO, WEDNESDAY, AUGUST 2, 1933 — SIXTEEN PAGES.   NO. 19,174.

BALMY BEACH DANCE HALL CLOSED TO AVERT SWASTIKA ROW
"Nazi" Parade Tours Boardwalk Singing Anti-Jewish Doggerel

Temperature Tumbles But Toronto Is Robbed Of Relief by Humidity

Mercury Drops Nearly 10 Degrees in Four Hours From High of 94.4.

ONLY TRACE OF RAIN CROPS ARE BENEFITED

Two Deaths Attributed to Heat Wave of Past Few Days.

SHOT AT IN CELL, BUCK TELLS COURT

Guards' Bullets Grazed Him, Red Leader Testifies.

EVIDENCE OF RIOT

Another Convict Gets Added Sentence at Kingston.

NINE-CENT GAIN IN WHEAT PRICES

Smashing Upturn as News of Frosts in West Received.

HEAVY ON EXPORTS

RED OBSERVANCES CAUSE DISORDERS

Bandits Hold Up Clerk And Rob Jewelry Store of $100,000 in Gems

WILL JAIL GANDHI THEN RELEASE HIM

Mahatma to be Taken to Yeruda Prison and Freed Under Conditions.

MUST DROP ACTIVITY

Will be Ordered to Stay in District or Face Public Trial

Police Called in as Noisy Throngs Threaten Disturbance at Canoe Club
Hitler Emblems Stir Jewish Protest

Mayor to Ask for Report From Chief Draper on Demonstration.

CANNOT FLOUT ORDER

Won't Tolerate Any Group Taking Law into Its Own Hands, He Says.

Commander Disperses Dancers as Officers Clear Crowds, Station Guards at Clubhouse Entrance—Swastika Organization Officials Deny Campaign Against Hebrews, But Self-styled Followers Demand Exclusive Use of Beaches by Gentiles — Second Demonstration Threatened for Sunday.

Deep Sea Divers Search At Bottom of Coal Mine

THE TORONTO DAILY STAR

TORONTO, FRIDAY, AUGUST 11, 1933 — 40 PAGES.   TWO CENTS

SWASTIKA CLUB WILL GIVE UP EMBLEM

TENDER-HEARTED BODY TRIBUTE OF HER SISTER TO MRS. ROSE CADEAU

"Must Have Been Temporarily Insane If She Shot Tenant"

HAS HAD HARD LIFE

HOME AND SPORT EDITION

CUBANS PROPOSE HERRERA BECOME NEW PRESIDENT

Government Has Made a Counter-Proposal to the U.S., Report Says

MACHADO WILLING

HITLER'S AIDE DENIES BERLIN MEDDLING HERE

"Absurd to Blame Nazis for Canadian Anti-Jewish Outbreak"

CABLES DAILY STAR

Says German Fascist Never Has Meddled With Any Other Country"

IS "CALLED" TO SCENE BUT IS "PUT ON SPOT"

DISASTER INEVITABLE IF INDIA RULES SELF LORD LLOYD ASSERTS

SHIP MANS FIRE IN WELLAND LOCK

WORLD TO SUFFER

QUEEN'S PARK EX-EMPLOYEE ADMITS EXAM. PAPER THEFT

WORKLESS 6 MONTHS GETS JOB AND DIES

BOTH GIVEN BAIL

INDIA'S SUCKER HARVEST SETS HIGH FOR ALL TIME

America's Cure - Alls Pale Beside Remedies Offered

GETS FINAL DIVORCE FROM BUSTER KEATON

R.C.M.P. INVESTIGATE

The Yiddish headline from *Der Yiddisher Zhurnal* reads: "Swastika Attacks Call Forth Great Panic in City—Mayor Stewart Promises Swift Action Against Nazis, Draper Called to Report."

Notes

Introduction

1 Ferdinand Kroh, "Durchhalten im Untergrund," *Die Zeit* (Canadian edition), No. 48, 30 November 1984.

2 Christie Pits was officially given the name Willowvale Park by City Council more than seventy-five years ago. In November 1983, Willowvale Park was officially renamed Christie Pits. (Information supplied by Mrs. G. Olive Taylor.)

3 In December 1952, the Bassett family acquired the Toronto *Evening Telegram*. Under John Bassett's direction, the *Tely* was kept free of the antisemitic tone that had characterized it in the thirties.

4 It is useful to note that the Christie Pits riot was not born of conditions obtaining only within the city limits of Ontario's capital. In fact, the opposite was more likely the case. As Morley Callaghan has written, Toronto in the 1930s was typically and proto-typically Canadian:

> As a city Toronto had a reticent coldness. In other Ontario towns and in the West they jeered at Toronto. But he had soon learned that many of these places were simply smaller Torontos. The more bitterly they mocked at Toronto the more conscious they seemed to be that the Toronto spirit was a skeleton hidden in their own closets. (Morley Callaghan, *The Varsity Story* [Toronto: Macmillan, 1948], 11.)

If anti-Jewish outbursts did not achieve the same force in Winnipeg and Montreal, two other major centres of Jewish life at the time, this did not mean Toronto was more antisemitic than elsewhere. Similar kinds of antisemitic feelings were indeed present in other parts of the country at the time but did not erupt in the fashion of the Christie Pits violence simply because certain demographic, geographic, ethnic, and political conditions coincidentally present in Toronto resulted in a situation more conducive to mass ethnic violence.

5 David Rome, *Clouds over the Thirties*, Section 3 (Montreal: Canadian Jewish Congress, 1977), 2–3.

6 Arnold Ages, "Antisemitism: The Uneasy Calm," in Morton Weinfeld, William Shaf-

fir, and Irwin Cotler, eds., *The Canadian Jewish Mosaic* (Toronto: John Wiley and Sons, 1981), 383–84.

7   Lita-Rose Betcherman, *The Swastika and the Maple Leaf: Fascist Movements in Canada in the Thirties* (Toronto: Fitzhenry and Whiteside, 1975).

8   *Le Goglu*, 10 February 1933, as cited in Betcherman, *The Swastika and the Maple Leaf*, 29.

9   *Ibid.*

10   *Ibid.*, 52.

11   Rome, *Clouds over the Thirties*, Section 2, 19.

12   *Ibid.*

13   *Der Yiddisher Zhurnal*, 14 February 1933, 4.

14   "Race Prejudice Is Fatal to Nation, Singer Warns," *Toronto Daily Star*, 14 March 1933, 1.

15   *Ibid.*

16   It should not be forgotten that there was considerable discrimination and prejudice shown towards Englishmen in Toronto during the thirties, even though the vast majority of the population was British in origin and staunchly supported the British Empire.

17   "*Yidn darfn oismeidn di antisemitishe pletzer*," *Der Yiddisher Zhurnal*, 28 June 1933, 4.

18   Yaacov Glickman, "Anti-Semitism and Jewish Social Cohesion in Canada," in R. M. Bienvenue and J. E. Goldstein, eds., *Ethnicity and Ethnic Relations in Canada: A Book of Readings*, 2nd ed. (Toronto: Butterworth, 1985).

19   Irving Abella and Harold Troper, *None Is Too Many* (Toronto: Lester & Orpen Dennys, 1982).

20   Louis Rosenberg, *Canada's Jews: A Social and Economic Study of the Jews in Canada* (Montreal: Canadian Jewish Congress, 1939), 37.

21   Rome, *Clouds over the Thirties*, Section 1, 17–18.

22   *Ibid.*, Section 3, 10.

23   One does well to remember that the antisemitism in Toronto during the thirties was experienced differently by the older and the younger generations of Jews. Young Jews, many of them born in Canada, appear to have been more aware of the intensity and extensiveness of antisemitism in Toronto than their parents. The older generation, living a cloistered life within the confines of the Jewish ghetto, had enjoyed and sought fewer opportunities to interact with Gentiles in the larger community. Quite naturally, the young people's activities brought them into greater and closer contact with institutions in the larger society—public schools, social clubs, dance halls, etc.—precisely the points at which they would most realize the degree to which they were singled out for special consideration. More important, younger Jews were simply unfamiliar with the vicious antisemitism that had impelled their parents to leave eastern Europe. By comparison, anti-Jewish sentiment

in Toronto was a minor inconvenience. As one of our respondents put it:
We lived in a ghetto. My father thought that this [Toronto] was paradise because he didn't speak English. Where he was in the Ukraine...
he wasn't allowed to walk the street and if they [the police] killed a
Jew, then they didn't have to make out a report. They [my parents]
came here and...they weren't beaten up on the street. And [if]...a guy
called them a fucking Jew, my father wouldn't know what the hell he
was saying to start with.

24   Abella and Troper, *None Is Too Many*.

Chapter 1: Toronto the Good—1933

1   *Evening Telegram,* 4 March 1933, 6.

2   Louis Cauz, *Baseball's Back in Town* (Toronto: CMC, n.d.), 77.

3   Bruce West, *Toronto* (Garden City, NY: Doubleday, 1967), 268.

4   "Most suburbs suffered more than the city; in East York 45 per cent of the population were on the dole and working residents paid much of the cost." James Lemon, *Toronto Since 1918: An Illustrated History* (Toronto: Lorimer, 1985), 59.

5   Hugh Garner, *Cabbagetown* (Toronto: McGraw-Hill Ryerson, 1968), 70–71.

6   Lemon, *Toronto Since 1918,* 60. It appears that this "minimum wage" referred to by Lemon was higher than the one received by many office workers. One respondent reported that a relative received eight dollars a week for working in a dentist's office in 1940–41. Others received five dollars a week or less.

7   According to the figures from the 1931 census, Toronto was composed of eight wards with a combined population of 631,207. (Including the satellite communities of East York, Etobicoke, Forest Hill, Long Branch, Mimico, New Toronto, North York, Scarborough, Swansea, Weston, and York Township, the population of Greater Toronto was 818,383 in that same year.) There were 510,432 persons of British descent in the eight wards, constituting 80.8 per cent of the whole.) In the wards, there were 45,305 Jews representing 7.2 per cent of the population. (There were 46,751 Jews in Greater Toronto; 5.7 per cent of the population.) Of the ethnic groups the Italians had the second greatest population—13,015 in the wards (2.6 per cent), 15,504 in Greater Toronto (1.9 per cent). Next came: the French—in the wards, 10,869 (1.7 per cent), in Greater Toronto, 13,544 (1.7 per cent); the Germans—in the wards, 9,343 (1.5 per cent), in Greater Toronto, 11,718 (1.4 per cent); the Poles—in the wards, 8,484 (1.3 per cent), in Greater Toronto, 9,383 (1.1 per cent). (For a breakdown of the population for both the wards and Greater Toronto by ethnic group see Appendix B, Table 9.) The two "ethnic" wards in the city were Ward 4 (52.2 per cent non-British) and Ward 5 (35.4 per cent non-British).

8   Irving Abella and Harold Troper, *None Is Too Many* (Toronto: Lester & Orpen Dennys, 1982).

9   M. Horn, "Keeping Canada 'Canadian'": Anti-Communism and Canadianism in Toronto 1928–29," *Canada* 3:1 (1975), 44; see also Lita-Rose Betcherman, *The Little Band* (Ottawa: Deneau, 1982), 7.

10 R. Donegan, *Spadina Avenue* (Vancouver and Toronto: Douglas and McIntyre, 1985), 19.

11 Betcherman, *The Little Band*, 1–13.

12 Horn, "Keeping Canada 'Canadian,'" 36; see also Betcherman, *The Little Band*, 19–28.

13 John Gray, in William Kilbourn, ed., *Toronto Remembered: A Celebration of the City* (Toronto: Stoddart, 1984), 146.

14 Kilbourn, *ibid.*, 222.

15 Aleister Crowley, *c.* 1906, "The Confessions of Aleister Crowley: An Autohagiography," in Kilbourn, *ibid.*, 141.

16 Betcherman assesses the participation of Jews in the Communist movement as follows: "Although Jews were indelibly associated in the popular mind with communism, they actually formed only a small part of the movement. The Jewish working class was employed in the needle trades, and this industry, with the exception of the dressmakers, was organized by two big anti-Communist American unions." *The Little Band*, 10.

17 Stephen Speisman, *The Jews of Toronto: A History to 1937* (Toronto: McClelland and Stewart, 1979), 319.

18 Horn, "Keeping Canada 'Canadian,'" 36.

19 *Evening Telegram*, 5 June 1933, 14.

20 *Toronto Daily Star*, 27 July 1933.

21 Horn, "Keeping Canada 'Canadian,'" 39.

22 Kilbourn, *Toronto Remembered*, 206.

23 Garner, *Cabbagetown*, 68.

24 C. J. Houston and W. J. Smyth, *The Sash Canada Wore* (Toronto: University of Toronto Press, 1980), 156–57.

25 Kilbourn, *Toronto Remembered*, 208.

26 Houston and Smyth, *The Sash Canada Wore*, 18.

27 *Ibid.*, 15–16.

28 *Ibid.*, 49.

29 *Ibid.*, 120.

30 Arnold Ages, "Antisemitism: The Uneasy Calm," in Morton Weinfeld, William Shaffir, Irwin Cotler, eds., *The Canadian Jewish Mosaic* (Toronto: John Wiley and Sons, 1981), 386.

31 The power of the Orange Order declined dramatically after the Second World War. Perhaps it had something to do with the new spirit of tolerance that arose out of the struggle against Nazism and the horrors racism had wrought upon the world.

Our colleague Robert Storey believes that the Legion halls provided veterans with an alternate location where they could meet socially after the Second World War. For many, the Legion Hall replaced the Orange Hall, just as the spirit of tolerance had replaced that of bigotry.

32   In 1933, Ward 4 included the area of the city bounded by Lake Ontario on the south, Simcoe Street, University Avenue, Queen's Park Crescent, and Avenue Road on the east, Bathurst Street on the west, and the streets just north of St. Clair Avenue on the north. Ward 5 included that area bounded by the lake on the south, Bathurst on the east, Atlantic Avenue, Dovercourt Road, and Oakwood Avenue on the west, and the city limit just north of St. Clair Avenue on the north. At the time Ward 8 included all the territory enclosed by the lake on the south, Victoria Park Road on the east, Greenwood Avenue on the west, and the city limit just north of the Danforth on the north.

33   Salutin in Donegan, *Spadina Avenue*, 15–16.

34   It would be a mistake to see the secularism of the working-class community opposed to or apart from the traditionalist and orthodox elements of the community. Many socialist Jews observed *kashruth* (more or less strictly), many rank-and-file supporters of the *Bund* went to synagogue services on the Sabbath, and many Communists said *kaddish* (memorial prayer for the dead) and observed the *yorzeit* (annual memorial for the dead) memorial. The tension between secularism and Jewish tradition was not nearly as great in the working-class and petty-bourgeois Jewish milieu then as it is today in the relatively affluent Jewish community. In the "Belfast of Canada" during the Depression there was a practical communitarian Jewishness that encompassed secular and traditional Jews alike.

35   The tax assessment rolls for 1933 show little class differentiation among those living in the "Jewish area" south of Bloor Street, in the non-Jewish area north of Bloor Street, and in the Beaches. Selecting a typical street for each area, we see that the only apparent difference in the large proportion of "Jewish" occupations practised by those in the Jewish area. Kippendavie Avenue—the Beaches (every seventh residence): machine operator, rubber worker, labourer, merchant, TTC motorman, printer, clerk, carpenter, diamond setter, butcher, hoisting engineer, salesman; Euclid Avenue—non-Jewish area north of Bloor Street (every seventh residence): bricklayer, shipper, cleaner, plasterer, chauffeur, mechanic, salesman, manufacturer, designer, clerk, mechanic, wood carver, barber, truck driver, CPR yardman, merchant, distributor, cutter, pattern maker, salesman; Euclid Avenue—Jewish area between College and Bloor Streets (every seventh residence): upholsterer, tailor, merchant, tailor, tailor, shoemaker, newsdealer, foreman, plumber, presser, tailor, tailor, musician, milliner, clothier, farmer, theatre proprietor, garage man, labourer, vocal teacher, tailor, chef, painter, salesman, CPR conductor, caretaker.

36 B. G. Kayfetz, "Only Yesterday" (Paper presented to the Toronto Jewish Historical Society, May 1972).

37 *Ibid.*, 4–5.

38 David Rome, *Clouds over the Thirties,* Section 2 (Montreal: Canadian Jewish Congress, 1977), 53.

39 Betcherman, *The Little Band,* 50–51. Although at least half of our respondents and the *Yiddisher Zhurnal* at the time referred directly to signs bearing the inscription "No Jews or Dogs Allowed," Ben Kayfetz remains skeptical as to their existence in Ontario during the early thirties. There is, in fact, no hard evidence to prove that they did exist, although when challenged, several of our respondents emphatically asserted that they had seen them with their own eyes.

40 Speisman, *The Jews of Toronto,* 120–21.

41 Rome, *Clouds over the Thirties,* 48.

42 *Ibid.*

43 "Race Prejudice Is Fatal to Nation, Singer Warns," *Toronto Daily Star,* 14 March 1933, 1. Ben Kayfetz emphasizes that, by and large, Jewish students had no great difficulty in entering medical schools in Ontario if they had the required grades. They did, however, face serious obstacles in obtaining positions as interns at Canadian hospitals. Quotas did arise, according to Kayfetz, in 1939 when the government offered subsidies to medical students and there was an ensuing rush to take advantage of this generosity by large numbers of applicants. Similarly, the situation of Jewish applicants to the faculty of dentistry was considerably worse during the early forties than it had been ten years earlier. In fact, with the outbreak of war the employment prospects for Jews generally deteriorated until the institution of fair employment legislation.

> As a wartime measure all employment, particularly in war industries, was being channelled through Selective Service. This government agency would in its procedures often uncritically acquiesce in employers' prejudices and keep Jews from filling certain jobs. Thus, there arose an uncomfortable feeling that now the government itself was not only sanctifying but also participating in and promoting wilful religious discrimination. As bad as the situation was before, it was now worse, since the government itself was directly involved. (See Ben Kayfetz, "Ontario Region," in *Pathways to the Present: Canadian Jewry and Canadian Jewish Congress* (Montreal: Canadian Jewish Congress, 1986), 30).

44 Louis Rosenberg, *Canada's Jews: A Social and Economic Study of the Jews in Canada* (Montreal: Canadian Jewish Congress, 1939), 193.

45 Sammy Luftspring, *Call Me Sammy* (Scarborough, ON: Prentice-Hall Canada, 1975), 5.

46   *Ibid.*

47   Jacob Moneta, "Mehr Gewalt für die Ohnmächtigen," *Kursbuch* 51 (March 1978), 44.

48   "Baby" Yack's name was not really Norman. He was named Binyamon (Yiddish/ Hebrew), which became "Nyamin," which in turn became "Numan," and finally Norman (according to Ben Kayfetz).

49   Luftspring, *Call Me Sammy*, 19. Yaponchik (whose name, we were told, was Harry Hartman) used to sell newspapers in front of the Labor Lyceum at the corner of Spadina and St. Andrew's. Ben Kayfetz recalls that he had oriental features, hence the nickname Yaponchik, meaning "Jap" in colloquial Yiddish.

50   Robert Harney, ed., *Gathering Place: People and Neighbourhoods of Toronto* (Toronto: Multicultural History Society of Ontario, 1985), 14.

51   For the concept of the "cognitive map" see Kevin Lynch, *The Image of the City* (Cambridge, MA: Technology Press, 1960).

52   Harney, *Gathering Place*, 15.

53   Kilbourn, *Toronto Remembered*, 231. Ben Kayfetz remarked on this point: "Odd that Rasky had the feeling that he was entering alien territory, because that's the feeling (I recall it vividly) the first time I walked on St. Clair West—which, as I learned later, was Rasky's own turf. To me it was part of the goyish *terra incognita*."

54   Harney, *Gathering Place*, 16.

55   Garner, *Cabbagetown*, 32–35.

56   *Der Yiddish Zhurnal*, 17 August 1933, 1.

57   *Ibid.*

58   "Family Reunion Rekindles Past," *Canadian Jewish News*, Toronto edition, 4 July 1985, 16. Over the years, the riot has been mentioned in several stories in the *Canadian Jewish News*. In the last two years, one story identified the riot as having occurred in 1937; another story situated it in 1940 or 1941.

Chapter 2: "Every Evil is Jewish"

1   See Deborah E. Lipstadt, *Beyond Belief: The American Press and the Coming of the Holocaust 1933–1945* (New York: Free Press, 1986); Walter Laqueur, *The Terrible Secret* (Boston and Toronto: Little, Brown, 1980) 8–9.

2   Laqueur, *ibid.*, 7–8.

3   "The *Star* had labour beginnings and, under Joseph Atkinson, it generally supported the federal Liberals, notably W.L.M. King, and, locally, Sam McBride. It favoured economic growth; freedom of speech; social welfare to a degree; free trade; and, for a while, the provincial United Farmers party under Premier E.C. Drury." J. Lemon, *Toronto Since 1918: An Illustrated History* (Toronto: Lorimer, 1985), 33; "Of the daily newspapers only one, Joseph Atkinson's *Star*, argued consistently that the expression of communist views was not a crime, and that if it were it should be

prosecuted in the courts, not forcibly prevented by the police. The *Star* also argued that, in view of its small readership and weak organization, the CPC was no genuine menace to law and order or to constituted authority." M. Horn, "'Free Speech within the Law': the Letter of the Sixty-Eight Toronto Professors, 1931," *Ontario History*, LXXII: 1 (March 1980), 28; see also Horn, "Keeping Canada 'Canadian': Anti-Communism and Canadianism in Toronto 1928–29," *Canada*, 3:1 (September 1975), 37.

4   Lemon, *Toronto Since 1918*; Horn, "'Free Speech within the Law'," 28, and "Keeping Canada 'Canadian,'"37.

5   Horn, "Keeping Canada 'Canadian,'" 37.

6   Stephen Speisman, *The Jews of Toronto: A History to 1937* (Toronto: McClelland and Stewart, 1979), 239–40.

7   *Ibid.*, 242.

8   *Ibid.*, 241. Speisman points out that Shapiro was a Conservative, yet tended to support whichever party was in power "probably in order to maintain government advertising." He opposed the election of Tommy Church, a Tory, in the 1930 civic campaign, for example. In the politics of the Jewish community he was a labour Zionist.

9   One of the most popular Yiddish dailies was the socialist paper from New York—*Der Forverts (The Forward)*—which addressed itself to the trials and tribulations of Jewish immigrants in the New World.

10   This is not to suggest that the young people at the Beaches or members of the Pit Gang were faithful readers of the newspapers. Yet it is probable that some of them or their parents would have read the *Telegram* on occasion, especially since the newspapers were the only source of news and sports reports in those years.

11   The Central-Verein Deutscher Staatsbürger Jüdischen Glaubens or Central Union of German Citizens of the Jewish Faith was founded in Berlin in 1893 to combat antisemitism. It had the support of the majority of Germany's Jews and was looked upon as the major Jewish organization concerned with civil, political, and social rights of Jews.

12   The *Evening Telegram*, in its 5 April edition, also carried the story of the ban on ritual slaughtering rites. *Der Yiddisher Zhurnal* had already carried the stories on local bans on "*shechita*" or ritual slaughtering.

13   The same day, 12 June, the *Zhurnal* carried a statement from Max Reinhardt, who painted a rather optimistic picture of the future of Germany's Jews. He argued that "In about ten years our people will look back on the current period as the time when Jewish art in Germany had begun to flourish again.... In the middle ages the Jews flourished under adversity when they transformed the initial atrocities of their enemies into the finest songs."

Chapter 3: "Keep the Beaches Clean"

1   *Daily Mail and Empire*, 2 August 1933, 2.

2   Toronto City Archives. On 7 July the Commissioner of Parks sent a memo to the Superintendent of Parks for the Eastern District:

> We have been requested to place a limited number of picnic tables under the trees in Kew Gardens…. Please report, if, in your opinion, it would be advisable to make provisions there for next year.

The response to this memo, dated 12 July, stated:

> I beg to report that owing to the increased demand for accommodation I respectfully recommend that an additional 20 tables be constructed in 1934.

3   *Evening Telegram*, 2 August 1933, 2.

4   *Toronto Daily Star*, 2 August 1933, 11.

5   *Ibid.*, 1.

6   *Daily Mail and Empire*, 2 August 1933, 1.

7   *Globe*, 2 August 1933, 1.

8   *Ibid.*

9   *Evening Telegram*, 1 August 1933, 2.

10   *Daily Mail and Empire*, 2 August 1933, 1.

11   *Evening Telegram*, 1 August 1933, 1.

12   *Evening Telegram*, 2 August 1933, 1.

13   *Daily Mail and Empire*, 2 August 1933, 1.

14   *Der Yiddisher Zhurnal*, 2 August 1933, 1.

15   *Ibid.*, 4.

16   *Daily Mail and Empire*, 2 August 1933, 1.

17   *Toronto Daily Star*, 2 August 1933, 1

18   *Globe*, 2 August 1933, 1.

19   *Toronto Daily Star*, 2 August 1933, 1.

20   *Daily Mail and Empire*, 2 August 1933, 1.

21   *Ibid.*

22   *Evening Telegram*, 1 August 1933, 2.

23   *Ibid.*

24   *Ibid.*

25   *Toronto Daily Star*, 2 August 1933, 1.

26   *Ibid.*, 3 August 1933, 8.

27   *Ibid.*, 2 August 1933, 1.

28   Alderman John J. Glass (1897–1973) and Nathan Phillips (1892–1976) were both Jews who were popular in the Jewish community. Nathan Phillips went on to become the first Jewish mayor of Toronto, "Mayor of all the people," as he was called. It was Phillips who ruled Toronto during the period of transition from provincial

town to world-class city. It was under his direction that the city got its subway system and the new city hall, in front of which is the square that bears his name. John Glass had served on the Board of Education from 1928–30. He was elected to the Ontario Legislature in 1934 where he served as a Liberal member until 1943. He was also active in the Zionist movement.

29   *Daily Mail and Empire*, 2 August 1933, 1.

30   *Evening Telegram*, 2 August 1933, 1.

31   *Ibid.*, 2 August 1933, 2.

32   *Ibid.*

Chapter 4: "Jews Flee in Terror from Nazi Torture"

1   *Evening Telegram*, 23 March 1933, 23.

Chapter 5: "Swastika Club Must Be Outlawed"

1   *Daily Mail and Empire*, 3 August 1933, 4.

2   *Globe*, 3 August 1933, 9.

3   *Evening Telegram*, 2 August 1933, 2.

4   *Daily Mail and Empire*, 3 August 1933, 4.

5   *Der Yiddisher Zhurnal*, 3 August 1933, 1.

6   *Ibid.*, 5.

7   *Ibid.*

8   *Daily Mail and Empire*, 3 August 1933, 4.

9   *Der Yiddisher Zhurnal*, 6 August 1933, 4.

10   Headlines in the *Globe* on Monday, 31 July 1933 proclaimed: "Ten Deaths Mark Toll of Sweltering Week-End/Ontario Folk Gasp for Breath as Thermometer Hovers Near 100 Mark."

11   *Globe*, 3 August 1933, 9.

12   *Evening Telegram*, 3 August 1933, 2.

13   *Ibid.*

14   *Ibid.*, 6. The reference here to Queen's Park concerns the anti-Fascist march organized by Jewish workers' and leftist groups on 11 July 1933.

15   *Evening Telegram*, 4 August 1933, 2.

16   *Jewish Standard*, 4 August 1933, 2.

17   *Toronto Daily Star*, 5 August 1933, 3. "It is generally accepted fact among folklorists in the vicinity of Toronto, Canada, that the primitive American tribes used this symbol to ornament their canoes and implements of warfare; however, William F. Poroless, Secretary of the Six Nations Council, Oshweken, Ontario, says:

It appears to have been in use by our ancestors in the distant past but apparently has been forgotten and does not appear in any legends that I have ever read.

Mr. Poroless also made enquiries relevant to the swastika among the older members of his tribe, but was unable to obtain any further information.

It might be of interest that almost the identical circumstances prevail among the Algonquins in the environs of Swastika, Ontario—a community named after the Swastika Mine of James Dusty. According to Dr. J. F. Edis, an authority on the lore and anthropological backgrounds of this tribe, "what little they know [about] or use [they make of] the Swastika they have adopted from the white man." (J. F. Doering, *The Swastika: A Link between the Old World and the New?* Kitchener, Ont.: Commercial Printing Co., 1936), 1–2.

18   *Toronto Daily Star*, 5 August 1933, 3.
19   *Jewish Standard*, 4 August 1933, 2.
20   *Daily Mail and Empire*, 4 August 1933, 1.
21   *Ibid.*
22   *Der Yiddisher Zhurnal*, 6 August 1933, 1.
23   *Ibid.*, 4.
24   *Toronto Daily Star*, 5 August 1933, 1.
25   *Ibid.*
26   *Evening Telegram*, 5 August 1933, 1, 2.
27   *Toronto Daily Star*, 8 August 1933, 1.
28   *Globe*, 7 August 1933, 1.
29   *Daily Mail and Empire*, 7 August 1933, 1.
30   *Evening Telegram*, 8 August 1933, 1.
31   *Toronto Daily Star*, 8 August 1933, 1.
32   *Evening Telegram*, 8 August 1933, 1.
33   *Daily Mail and Empire*, 7 August 1933, 1.
34   *Der Yiddisher Zhurnal*, 7 August 1933, 1.
35   *Ibid.*
36   *Der Yiddisher Zhurnal*, 8 August 1933, 4.
37   *Toronto Daily Star*, 8 August 1933, 2.
38   *Ibid.*
39   *Ibid.*, 8 August 1933, 2.
40   *Ibid.*
41   *Ibid.*, 9 August 1933, 2nd section, 1.
42   *Ibid.*, 8 August 1933, 2.
43   *Ibid.*
44   *Ibid.*, 10 August 1933, 6.
45   *Globe*, 8 August 1933, 1. It is interesting to note that Rabbi Samuel Sachs of the Goel Tzedec (University Avenue Synagogue) appears to have played a larger role in community relations in 1933 than Rabbi Maurice N. Eisendrath of the Holy Blossom Temple, during that period in which the Canadian Jewish Congress was in

the process of being reconstituted. After the first national assembly of the new Congress, Rabbi Eisendrath became chairman of the high-profile public relations committee, while Rabbi Sachs was entrusted with the committee on education and culture. For further information on the reconstitution of the CJC, see Ben Kayfetz, "Ontario Region," in *Pathways to the Present: Canadian Jewry and Canadian Jewish Congress* (Montreal: Canadian Jewish Congress, 1986), 26–62.

46 *Der Yiddisher Zhurnal*, 9 August 1933, 2.

47 *Daily Mail and Empire*, 10 August 1933, 1.

48 *Globe*, 10 August 1933, 9.

49 *Evening Telegram*, 10 August 1933, 9.

50 *Jewish Standard*, 11 August 1933, 15.

51 *Ibid.*

52 *Globe*, 10 August 1933, 4.

53 *Toronto Daily Star*, 11 August 1933, 1.

54 *Ibid.*

55 *Evening Telegram*, 11 August 1933, 1.

56 *Ibid.*, 2.

57 *Der Yiddisher Zhurnal*, 11 August 1933, 4.

58 *Toronto Daily Star*, 14 August 1933, 2.

59 *Ibid.*

60 *Ibid.*

61 *Daily Mail and Empire*, 14 August 1933, 1.

62 *Toronto Daily Star*, 14 August 1933, 1.

63 *Evening Telegram*, 14 August 1933, 1.

64 *Toronto Daily Star*, 14 August 1933, 2.

65 *Ibid.*

66 *Evening Telegram*, 15 August 1933, 1.

67 *Ibid.*

68 *Ibid.*

69 *Toronto Daily Star*, 15 August 1933, 2.

70 *Evening Telegram*, 15 August 1933, 1.

71 *Toronto Daily Star*, 15 August 1933, 2.

72 *Evening Telegram*, 15 August 1933, 1.

73 *Der Yiddisher Zhurnal*, 15 August 1933, 1.

74 *Ibid.*, 4.

Chapter 6: Kipling or Hitler?

1 *Evening Telegram*, 15 August 1933, 2.

2 *Toronto Daily Star*, 18 August 1933, 11.

3 *Ibid.*, 1.

4   *Ibid.*, 11.

5   Lita-Rose Betcherman claims that J. Fair of the SWC was none other than J. C. Farr, a notorious antisemitic and Fascist leader in the late thirties. See *The Swastika and the Maple Leaf* (Toronto: Fitzhenry and Whiteside, 1975), 60.

6   *Evening Telegram*, 19 August 1933, 1.

7   *Daily Mail and Empire*, 18 August 1933, 1.

8   *Ibid.*, 1.

9   Joachim Riedl, "Hitlers Lehrmeister," *Die Zeit* (Canadian edition), No. 24, 13 June 1986, 9.

10   Simply because the swastika became emblematic for certain groups, many in the community failed to differentiate sufficiently between Swastika Club and Pit Gang members on the one hand, and German storm troopers on the other. This is in line with a disquieting trend in recent literature on antisemitism and the Holocaust. Everyone appears to share the responsibility for the destruction of European Jewry. We know that the Allies could have bombed, but they did not, the rail lines to Auschwitz. But it would be a grave error to put the blame for the Nazi genocide upon the Allies. Canadian political leaders and government officials who demonstrated their antisemitism in the practical, and largely successful, attempts to keep Jewish refugees out of Canada in the thirties and forties were not of the same ilk as Hitler, Eichmann, Streicher, and Himmler. Frederick C. Blair was, to be sure, a nasty little antisemite who consciously blocked every attempt by Jews to enter Canada, condemning them, indirectly, to death. But it would never have crossed his mind to participate in rounding up Jews in Montreal, Toronto, and Winnipeg and shipping them in CPR cattle cars to mass extermination camps in northern British Columbia. This is not to whitewash the poor record of the Canadian and other governments in relationship to the rescue of European Jews from the Nazis. But it is indeed unfortunate that much of the recent literature on the Holocaust gives the impression that everyone is to blame for the death camps *but* the Nazis. Canadians as a whole did not share the same kind of Jew-hatred that was being cultivated by the newly formed German government under Hitler. Neither was Toronto about to become a Nazified city in a country terrorized by storm troopers and brownshirts.

11   *Toronto Daily Star*, 17 May 1933, 3.

12   *Ibid.*, 30 June 1933, 17.

13   *Evening Telegram*, 27 March 1933, 21.

14   *Ibid.*, 1 April 1933, 2.

15   Hugh Garner, *Cabbagetown* (Toronto: McGraw-Hill Ryerson, 1968), 201–02. After describing the fighting between the two sides, Garner has a group of Fascists meet to discuss the battle:

     "Hello, East, how did you make out?" Jack asked.

"We drove a kike into the lake," Theodore answered. "You should have seen him standing in the water crying. It was the funniest damned thing I ever saw."

"Good stuff! I managed to get one of the dirty sheenies. Look at my hand where I hit him!" Theodore glanced at the skinned knuckles of Sharpe's hand

"I didn't get a chance to get that close," Theodore said. "I sure bounced some rocks off the one in the water though." (207)

Sally Gibson recalls the situation on Toronto's islands in the early thirties:

There may have been no Swastika Clubs or riots on the Island, but there was open anti-Semitism. Ward's Island—that self-proclaimed happy, tolerant, welcoming little community, where newcomers were counselled to join the WIA in order to preserve their "self-respect"—Ward's Island was "restrictive." "Jewish people couldn't get on," one former tenter commented with a mixture of astonishment and embarrassment. "I don't know how they got away with that. But if they did get over here," she continued, "there was no way they could join the [Ward's Island] Association…. It was pretty bad."

It was pretty bad over at Centre, too. As early as 1929, Jewish Alderman Nathan Phillips had protested against a sign on an Island hotel which advertised that it catered to "Gentiles of refinement only." With little effect. By the mid-thirties, signs saying "Restricted" or "Gentiles Only" were popping up in front of rooming houses and big hotels like the Manitou on Manitou Road. J. J. Glass, a Jewish alderman and chairman of the Parks and Exhibition Committee, managed to have a clause inserted into Island leases that no sign could be erected without City approval. But [the] signs were like weeds and kept springing up.

…One summer a number of Jewish women were attacked. One day a friend of this same woman's mother "came down the walk in front of her rented house and a man jumped out from behind a hedge and beat her up." There was also a "fair amount of vocal anti-Semitism." "One day, for example, my father—who was very athletic and very strong and impulsive—was coming over to work on the ferry in the morning. And a man brushed up against him and said, 'You kikes ought to go back where you came from.' And my father tried to restrain himself from getting into a fight. But he couldn't help it when the man kept making a lot of comments and as the ferry docked, my father grabbed the guy, punched him out and I think threw his bicycle in the harbour." (Sally Gibson, *More Than an Island: A History of the Toronto Island* (Toronto: Irwin Publishing, 1984), 190)

16　*Toronto Daily Star*, 12 August 1933, 7.

Chapter 7: "Take Me Out to the Ballgame"

1   *Daily Mail and Empire*, 15 August 1933, 1.

2   *Ibid.* Having interviewed many of the players from the Harbord team and two from the St. Peter's, we firmly believe that the ball teams themselves had nothing whatever to do with the provocation, or with the violent encounters.

3   *Toronto Daily Star*, 15 August 1933, 1.

4   *Ibid.*, 27.

5   *Ibid.*

6   *Ibid.*

7   *Daily Mail and Empire*, 16 August 1933, 4.

8   *Toronto Daily Star*, 17 August 1933, 1. By far the most dramatic story of the day's newspaper reports relating to the riot was featured by the *Telegram* in a story headlined "Claim Armed U.S. Thugs Seeking Lives of Swazis Blocked by Jewish Heads." According to the paper, four gunmen from the United States had visited Toronto two weeks earlier with the objective of "taking for a ride" leaders of the east end Swastika Club. The quartet from Buffalo, who had heard of the Swastika movement in Toronto, visited the Beaches boardwalk and asked for Garner and Mackay to be pointed out to them "so that they could be looked after in the approved gangster manner." According to a prominent Jewish citizen, reported the *Telegram*, the gunmen were asked to leave the city by Jewish leaders, as they would only make matters worse if they remained.

In connection with this story, the *Telegram* also reported that three hoodlums were searching for a crack boxer who had fought against the Jewish boys at Christie Pits: "Three hoodlums spent the better part of the night searching the city for a coloured Toronto amateur boxer, who, they claim, put three Jews in the hospital last night as a result of the Willowvale episode...." This latter report puzzled us initially in light of the friendly and supportive relationships that were said to exist in the city between Jewish and black youth. And yet, several of our respondents independently referred to a black boxer who was seen fighting against the Jews. One explanation was offered by another black athlete, a friend of the amateur boxer in question, who witnessed the incident. He recalled seeing two trucks of Jewish boys pull up to the Pits. The Jewish boys piled out and began to attack indiscriminately. The fighting had turned into a free-for-all, and the black boxer was caught in the middle. In defending himself from the attack, he landed blows upon Jewish participants, not because he was taking sides against the Jews, but simply to protect himself in the wild mêlée. (We would like to thank Sheldon Taylor for this information.) Our respondents, however, were unconvinced by this explanation. In their view, this black boxer was a turncoat.

9   *Toronto Daily Star*, 17 August 1933, 3.

10 *Ibid.*

11   *Ibid.*

12   *Ibid.*

13   *Evening Telegram*, 17 August 1933, 2.

14   *Ibid.*

15   *Ibid.*

16   *Globe*, 17 August 1933, 1.

17   *Toronto Daily Star*, 17 August 1933, 3.

18   *Daily Mail and Empire*, 17 August 1933, 1.

19   *Toronto Daily Star*, 17 August 1933, 3.

20   *Ibid.*

21   *Evening Telegram*, 17 August 1933, 2.

22   *Toronto Daily Star*, 17 August 1933, 1.

23   *Der Yiddisher Zhurnal*, 17 August 1933, 5.

24   *Daily Mail and Empire*, 17 August 1933, 1.

25   *Toronto Daily Star*, 17 August 1933, 3.

26   *Ibid.*

27   *Ibid.*

28   *Ibid.*, 1.

29   *Daily Mail and Empire*, 17 August 1933, 1.

30   *Evening Telegram*, 17 August 1933, 2.

31   *Ibid.*

32   *Ibid.*

33   *Globe*, 17 August 1933, 1.

34   *Evening Telegram*, 17 August 1933, 2.

35   *Ibid.*

36   *Ibid.*

37   *Ibid.*, 1, 2.

38   Ibid., 1.

39   *Ibid.*

40   *Ibid.*

41   *Daily Mail and Empire*, 17 August 1933, 1.

42   *Toronto Daily Star*, 17 August 1933, 3.

43   *Saturday Night*, 26 August 1933, 48:42, 1.

44   *Globe*, 18 August 1933, 3.

45   *Daily Mail and Empire*, 18 August 1933, 3.

46   *Toronto Daily Star*, 18 August 1933, 3.

47   *Daily Mail and Empire*, 18 August 1933, 3.

48   *Globe*, 18 August 1933, 1.

49   *Toronto Daily Star*, 18 August 1933, 3.

Chapter 8: "Dismissed All Charges"

1   *Evening Telegram*, 18 August 1933, 6.

2   *Globe*, 18 August 1933, 4.

3   *Daily Mail and Empire*, 18 August 1933, 6.

4   *Toronto Daily Star*, 18 August 1933, 6.

5   *Der Yiddisher Zhurnal*, 18 August 1933, 4. Chief Draper had not had a good year, for he had come under fire from a royal commission investigating the claims of a convict that he had been framed in a bank robbery by a police informer acting under orders from Chief Draper. In the so-called Dorland case, Albert Dorland claimed he was framed by William Toohey acting on Draper's orders. This had caused quite a stir in the Toronto papers during the first six months of 1933, and brought cries for Draper to resign.

6   *Der Yiddisher Zhurnal*, 21 August 1933, 4.

7   *Toronto Daily Star*, 18 August 1933, 1.

8   *Ibid.*

9   *Ibid.*

10   *Ibid.*

11   *Ibid.*

12   *Ibid.*

13   *Daily Mail and Empire*, 19 August 1933, 1.

14   *Toronto Daily Star*, 19 August 1933, 2.

15   *Evening Telegram*, 19 August 1933, 2.

16   *Ibid.*

17   *Toronto Daily Star*, 19 August 1933, 2.

18   *Ibid.*

19   *Ibid.*

20   *Ibid.*

21   Robert Harney, "The Italian Community in Toronto," in J. Elliot, *Two Nations, Many Cultures* (Scarborough, ON: Prentice-Hall Canada, 1979), 223–24.

22   Hester Howe School was on Elizabeth Street north of Dundas.

23   *Globe*, 21 August 1933, 1.

24   *Evening Telegram*, 19 August 1933, 1.

25   *Der Yiddisher Zhurnal*, 22 August 1933, 4.

26   *Ibid.*, 23 August 1933, 5.

27   *Ibid.*

28   *Ibid.*

29   *Toronto Star*, 17 August 1933, 3.

30   Jonathan F. Wagner, *Brothers Beyond the Sea: National Socialism in Canada* (Waterloo, ON: Wilfrid Laurier University Press, 1981).

31   Magistrate Brown had played an important role in prosecuting free-speech viola-

tions in the years prior to the Christie Pits riot. Betcherman describes him as a former policeman. A tall and impressive figure in a morning coat, he presided over his court with all the pomp and circumstance of a chief justice. A Crown Attorney recalls it as "a real performance." Reactionary even by contemporary standards, Browne was accused, not without reason, of being anti-labour, anti-female, and, of course, extremely anti-Communist. (See Lita-Rose Betcherman, *The Little Band* (Ottawa: Deneau, 1982), 28.)

Chapter 9: Protest

1   *Toronto Daily Star*, 8 May 1933, 11.
2   *Evening Telegram*, 11 May 1933, 3.
3   *Toronto Daily Star*, 19 May 1933, 5.
4   *Evening Telegram*, 25 May 1933, 1; *Toronto Daily Star*, 25 May 1933, 23.
5   *Evening Telegram*, 25 May 1933, 3.
6   Cf. "Nazis' Fistic Rulers Oust Jewish Boxers Suspend All Aliens: Union of German Professional Boxers Joins in 'Purging': Managers Out Too," *Toronto Daily Star*, 25 August. 1933, 19; "Jewish Boxers Forced to Quit," *Evening Telegram*, 25 August 1933, 34.
7   *Evening Telegram*, 29 March 1933, 20.
8   Baer went on to take the heavyweight championship from Primo Carnera in 1934, only to lose it to James J. Braddock a year later.
9   *Der Yiddisher Zhurnal*, 11 June 1933, 5.
10 The meeting especially focused on the arrest of Jakob Lestschinsky, sociologist, economist, and demographer, who was the Berlin correspondent for the New York Yiddish daily *Forverts*.
11 *Evening Telegram*, 28 March 1933, 1.
12 *Ibid.*, 29 March 1933, 2.
13 *Toronto Daily Star*, 3 April 1933, 5.
14 *Evening Telegram*, 6 April 1933, 18.
15 *Ibid.*, 12 July 1933, 19.

Chapter 10: "…Lies, Lies, Lies"

1   Deborah E. Lipstadt, *Beyond Belief: The American Press and the Coming of the Holocaust 1933–1945* (New York: Free Press, 1986), 18.
2   The prejudice of the *Evening Telegram* in the thirties can perhaps best be seen in its coverage of cases tried in police court. Allusions to the defendant's race or religion—such as "a most celestial gentleman" for a Chinese or "a man of Hebrew persuasion" for a Jew—would often be part of the description of the court proceedings.

3   *Evening Telegram*, 31 March 1933, 17.

4   We were fortunate enough to find Kantorowicz's file and party book in the American Documentation Center on Nazi War Criminals in West Berlin. Apparently Kantorowicz returned to Berlin shortly after giving these interviews to the Toronto newspapers, for he was crossed off the party list in Berlin in October 1933. He was readmitted in December of that year, but expelled in July 1934. It is possible that he was dismissed from the party on account of the lack of racial credentials. *Der Yiddisher Zhurnal* pointed out that after all Kantorowicz is a relatively common Jewish name. But this is pure speculation.

5   According to Albert Brandt, Viereck was "the real brain-trust of Nazi propaganda in America. It is Viereck who sends an indignant letter of protest to the editor whenever an American publication exposes the machinations of Nazidom here. It is Viereck who censors all the Nazi publicity materials in this country." See Albert Brandt, "The Invasion of America," in Pierre van Paassen and James Waterman Wise, eds., *Nazism: An Assault on Civilization* (New York: Smith and Haas, 1934), 241.

6   Matthew Henry Halton (1904–56) was a schoolteacher from Alberta before becoming a correspondent for the *Toronto Daily Star*. In the mid-thirties he predicted the outbreak of the Second World War and believed that Germany and Japan would be ranged against the Allies. During the war he was one of Canada's most celebrated war correspondents.

7   *Evening Telegram*, 25 March 1933, 13.

8   *Ibid.*, 22 April 1933, 12.

9   *Toronto Daily Star*, 4 May 1933, 6.

Conclusion

1   *Toronto Star*, 22 April 1965, 22.

2   Although our story ends in the summer of 1933, the question arises concerning the situation at the Beaches and in Christie Pits during the rest of the decade. Most of our respondents agree that the fight represented a victory for the Jewish boys and their allies, and that the Pits was quiet for a while. However, the Pit Gang soon returned to its bullying ways, and Jews still had to beware when venturing into the park alone or in small groups. There was, however, no repeat of the riot of August 1933. Happily, the situation at the Beaches improved. By the summer of 1934, the large crowds of the previous year had dwindled, and the disorder that provided the excuse and some popular support for the Swastika Club did not repeat itself. Fascism and National Socialism continued to grow, especially in Quebec and in western Canada, but they failed to make substantial inroads into mainstream politics. The outbreak of the Second World War and the internment of Fascist leaders

led to the collapse of the movement. For a fuller description of the vicissitudes of Fascism in Canada during the thirties, see Lita-Rose Betcherman, *The Swastika and the Maple Leaf* (Toronto: Fitzhenry and Whiteside, 1975).

Postscript

1   Judea Pearl, "Is Anti-Zionism Hate?" *The Los Angeles Times*, 15 March 2009.

Appendices

APPENDIX A:1

Minutes of a Special Meeting of the Board of Commissioners of Police held on Thursday, August 17, 1933, at 10.30 a.m. In the office of His Worship the Mayor, City Hall.

Present: His Worship W. J. Stewart, Chairman, His Honour Judge Parker.

The Chief Constable was also present.

His Worship Magistrate Coatsworth was not notified of the meeting on account of being out of the city on vacation.

Meetings in parks etc.

His Worship the Mayor explained that the meeting was called for the purpose of considering what action could or should be taken to prevent a repetition of the disturbance in Willowvale Park on the evening of Wednesday, August 16th. He stated further that he proposed to give out the following statement:

> From recent occurrences in our city it must be apparent that the display in any form of the "Swastika" Emblem is provocative and tends to incite riotous conduct and a disturbance of the peace which is not at all in keeping with the good name of our city or for the public good.
>
> I therefore wish to warn all citizens that such use of this "Swastika" Emblem will render the person so using same liable to prosecution to the full extent of the law.
>
> I also wish to warn all persons against taking the law in their own hands or taking part in unlawful assembly. Peace, order and good government is my desire—I invite co-operation.

This statement was endorsed by the members of the Police Commission present.

It was ordered that a copy of the statement be given to the Chief Constable and that he be instructed to see that the purport of this statement is carried into effect.

The Board also considered it advisable for the Mayor to call on some of the leaders among the Jewish citizens for the purpose of having them urge their people to restrain themselves from any acts of violence or from becoming part of any unlawful assembly in cases where the "Swastika" Emblem may be displayed.

The Chief Constable read the reports made by Chief Inspector George Guthrie and Inspector Anderson in regard to the disturbance. The Chief Constable was asked as to whether he had knowledge of an assembly on Spadina Avenue of a crowd of about one hundred persons who were armed and who proceeded from there to the vicinity of Willowvale Park. He was instructed to submit a report with reference to this alleged assembly, stating whether or not there was any evidence as to whether the party was armed and as to where they were about to proceed and stating also that if there was such evidence, why this crowd was permitted to proceed.

The meeting was then adjourned.

APPENDIX A:2

On 26 August, 1933, the German Consul-General in Montreal, Ludwig Kempff, sent a dispatch to Berlin. It arrived on 8 September and was filed as document IIIE 2249 by the foreign office. (The document was found in the archives of the *Aussenamt* in Bonn, Federal Republic of Germany. It was part of a collection of papers in a folder entitled: *Faschistische Bewegungen in Ontario*—fascist movements in Ontario. We are grateful to Frau Dr. Keipert and her staff, without whose generous assistance the document could not have been located.) The report contained a description of several events in Ontario during the month of August that the Consul-General felt were important enough to review for his superiors in Berlin. All of Kempff's information appears to have been taken directly from Toronto newspaper reports of the incidents, although he distorted certain aspects of the stories, probably to impress his superiors in the foreign office. This is what Kempff wrote:

1) Toronto: In mid-July the press reported that a "National State Party" had been constituted in Toronto, which had a fascist program. On 24 July 2 copies of this program and a preamble were sent to the General Consulate without accompanying letter. A copy of this printed matter is enclosed here. From the beginning of August on, press reports from Toronto about the Fascist movement and about the displaying of swastikas and the resulting disturbances multiplied. Chiefly involved in this regard were 2 separate events:

I

At various beaches in the Toronto vicinity swastikas were displayed. In particular, swastikas were put up on the building and in the area of a canoe club and what is more with the words "Hail Hitler." In addition, many persons on the beach wore swastikas on their leather windbreakers, raincoats and sweaters, or they wore a button with a swastika. Furthermore, notices were posted on the beach to the effect that undesirables should stay away. These demonstrations originated with the so-called Swastika Club. This was a voluntary association which had no functionaries—no president and no secretary—and raised no membership dues. The members only wore a swastika as an emblem. No speeches were to be held and no parades were to take place. The wearing of the emblem was to have the desired effect. It was assumed that this was within the law and that nothing could be undertaken against it.

The appearance of the swastika excited the Jewish population exceedingly and repeated clashes occurred. The police first took the position that they couldn't remove the swastikas which were placed on private property; on the other hand, they took the view that they did have the authority to remove them if these were placed on other than private property. Later, the mayor of Toronto, Stewart, sought expert opinion from his legal counsel as to whether the police could order those wearing the swastika to take it off. Counsel concluded in this regard that the police would be justified in intervening if, in their view, peace were to be threatened by some demonstration. Various meetings were held at the mayor's office in which representatives of the Swastika Club and representatives of Jewry participated. In the course of these meetings it was said that the members of the club and other respectable people on the beach were affronted by the fact that a part of the public coming to the beach to swim conducted themselves indecently. They were mostly Jews. The men took off their pants on the sidewalk. The women disrobed in the trucks which brought them to the beach. Apologetically, one of the representatives of Jewry indicated that these were Jews who came fresh from Russia, and who in their enthusiasm over their being able to swim freely at the beach in a democratic country went too far and caused trouble. It was conceded that there were non-Jews as well among those who did not act with decorum.

At the request of the mayor, the Swastika Club proclaimed its dissolution. It was decided to found a new society to protect the beach. To this purpose, several committee meetings as well took place. The result was the giving up on the founding of such a society.

II

In mid-August there was a baseball game in the northwest part of the city. During the game, not far from the baseball field, a white sheet was displayed by four young people upon which there was a swastika. The numerous Jews present attacked the young people and this led to a riot which necessitated police intervention. This incident had called forth great apprehension in Toronto, and the Mayor called a meeting of the Board of Police Commissioners to review the situation. After the meeting ended, the Mayor proclaimed the following order of the Board of Police Commissioners:

From recent occurrences in our city it must be apparent that the display in any form of the "Swastika" Emblem is provocative and tends to incite riotous conduct and a disturbance of the peace which is not at all in keeping with the good name of our city or the public good.

I therefore wish to warn all citizens that such use of this "Swastika" Emblem will render the person so using same liable to prosecution to the full extent of the law.

I also wish to warn all persons against taking the law in their own hands or taking part in unlawful assembly. Peace, order and good government is my desire—I invite co-operation.

On the same day a Jewish deputation made for the mayor and expressed their appreciation for his prompt and effective intervention.

A large number of citizens appeared not to have been in agreement with the mayor's decision. Numerous members of the Swastika Club mentioned in I, who wished to ensure order on the beach, were supposed to have joined a new Swastika organization, according to newspaper reports, which bore the name: "Swastika Association of Canada." The purpose of this society was to call a movement to life which would reach across the entire dominion to oppose "all those who prevent the advancement of the rights of Christians in our own country by deception and unscrupulous business practices". At the head of this organization stands a Mr. E. Hull [sic]. The names and addresses of the other members are, as the press reports, not revealed out of fear of violence from the side of the opposition party. Some headlines in Canadian newspapers have come out against an antisemitic movement of that kind.

I note too, that according to the census of 1931 the city of Toronto has 631,200 inhabitants of which 45,300 are Jews.

2) Kitchener: In Kitchener too, there were signs, albeit weak ones, of Fascist activity. It was directed by a German named O. E. Becker who sent the enclosed program for a meeting on 14 August and a circular (also enclosed here) addressed to the citizens of Kitchener and Waterloo County. The meeting took place. The chair was occupied by one of those persons who had particularly distinguished himself in the Swastika Club in Toronto. There were supposedly 250 persons in attendance there. Becker was supposed to have spoken in broken English and to have had the chairman read out a number of newspaper clippings. Those present, among whom were found socialists and Communists as well, were supposed to have become unruly. On the advice of the supervising police officials the meeting was adjourned. Becker announced that a second meeting would occur a few days later. This too was postponed, and Becker is at this time being deported to Germany. The deportation was not carried out on account of his political activity, but rather on grounds of an application made by Becker several weeks ago. Becker was unemployed, drew public support and wanted to return to Germany.

The local *Star* of 16 August printed a telegram from Toronto according to which a Mr. F. K. M. Seigert explained that members of the German Nazi party who live outside of Germany are duty bound to obey the laws of the land in which they live and to keep out of the politics of their host country. Therefore, no member of the Nazi party could take part in such a meeting as was held in Kitchener. Mr. Seigert was supposed to have shown as well the entry in the special Nazi passports which contains the above-mentioned directives.

The *Toronto Star* of 11 August took note of a question directed to the Reichskanzler by the *Star* in a telegram, whether the rumours currently in circulation in Toronto that the antisemitic movement in Canada is allied with the German Fascists have substance. In reply Mr. Ernst Hanfstaengl wired back that it is absurd to say that Canadian antisemitic outbreaks are in any way related to the Nazi movement in Germany. The Nazi movement is purely German and not tied to any other country.

3) Orillia: A somewhat humorous event was reported by the press last weekend out of Orillia. Orillia is a city of 8,000 situated on a beautiful lake 86 miles from Toronto. All the Jewish inhabitants of Orillia were supposed to have received a letter on the Saturday of the previous week, in which they were warned not to appear on the beach on Saturday, 20 August. The letter was signed "O.S.C." The result was that on Saturday not a single Jew was at the beach. Of course, there were no swastikas to be seen either.

Kempff

APPENDIX B

Table 1

WARDS	BRITISH		JEWISH		ITALIAN	
	Number	%	Number	%	Number	%
4	31,893	47.8	20,329	30.5	1,070	1.6
5	57,802	64.6	16,665	18.6	4,264	4.6
3	53,770	83.9	1,817	2.8	1,395	2.2
7	40,068	85.3	1,105	2.3	1,218	2.6
6	101,451	88.6	2,382	2.0	2,637	2.3
2	80,273	86.2	1,754	1.9	999	1.0
8	76,823	93.6	677	0.8	690	0.8
1	68,352	91.6	576	0.8	742	1.0
ALL	510,432	80.8	45,305	7.2	13,015	2.6

Table 2

Languages spoken by Jewish population 10 years of age and over in Toronto in 1931

Yiddish Only	English Only	French Only	English & French	English & Yiddish	Yiddish & French	Yiddish, English & French	TOTAL POP.
1,366	785	—	20	34,895	3	744	37,813

Table 3

Percentage distribution of Jews in Toronto 1931 by language spoken

English Speaking	Yiddish Speaking	French Speaking	English Only	Yiddish Only
96.38	97.87	2.03	2.08	3.61
English & French Only	English & Yiddish Only	French & Yiddish Only	English, French & Yiddish	
0.05	92.28	0.01	1.97	

Table 4

Percentage distribution of Jews (both sexes) gainfully employed among
the various occupational groups as compared with the total populations
of all origins in Toronto, 1931

OCCUPATIONAL GROUP	JEWS	ALL ORIGINS
Merchandising	25.93	13.52
Manufacturing	40.93	19.96
Clerical	9.59	13.81
Professional	4.08	8.74
Personal Service	3.17	11.64
Building Construction	3.88	6.79
Transportation & Communication	2.59	7.76
Labourers & Unskilled	2.71	8.91
Laundering, Cleaning, Dyeing & Pressing	3.72	1.38
Primary Industries	0.09	0.81
Warehousing & Storage	1.47	2.20
Insurance & Real Estate	1.02	1.26
Entertainment & Sports	0.56	0.34
Finance	0.13	0.73
Public Administration & Defence	0.03	1.13
Electric Light & Power	0.02	0.90
Unspecified	0.07	0.12

Table 5

Percentage of Jews (both sexes) of all persons gainfully employed in each occupational group in Toronto, 1931

OCCUPATIONAL GROUP	% JEWS
Commerce	12.42
Manufacturing	13.29
Laundering, Dyeing & Cleaning	17.45
Entertainment & Sports	10.72
Insurance & Real Estate	5.28
Clerical	4.49
Warehousing & Storage	4.33
Professional	3.01
Building & Construction	3.70
Transportation & Communication	2.16
Finance	1.11
Labourers & Unskilled Workers	2.00
Personal Service	1.76
Primary Industries	0.75
Electric Light & Power	0.12
Public Administration & Defence	0.19
All Occupations	6.47

Table 6

Comparative percentage distribution of Jewish and total population of all origins by specified age groups

AGES	JEWS	ALL
0–4	7.27	7.16
5–14	20.05	15.92
15–19	13.24	8.9
20–29	21.8	18.45
30–39	13.98	16.53
40–49	12.13	14.70
50–59	6.89	9.67
60–69	3.24	5.43
70+	1.4	3.24

Table 7

Religious affiliation of households on selected streets, south of Bloor street, Toronto 1933 (adapted from the Toronto tax assessment rolls, 1933)

STREET	PROTESTANT	CATHOLIC	JEWISH
Euclid (between College & Harbord)	34	5	125
Euclid (between Harbord & Bloor)	56	13	28
Manning (between College & Harbord)	32	12	91
Manning (between Harbord & Bloor)	41	7	34
Clinton (between College & Harbord)	112	21	27
Clinton (between Harbord & Bloor)	94	15	34
Grace (between College & Harbord)	28	7	123
Grace (between Harbord & Bloor)	40	5	31
Montrose (between College & Harbord)	71	12	45
Montrose (between Harbord & Bloor)	93	14	9
Crawford (between College & Harbord)	80	14	46
Crawford (between Harbord & Bloor)	131	15	14
Shaw (between College & Harbord)	65	10	13
Shaw (between Harbord & Bloor)	91	7	11

Table 8

Same as Table 7, but north of Bloor Street

STREET	PROTESTANT	CATHOLIC	JEWISH
Euclid (north of Bloor)	90	28	21
Manning (between Bloor & Dupont)	187	28	13
Clinton (between Bloor & Dupont)	213	20	7
Christie (between Bloor & Dupont)	183	19	5
Crawford (north of Bloor)	50	3	0
Shaw (between Bloor & Dupont)	224	9	8
Barton (between Euclid & Shaw)	81	11	0
Pendrith (between Christie & Shaw)	94	15	4
Essex (between Christie & Shaw)	73	9	0

Table 9

Ethnic origin of population of Greater Toronto by wards and satellite communities, 1931

WARDS	BRITISH NO.	BRITISH %	JEWISH NO.	JEWISH %	ITALIAN NO.	ITALIAN %	FRENCH NO.	FRENCH %	GERMAN NO.	GERMAN %	POLISH NO.	POLISH %	SUNDRY NO.	SUNDRY %
Ward 4	31,893	47.8	20,329	30.5	1,070	1.6	779	1.1	1,248	1.8	2,517	3.7	8,754	13.5
Ward 5	57,802	64.6	16,665	18.6	4,264	4.6	1,140	1.3	1,067	1.2	3,585	4.0	4,861	5.7
Ward 3	53,770	83.9	1,817	2.8	1,395	2.2	1,193	1.8	1,083	1.6	338	0.5	4,487	7.2
Ward 7	40,068	85.3	1,105	2.3	1,218	2.6	608	1.3	787	1.6	796	1.7	2,369	5.2
Ward 6	101,451	88.6	2,382	2.0	2,637	2.3	1,730	1.5	1,714	1.5	574	0.5	3,969	3.6
Ward 2	80,273	86.2	1,754	1.9	999	1.0	2,614	2.8	1,496	1.6	524	0.5	5,439	6.0
Ward 8	76,823	93.6	677	0.8	690	0.8	1,143	1.3	1,044	1.2	73	*	1,558	2.4
Ward 1	68,352	91.6	576	0.8	742	1.0	1,662	2.2	904	1.2	76	0.1	2,323	3.2
ALL WARDS	510,432	80.8	45,305	7.2	13,015	2.6	10,869	1.7	9,343	1.5	8,483	1.3	33,760	4.9
Satellite Communities														
Forest Hill	4,587	88.1	178	3.4	11	0.2	80	1.5	89	1.7	4	0.1	258	5.0
York Township	63,498	91.3	1,088	1.6	1,246	1.8	773	1.1	770	1.1	216	0.3	2,002	2.8
New Toronto	5,521	77.2	42	0.6	82	1.1	309	4.3	143	2.0	229	3.2	820	11.6
Long Branch	3,667	92.6	19	0.5	16	0.4	77	1.9	54	1.4	11	0.3	118	2.9
Scarborough	19,164	92.6	24	0.2	186	0.9	331	1.6	246	1.2	60	0.3	671	3.2
Etobicoke	12,354	89.7	18	0.2	205	1.5	264	1.9	240	1.7	127	0.9	561	4.1
East York	34,382	95.3	41	0.1	339	0.9	516	1.4	344	0.9	47	0.1	411	2.3
North York	12,099	91.6	16	0.1	233	1.8	102	0.9	134	1.0	21	0.2	605	4.4
Mimico	6,226	91.6	10	0.1	118	1.7	94	1.4	105	1.5	40	0.6	207	3.1
Weston	4,351	92.1	6	0.1	27	0.6	41	0.9	131	2.8	7	0.1	160	3.4
Swansea	4,510	89.6	4	0.1	14	0.3	72	1.4	100	2.0	133	2.6	198	4.0
GREATER TORONTO	681,640	84.3	46,751	5.7	15,504	1.9	13,544	1.7	11,718	1.4	9,383	1.1	39,808	3.9

APPENDIX C

As far as we are able to ascertain, the following are the names of some of the boys who played for Harbord Playground and St. Peter's on the night of the riot in Christie Pits:

HARBORD PLAYGROUND

Sam Brooks	Pitcher
Ruby Stein	Pitcher
Irv Letofsky (Lasky)	Catcher
Louis Book	First Base
Ben Lockwood	First Base
David Gollom	Second Base
Snooky Rubenstein	Short Stop
Max Yarmolinsky	Third Base & Outfield
Lou Rubin	Left Field
Mickey Bockner	Centre Field
Bill Simon	Right Field
Harold Cooper	Right Field

ST. PETER'S

Gerry Burke	Pitcher
Steve Hill	Catcher
Jack Ebach	First Base
Bill Lonergan	First Base
Elmer Querques	First Base
Page	Second Base
Tom Wilson	Second Base
Gord Noble	Short Stop
George Lunt	Third Base
W. Smith	Third Base
J. Burke	Left Field
M. MacNamara	Outfield
Bill Marr	Outfield
Murphy	Outfield

Bibliography

Abella, Irving, and Harold Troper. *None Is Too Many*. Toronto: Lester & Orpen Dennys, 1982.

Ages, Arnold. "Antisemitism: The Uneasy Calm," in Morton Weinfeld, William Shaffir, Irwin Cotler, eds. *The Canadian Jewish Mosaic*. Toronto: John Wiley and Sons, 1981.

Betcherman, Lita-Rose. *The Swastika and the Maple Leaf*. Toronto: Fitzhenry and Whiteside, 1975.

———. *The Little Band*. Ottawa: Deneau, 1982.

Callaghan, Morley. *The Varsity Story*. Toronto: Macmillan, 1948.

———. *Strange Fugitive*. New York: Grosset and Dunlap, 1928.

Cauz, Louis. *Baseball's Back in Town*. Toronto: CMC, n.d.

Donegan, Rosemary. *Spadina*. Vancouver and Toronto: Douglas and McIntyre, 1985.

Garner, Hugh. *Cabbagetown*. Toronto: McGraw-Hill Ryerson, 1968.

Gibson, Sally. *More Than an Island: A History of the Toronto Island*. Toronto: Irwin, 1984.

Glickman, Yaacov. "Anti-Semitism and Jewish Social Cohesion in Canada," in Rita M. Bienvenue and Jay E. Goldstein, eds. *Ethnicity and Ethnic Relations in Canada: A Book of Readings*. 2nd ed. Toronto: Butterworth, 1985.

Goldfarb (Martin) Consultants. *Jewish Canadians*. A study conducted for the *Toronto Star*. Photocopy. 1985.

Harney, Robert, ed. *Gathering Place: People and Neighbourhoods of Toronto*. Toronto: Multicultural History Society of Ontario, 1985.

———. "The Italian Community in Toronto," in J. Elliot, ed., *Two Nations, Many Cultures*. Scarborough: Prentice-Hall Canada, 1979.

Horn, Michiel. "'Free Speech within the Law': The Letter of the Sixty-Eight Toronto Professors, 1931," *Ontario History* LXXII:1 (March 1980).

———. "Keeping Canada 'Canadian': Anti-Communism and Canadianism in Toronto 1928-29," *Canada* 3:1 (Sept. 1975).

Houston, Cecil J., and William J. Smyth. *The Sash Canada Wore*. Toronto: University of Toronto Press, 1980.

Kayfetz, Ben. *Only Yesterday.* Paper presented to the Toronto Jewish Historical Society, May 1982.

———. "Ontario Region," in *Pathways to the Present: Canadian Jewry and Canadian Jewish Congress.* Montreal: Canadian Jewish Congress, 1986.

Kilbourn, William, ed. *Toronto Remembered: A Celebration of the City.* Toronto: Stoddart, 1984.

Laqueur, Walter. *The Terrible Secret.* Boston and Toronto: Little, Brown, 1980.

Lemon, James. *Toronto Since 1918: An Illustrated History.* Toronto: Lorimer, 1985.

Lipstadt, Deborah E. *Beyond Belief: The American Press and the Coming of the Holocaust 1933–1945.* New York: The Free Press, 1986.

Luftspring, Sammy, with Brian Swarbrick. *Call Me Sammy.* Scarborough: Prentice-Hall Canada, 1975.

Lynch, Kevin. *The Image of the City.* Cambridge, MA: Technology Press, 1960.

Mannheim, Karl. *Essays on the Sociology of Knowledge.* London: Routledge and Kegan Paul, 1952.

Moneta, Jacob. "Mehr Gewalt für die Ohnmächtigen," *Kursbuch,* 51 (March 1978), 43–57.

(The) Review of Anti-Semitism in Canada, 1983. Toronto: League for Human Rights of B'nai B'rith, 1984.

(The) Review of Anti-Semitism in Canada, 1984. Toronto: League for Human Rights of B'nai B'rith, 1985.

(The) Review of Anti-Semitism in Canada, 1985. Toronto: League for Human Rights of B'nai B'rith, 1986.

Rome, David. *Clouds over the Thirties.* Section 3. Montreal: Canadian Jewish Congress, 1977.

Rosenberg, Louis. *Canada's Jews: A Social and Economic Study of the Jews in Canada.* Montreal: Bureau of Social and Economic Research, Canadian Jewish Congress, 1939.

———. "Two Centuries of Jewish Life in Canada," in *American Jewish Yearbook* 62 (1961), 28–49.

Speisman, Stephen A. *The Jews of Toronto: A History to 1937.* Toronto: McClelland and Stewart, 1979.

van Paassen, Pierre, and James Waterman Wise, eds. *Nazism: An Assault on Civilization.* New York: Harrison Smith and Robert Haas, 1934.

Wagner, Jonathan F. *Brothers Beyond the Sea: National Socialism in Canada.* Waterloo: Wilfrid Laurier University Press, 1981.

Weimann, Gabriel, and Conrad Winn. *Hate on Trial.* Oakville: Mosaic Press, 1986.

West, Bruce. *Toronto.* Garden City, NY: Doubleday, 1967.

Index

18 19 20 21 22 · 5 4 3 2 1